Faith's Knowledge

Faith's Knowledge

*Explorations into the Theory
and Application of Theological Epistemology*

PAUL G. TYSON

☙PICKWICK *Publications* • Eugene, Oregon

FAITH'S KNOWLEDGE
Explorations into the Theory and Application of Theological Epistemology

Copyright © 2013 Paul G. Tyson. All rights reserved. Except for brief quotations in critical publications or reviews, no part of this book may be reproduced in any manner without prior written permission from the publisher. Write: Permissions, Wipf and Stock Publishers, 199 W. 8th Ave., Suite 3, Eugene, OR 97401.

Pickwick Publications
An Imprint of Wipf and Stock Publishers
199 W. 8th Ave., Suite 3
Eugene, OR 97401

www.wipfandstock.com

ISBN 13: 978-1-61097-818-7

Cataloguing-in-Publication data:

Tyson, Paul G.

Faith's knowledge : explorations into the theory and application of theological epistemology / Paul G. Tyson.

viii + 202 pp. ; 23 cm. Includes bibliographical references.

ISBN 13: 978-1-61097-818-7

1. Philosophical theology. 2. Knowledge, Theory of (Religion). I. Title.

BT40 T97 2013

Manufactured in the USA

Four of the chapters in this book have already appeared in print and I am very pleased to acknowledge those publications here:

"Transcendence and Epistemology" was published in *Modern Theology* 24/2 (April 2008) 245–70 © Blackwell.

"Plato against Ontotheology" was published as chapter 17 in *Belief and Metaphysics*, edited by Conor Cunningham and Peter Candler Jr. (London: SCM Press, 2007), 393–412.

"The Iron Cage Closes" was published in *Quadrant* 51/7–8 (July–August 2007) 55–58 (Sydney).

"Australian Universities in Transition" was published in the *Australian eJournal of Theology* 13 (March 2009).

Contents

Acknowledgments   vii

Introduction   1

Part One—Theory

1. Transcendence and Epistemology   13
2. Plato against Ontotheology   43
3. Faith in Plato and John   59

Part Two—Application

    What Is Applied Theological Epistemology?   85

4. The Iron Cage Closes   98
5. Australian Universities in Transition   109
6. A Post-Secular Approach to Understanding Religion and Global Security   130
7. Faith and Medicine   159

    Faith's Knowledge   181

Bibliography   193

Acknowledgments

FIRSTLY I WANT TO thank Paul Harrison and Gavin Kendall for their constant encouragement, assistance, and long conversations over the course of writing this work. It is a curious fact that these two simply beautiful paragons of humanity and scholarship are both ex-Catholic atheists and I could not have had better supervisors, though this work is entirely situated within Christian theology. Then there is the cricket-mad and astoundingly generous King Arthur of Nottingham (John Milbank) and his dazzling queen (Alison Milbank), the always merry Sir Gawain of the pure heart (Conor Cunningham) and his better half (Crystal Cunningham), the yet to be unveiled Sir Percival (Eric Lee), and—to badly mash my literary metaphor—the Lady Galadriel of Cambridge (Catherine Pickstock) from the 'Radical Orthodox' Camelot in that distant isle. Without your voice, your generous engagement and your friendship I would have felt very intellectually alone in the world. Many thanks. To Nathan Kerr in the United States, thank you very much for your ever-thoughtful engagement with my work. In Australia: Jo Rose, Catherine Althause, Matthew Tan, Ben Tarren, Tracey Rowland, Scott Stephens, and Richard Colledge have been wonderful intellectual friends. To Dave Andrews, Charles Ringma, and Ray Overend—many thanks for your pastoral care of my head/heart/hands. Most significantly, Annette, Daniel, Hannah, Claire, Aurora, Francis, Lucy, and Emma Tyson have all put up with my study for years with extraordinary good grace—thank you. To Karl and Ursula Wiethoff, many thanks for your generous assistance over the course of my studies. To Graham and Andrew Tyson, many thanks for your love and goodwill. To Peter Orchard, thank you so much for the many hours you put into formatting and preparing this work for the publishers. To Christian Amondson, Patrick Harrison, and Robin Parry at Wipf and Stock, many thanks for your encouragement and labors. To Nicola Barnett, many thanks for your sharp-eyed help with the text.

Introduction

THE QUESTION "WHAT IS true knowledge?" is a meta-epistemological question. That is, the question upon which all epistemological endeavors are premised is a metaphysical or theological question. All epistemological investigations that ask "can you know for sure that what you think is true really is true, and if so, how?" arise from some meta-epistemological stance. They presuppose some working meaning for truth and knowledge so that they can then proceed to see if a knowledge of truth can be justified. Yet meta-epistemology is not simply presupposed by any given epistemological exploration, for meta-epistemology and epistemology are dynamically related to each other in a complex feedback loop. That is, the depth presuppositions of any understanding of truth and any understanding of knowledge which makes any given epistemological investigation possible are typically brought into question by that epistemological investigation. Further, this loop's logic operates within the broader interpretive loop of culture which is shaped by relationships and powers that are embedded in space and time and by the evolving language and meaning narratives that structure and enliven collective and individual knowledge. Thus, all outlooks on truth and knowledge are a view from somewhere so the specific cultural, political, and relational contexts of knowers can never be separated from either epistemology or meta-epistemology. Thus theory and application, and epistemology and meta-epistemology are only notionally separable when it comes to any investigation of truth.[1]

Knowledge, then, displays many life forms and the lives and behaviors of these strange creatures are themselves only comprehensible in relation to the larger cultural biosphere in which particular forms of

---

1. This outlook upholding the interdependence of theory and practice can be well seen in a diverse range of recent scholarly movements, including Radical Orthodox theologians and the Marxism of Louis Althusser. See Smith, *Introducing Radical Orthodoxy*, 231–59; Althusser, *For Marx*, 169, 172.

knowledge live. Thus, meaningfully exploring the terrain of knowledge and of truth is very complex if, indeed, it is considered possible at all. For within such an exploration recognizing and accepting the particularity of the explorer's own appropriation of truth aspiring knowledge—with all its idiosyncrasies, relativities and contextual contingencies—is unavoidable. Here an obvious problem arises. If universality, objectivity, rational purity, demonstrable certainty etc. are deemed necessary for true knowledge, then the task for epistemology does indeed seems hopeless. And yet, if we do not believe that the meaning of the words "knowledge" and "truth" have some context transcending validity, then we find ourselves being tacitly committed to epistemological nihilism, to the anti-metaphysics of irrealism and to the suspicious hermeneutic bias that arises from the inherently problematic attempt to uphold a belief-suspending stance. Yet, definitionally, irrealism in meta-epistemology cannot be true because if the word truth is deemed devoid of *any* significance relative to reality, then all meta-epistemological commitments to irrealism must be entirely without truth. So it seems that the commitment to irrealism is premised on a dogmatic existentially asserted absurdism. This absurdism is a prior commitment to the meaninglessness of the very notion of true knowledge for—explicitly—no reason. Hence any existential refusal of onto-epistemic absurdism—that is, any commitment to at least the aim of a reasonable knowledge of truth—requires one to maintain at minimum a stance of meta-epistemological agnosticism in relation to the possibility of human linguistic signification and reality having some true relation. Here, where our knowledge *might* hold open the possibility of some form of true relationship to reality, then it seems inherent to the existential commitment to reason to have faith in that possibility, for reason is valued precisely as a function of truth. So, if we are interested in reasoning about knowledge and truth at all then it makes sense that we should show at least some confidence (good faith) in this process and in the words knowledge and truth. The hopeful searcher after true knowledge then endeavors to gain some view of the broader culturo-politico-linguistic-relational landscape in which the knower is situated, looking for suggestions of truth which in some manner transcends the context that enables us to be truth seeking knowers in the first place. In such an endeavor reason hopes to find at least analogical gestures of larger truths that rise beyond the specificity and incompleteness of all human knowledge, even though our knowledge can never be epistemologically divorced from the particular and contingent limits of its 'all too human' context.

Introduction

If we are prepared to approach questions of knowledge and truth with both hope and modesty, then, as never realized as such an endeavor is, the perennial fascinations of knowledge and truth need not be denied. And if, in full acceptance of their fragility and incompleteness, knowledge and truth are not denied, and are even taken up in good faith, then it is reasonable to believe that it is possible for even our all too human knowledge of truth to be sacraments of the kind of truth which is always embodied within human knowing and yet transcends the limits of human knowing; what theologians call revelation. That is, unless some larger suggestion of meaning than any of our linguistic meanings can capture undergirds our attempts at knowing and understanding reality, then we are indeed cut off from true knowledge of any sort.

In terms of some larger suggestion of truth, this book explores the possibility that Western epistemology has fallen into a credibility hole—with disastrous cultural consequences—because it is not grounded in an adequate meta-epistemology, because it is grounded in an inadequate theology. Following John Milbank's lead, this book seeks to ask the basic meta-epistemological question concerning what true knowledge itself is from within non-nominalist, somewhat Augustinian, orthodox Christian theology. From this explicitly theological epistemic view point, metaphysical and methodological assumptions about valid knowledge that pre-suppose some form of faith/reason dualism are considered neither Christian nor credible. That is, the outlook I seek to defend and develop maintains that rather than there being either a positive or a negative relationship between faith and reason, the only possible knowledge of truth is the knowledge of faith. This is not simply a Christian stance but, so this book argues, Plato too holds something like this stance.

Notably, however, the onto-epistemological stance where transcendentally warranted faith and truth are inextricably entwined is rejected by modernity. Yet even here, this rejection is not independent of faith but arises out of late medieval theology. Historically, the modern assumption that knowledge is a discretely rational or empirical apprehension of universally valid, indubitably factual, or pragmatically probabilistic truth arises from a specific development in Christian theology that enabled faith and reason to be treated as separate pathways to truth.[2] As this

---

2. Copleston, Pieper, and Gilson all draw attention to "the moment" in the history of Western belief that Aquinas fills, when the dogmatic certainties of the early Middle Ages are combined with Aristotelian philosophy, and it becomes possible to distinguish theology from philosophy, and possible to treat faith and reason as functionally

notional separation of faith from reason hardened into a deep cultural habit, a division between theology and dogmatics on the one hand, and philosophy and science on the other hand, came to define the meta-epistemological framework of belief in which modern Western epistemology now largely operates.

Yet, Modern epistemology has notoriously failed to justify truth in the universal, rational and empirical terms in which it approaches knowledge.[3] This means that our culturally embedded knowledge assumptions make it natural for us to accept pragmatic instrumentalism on the one hand and fundamental skepticism regarding questions of ontology and morality on the other hand. So seeking to re-think epistemology from a Christian meta-epistemological stance opens up new possibilities for epistemological and metaphysical optimism and also challenges the fundamental assumptions on which so much of the distinctive logic, politics and teleology of the modern world operates.

Thus, the overarching argument in these pages asks can the ontological and moral problems integral to modern Western epistemology be located in its meta-epistemological outlook which severs faith from reason, and is this severance valid? If this severance is not valid, could, then, a contemporary revival of Christian Neoplatonist conceptions of the meta-epistemological unity of faith and reason provide a 'postmodern' framework of approaching knowledge in such a manner as to give truth and substantive (though always incomplete) understandings of ontology and morality new life in Western culture?

The first three chapters of this book attempt to make a dent in some of the big meta-epistemological questions that concern both the problematic nature of the modern bifurcation of faith from knowledge as well as the difficulties of attempting to re-forge the conceptual unity of faith and knowledge via a post-secular Christian Platonist stance.

The first chapter seeks to locate the rift between faith and knowledge in the context of late medieval Aristotelianism. The move towards secular rationalism and secular empiricism is here argued as arising from the particular species of Aristotelianism that arose in the West

---

autonomous. Thus the delicate theological balance that Aquinas realizes in his approach to reason, is, as Copleston notes, "intrinsically precarious" and leads on to the proto-modern separation of faith from reason, and the emergence of philosophy as a discretely secular substitute for theology. See Copleston, *A History of Philosophy*, 423–34; Pieper, *Scholasticism*, 118–26; Gilson, *Christian Philosophy*, 321.

3. See Lyotard, *The Postmodern Condition*.

after Aquinas. That is, it is not Aristotle's philosophy itself or the type of synthesis of Aristotle and Christian faith found in Aquinas which births the modern Western separation of faith and knowledge, but rather it is explicitly late medieval Aristotelianism, along with its socio-politico-theological context, which generates the modern bifurcation of faith and knowledge. I argue that though the early modernists of our era typically saw themselves as reacting against Aristotelianism, even so the stance of nascent secular modernity—where the autonomy of the rational and the empirical from faith is assumed—is inherent within the university ethos of post 1277 medievalism. The prevalence of this stance, I argue, owes a great deal to the enormous influence of Aristotle from the thirteenth to the fifteenth centuries, and this stance is assumed by the early modern thinkers even whilst they reject key dogmas of medieval Aristotelian natural philosophy. However, this stance—and hence secular modernity—is seriously problematic. In contrast to the 'Aristotelian' trajectory of secular modernity I posit the conceptual advantages of a Platonist understanding of the unity of faith and knowledge. Having, hopefully, established the problematic nature of the birth of the modern autonomy of knowledge from faith and the ongoing viability of a unitary stance on faith and knowledge, the second chapter then looks at a well-known argument against the Platonist approach to knowledge. For in recent years it has commonly been claimed that Plato is the father of an unpardonable philosophical error, ontotheology.

Chapter two argues that whilst ontotheology—the substitution of living and lived religious belief for abstract philosophical speculation—is a serious charge against modern philosophy in general, this is not a charge that has any teeth when set to attack Plato. I seek to point out that Plato provides us with ample fuel against the hubris of modern ontotheology, yet he also calls into question the integrity of the anti-metaphysical trajectory out of which the modern critique of ontotheology arises. Whilst ontotheology is indeed something to be avoided, the rejection of any form of substantive metaphysical knowledge achieves the avoidance of ontotheology at the self-defeating expense of being unable to uphold any analogical belief in a true understanding of reality.

Chapters one and two seek to argue against the separation of faith and knowledge, and for a Platonist metaphysical vision that both unifies faith and knowledge and gives us some belief purchase on true and transcendentally meaningful reality. However, chapter three seeks to clarify some important differences between Platonism and Christian Platonism.

This chapter looks closely at how John's Gospel understands the dynamic of Christian belief and then compares that with how Plato understands the low epistemic categories of opinion (*doxa*), perception and historical particularity. This comparison—based on a textual survey of *pist-* stem words (the root common to the Greek words for faith and belief)—in both John and Plato shows a Christian understanding of the act of believing truth to have a distinct signature from a non-Christian Platonist stance. There is not so much direct contradiction—Plato's understanding of faith has good points of contact with a Johannine outlook—as a very conscious Christian embracing of the mystery of the divine choice of low epistemic categories as the medium of revelation. This chapter, I believe, clarifies the important epistemic ways in which Christian Platonism is distinct from the forms of Platonism which sit naturally within a pagan Classical intellectual milieu. As Hamann and Kierkegaard point out—not to mention Saint Paul and Christ Himself—there is always an offense to the high intellect, to the pride of mind, in Christian faith. Yet, so thinkers like Augustine maintain, once, by grace, one has come into faith, then only can truth be clearly understood and appropriated even if, pace Aquinas, that truth is always for us analogous rather than immediate, and always only ever partially appropriated.

The first three chapters seek to set up the basic outlines of a particular stance which both upholds the unity of faith and knowledge and which sees the modern secular Western understanding of truth as profoundly disintegrative and dysfunctional due to its bifurcation of faith and knowledge. Working from this stance, the rest of this book seeks to look more closely at how the separation of faith from knowledge plays out in a few selected contemporary contexts, and what the pathologies of this separation entails. Each of the chapters in this book were written as self-standing publishable articles so these chapters do contain a bit of conceptual repetition regarding the stance worked out in the first three chapters.

The second part of this book comes with something of an academic health warning. The approach to truth and knowledge which I draw on takes much from Plato, from John, and also from Kierkegaard. None of these thinkers would recognize strong lines of division between some discretely public and objective truth discourse and personal interestedness and religious belief. Hence, the applied section of this book does not seek to gloss over the existentially interested and the hermeneutically, politically and culturo-historically situated nature of any would-be knower of truth. As a result, most of the chapters in part two of this book are directly connected to events and communicative voices one might call personal. This is particularly evident in chapters four, five and seven.

Chapters four and five look at the concrete situation of my own university's decision to discontinue its Arts degree, to end its dedicated Humanities and Social Science offerings, and to close down the campus where Humanities and Social Science subjects were previously offered. I argue that the logic of this administrative choice reflects a particularly pragmatic outlook on knowledge embedded deeply in the meta-epistemological outlook of late modernity. I argue that the epistemological assumptions of my administration are faulty, resting on unsound meta-epistemological premises, and I analyze the logic of this administrative decision from the perspective of what I argue to be a more credible meta-epistemological set of terms and premises.

Chapter six critiques the assumed validity of secular knowledge as a good and progressive epistemological paradigm from which to approach global security. The politics of fear, premised on a view that secular politics and global power is rational and humane and that militant Islamic fundamentalism is evil precisely because it is not secular, rational and humane, has dominated Australian foreign policy since the destruction of the World Trade buildings in 2001. This outlook makes us unable to see how theologically premised modern Western secularism is, and for Australia—living next door to the most populous Islamic nation on earth—such a stance has all sorts of regional implications. The problems of contemporary geopolitical good will are very demanding but this chapter argues that the separation of faith from reason in our own minds in relation to international politics leads to peculiar blindnesses and biases regarding our own beliefs and actions.

Chapter seven explores the modern hospital and the modern church in terms of power, knowledge and faith. The Christian religion does not believe in a materialist cosmos, nor does orthodox Christian belief adhere to a strict division between nature and supernature. Thus, a Christian outlook and a secular materialist outlook approach untreatable terminal illness very differently, both in terms of the ultimacy or otherwise of physical death, and in terms of the possibility of a miracle. That is, different outlooks on reality entail different outlooks on knowledge, possibility and power. This chapter explores some of those differences and seeks to problematize the 'realism' of the dominant contemporary medical outlook at the same time that it seeks to note that contemporary

Western Christianity is typically fully at home within a modern secular materialist frame of reality assumptions and life practices.

This book is a work in theological epistemology. This book seeks to advocate and display a conceptual outlook that does not bifurcate faith and knowledge. Yet such a book runs at cross-purposes to the dominant epistemic categories of the modern secular West. So one must wonder why should such a book be written or read? The answer to that question is, I think, well put forward by Josef Pieper's remarkable book on scholasticism. Pieper argues that the highly demanding attempt at an integrative approach to faith and reason is not something that can be avoided if one believes that the Christian revelation is true.[4] All too easily modern Western Christianity has allowed the epistemic and metaphysical convictions of secular modernity—convictions premised on the asserted autonomy of knowledge from faith—to rob Christian thought of the very possibility of being situated within its own vision of truth. But the outlook of secular modernity cannot uphold *its* own vision of truth, so modern Western Christianity ends up trading its birthright for a passing onto-epistemic mess of potage when she uncritically accepts the validity of the modern faithless notion of knowledge. For secular modernity's universal, objective and empirically demonstrable notions of truth are, simply, fictions. Since the counter-Enlightenment it has been unavoidably clear that the truth discourse of secular modernity falls readily to an army of self-generated foes. These enemies of modern truth which modernity itself has given birth to are: the fundamental irrationalism of metaphysical irrealism; epistemological nihilism; moral relativism; amoral instrumental pragmatism and, as Plato well saw; brazen manipulative exploitation and sheer violent power.[5] So not only is an integral understanding of faith and knowledge basic to the Christian understanding of how we know truth, but—as Lyotard reported—the state of knowledge in modernity is in profound disarray and we are threatened by serious cultural entropy as a result.[6] So perhaps it is the way in which we understand knowledge itself which is so deeply at the core of the cultural pathologies of modernity. Perhaps, even, a post-secular Christian understanding of true knowledge offers a radical enough alternative to the belief and practice norms of our times as to make a spiritual renewal of Western culture a

---

4. Pieper, *Scholasticism*, 151–62.
5. Schindler, *Plato's Critique of Impure Reason*, 41–84.
6. Lyotard, *The Postmodern Condition*, xxiii–xxv.

possibility. If there is any credibility to these possibilities then the recovery of a genuinely Christian theological epistemology is a very important matter deserving serious attention.

PART ONE

Theory

1

Transcendence and Epistemology

We know by means of our intelligence that what the intelligence does not comprehend is more real than what it does comprehend. Faith is experience that intelligence is enlightened by love.[1]

—Simone Weil

Seeing is not believing, it is only seeing.[2]

—George MacDonald

MODERN SECULAR REASON IS grounded in epistemological foundationalism typically traced back to Descartes. Here, truth sits within the confines of what the autonomous human mind can indubitably know and those confines are defined by what can be validly demonstrated by human logic and/or perception. Whilst this approach to truth greatly facilitated the launch of the modern scientific method, it was philosophically unstable from the outset. Hume argued that metaphysical and theological speculation grounded in the modern conception of truth invariably collapses, for modern truth feeds into fundamental solipsistic doubt in a manner that is not only theologically destructive but that leads naturally to epistemological nihilism in relation to all realist conceptions of truth. "Truth" must hence be practical and skeptical and cannot be metaphysical or theological. Kant attempted to salvage Western metaphysics and theology from Humean doubt but his 'salvage' only deepened our problem.

1. Weil, *Gravity and Grace*, 128.
2. MacDonald, *The Princess and the Goblin*, 177.

Since the opening of the nineteenth century the West has been reeling in a cultural crisis of metaphysical and theological failure, what one scholar has called the "dis-enchantment of reason."[3] For Kant's powerful thinking makes it reasonable for us to believe that the Real, though it may exist, is substantively unknowable. Today, a profound spiritual skepticism underpins both modernism and postmodernism and this makes the very exploration of epistemology and transcendence difficult.

However, if modern epistemological foundationalism itself is grounded in a faulty set of onto-epistemological assumptions then a specific critique of those assumptions rather than the wholesale rejection of realist ontology and epistemology may open up the ideas of knowable transcendent truth and inherently meaningful reality to us again. The Radical Orthodoxy critique of secular reason, delving into the theological roots of the modern outlook, underlies the liberty this chapter takes in exploring the largely abandoned territory of epistemology and transcendence.

This chapter starts with Plato's approach to epistemology and transcendence and finds this powerful in its own right, compatible with orthodox Christian theology, and refreshingly outside of the onto-epistemological assumptions implicit in modern epistemological foundationalism. Christian Neoplatonist Aristotelianism—as developed in the *via antiqua* of Aquinas and Bonaventure—is argued as onto-epistemologically of one piece with Christian Platonism. So Augustine and Aquinas are seen as allies in theologically premised realism that is profoundly at odds with the *via moderna* that is heralded by Abelard, takes off with William of Ockham, leads through the Renaissance to Descartes, and then arrives at its striking Humean metaphysical dead end in the Enlightenment. However, this chapter argues that proto-modern Aristotelian epistemology, in contrast to Neoplatonic Aristotelianism, is integral to the *via moderna* and the metaphysical failure of modern truth. For the *via moderna* is under-girded by an epistemological revolution that can be traced back to the enormous influence of Aristotle's science, logic and metaphysics on the Middle Ages and the Renaissance. In this period of Aristotelian supremacy philosophy first delineated itself from theology and then slowly produced the secularized natural theology which emerges in Enlightenment metaphysics, finally giving progressive nineteenth century materialism its amazing theological confidence. The anti-Aristotelian epistemological invention of representation by Duns Scotus

---

3. See Harrison, *The Disenchantment of Reason*.

Transcendence and Epistemology

and William of Ockham is a critical development for the *via moderna*, but this chapter suggests that the background role of Aristotle's approach to perception and logic underpins Franciscan science, is a critical feature of proto-modern science, and underlies the mortal conflict between science and religion that was to flower in high modernity. For once nature and super-nature are fixedly separated by the nominalists, Aristotle's pagan natural theology creeps back into the West in a trajectory thoroughly at odds with both Aquinas' baptism of Aristotle's philosophy into dogmatic Christian theology *and* the delineated theological interests of the nominalists. Yet, modern scientific and naturalistic truth is a doomed enterprise. Naturalistic metaphysics without the Platonic belief in a transcendent reality beyond matter in which natural reality nevertheless ontically participates, becomes wrecked by the inherent unknowables of human perception and reason understood in *natura pura* and nominalist terms. So, this chapter argues, Aristotle is very important as an influence supporting the ontotheological hubris and metaphysical dead ends of modernity. Yet, the argument of this chapter suggests that this hubris and metaphysical failure can be discarded and a valid knowledge of transcendent truth can be regained if we can open up a new and post-secular chapter in epistemology that draws more directly on the epistemological traditions of Christian Platonism.

PLATO'S APPROACH TO TRUTH: FAITH IN DIVINE REASON

In his famous cave analogy Plato takes the flux, contingency and transience of all that we perceive to be but confused shadows of reality.[4] Equally, Plato sees the emptiness of merely cunning arguments. The instrumental and manipulative language games of the Sophists do not aim at truth, thus they are nothing but deceptive concoctions of semantic shadows. So to Plato, neither immediate perception nor mere argument delivers truth.[5] Given these limitations, the search for the true is hence a search away from the play of shadows on the cave wall towards the real things that produce the shadows, and ultimately to ecstatic union with the sun itself. But whilst the shadows of truth do, in their confused and illusive manner, stimulate us to seek real truth, truth is itself the cause of the shadows and this asymmetrical causal relationship can never be

4. Plato, *The Republic* 514–21.
5. Plato, *Sophist* 268c, d.

reversed. The realm of contingency and flux and the sophistic knots of constructed speculative language games can never, in those terms, divulge truth to us. Yet to Plato, this does not mean that we cannot know truth.

In *Theaetetus* Plato puts forward the notion that our knowledge of timeless universal truths—such as mathematics—cannot be derived from perception but must be directly apprehended by some capacity of the mind herself.[6] In Meno Plato puts forward the notion that because we do have an innate pre-recognition of universal and timeless truths, it stands to reason that our minds have a transcendent origin.[7] We can only recognize necessary truths if our minds already have truth and are, in some profound sense, akin to transcendent truth. To Plato, that we do grasp universal truths beyond the contingency and flux of the perceptual manifold indicates that our minds are not spawned from contingent fluctuating temporal nature. In this way Plato grounds the ordinary processes of thought in transcendence and makes perception a derivative knowledge grounded in the mysteries of transcendent reality, rather than seeing perception, or the internal structures of our mind, as the source of knowledge itself.[8]

Due to the asymmetry mentioned above, logical and empirical proofs constructed in the terms of our 'natural' epistemological capacities are not found in Plato. Whilst Plato is a master of dialectics and keen observation, these are merely tools to deflect distractions, untangle confusions, or undermine false confidence. The essence of his philosophy is what we would now call religious: when Plato is grasped by *Nous* in the context of intellectual love (desiring contemplation), there he gains

---

6. Plato, *Theaetetus* 185d, e.

7. Plato, *Meno* 85d, e.

8. This makes the entire idea of epistemology after Ockham and Descartes very different to the approach towards knowing truth native to the Platonic and Neoplatonic traditions of antiquity and the high Middle Ages. Whilst Aristotle is not a Neoplatonist and whilst Aristotle is far closer to the pre-Socratic *phusikoi* tradition than Plato—and hence his interests are more recognizably scientific to us than are the interests of Plato—yet even to Aristotle, the idea that epistemology should entail unequivocal demonstrations that perception and reason give us sure access to realist truth is dismissed out of hand. "Now some think that because one must understand the primitives there is no understanding at all; others that there is, but that there are demonstrations of everything. Neither of these views is either true or necessary" (Aristotle, *Posterior Analytics* 72b, 5–7). Here, tacitly, Platonist assumptions about our knowledge of truth, combined with a nearly pragmatic interest in simply doing science, is evident in Aristotle. We return to these themes later in the chapter.

divine insights that are spiritual, that can only be expressed in parables, in analogies, in poetic myths—for they are insights not of the transient sub-lunar world, but of the eternal Reality on which our comprehension and being, and the being of the perceived world, depends. Plato puts the heart of his philosophy forward in a way that must be grasped as inspired and searching spiritual analogies; never as definitive rational or scientific descriptions that replicate a simple correspondence with "reality" as some objective material thing. And yet, the rigor of contemplative thought in Plato is in no contradiction to the poetic imagery in which he seeks to express the mystical and spiritually erotic insights that ground his whole conception of the love of wisdom. Plato's onto-epistemological belief framework, as a blend of mystical insight, rigorous dialect, human warmth, literary art and broad learning, is subtle and profound. And it is essentially religious.

An examination of how Plato depicts Socratic wisdom, as found in *Apology*, brings out a twofold purpose in Plato's approach to the human situation in relation to the divine, and reveals Plato as a deeply theological thinker. Negatively, Plato critiques "human wisdom" grounded in immediate sensory knowledge, custom, status and power, and mere argument. Such "wisdom" cannot be adequately justified. But Plato's critique is not critique for its own sake. Positively, once merely human wisdom is found wanting, Plato seeks to bring divine wisdom into view; wisdom which cannot be grasped by merely human capacities, but must hence be received, in humility, from the god.

"The god" is pivotal to Plato's depiction of Socratic wisdom. In *Apology* 22e–23b the true wisdom of "Socratic ignorance" is clearly identified with Socrates' refusal to trust reputed "human wisdom," precisely *because* he serves the god of true and divine wisdom. At issue here is not simply a theory about wisdom and knowledge, but an approach to life that must be lived out in either good faith or bad faith to the god that the illusions of human certainty cannot grasp. Socrates discovers that such an approach to ignorance and wisdom is politically problematic. For as human wisdom cannot grasp divine wisdom in the terms of human "certainty" and "control," true wisdom, grounded in the divine, will always appear uncertain and subversive to those committed to merely conventional authority and the apparent immediacy and solidity generated by the perceptual manifold. The condemnation and execution of Socrates underlines the political problematic of life lived in devotion to the god of true wisdom.

Serving divine wisdom is a life of existential commitment, of political danger and most of all, of relational good faith in the god; it is never the discretely academic pursuit of mere dogmatic or abstract certainty.

Kierkegaard makes much of Socrates' reckless preparedness, in the face of his own pending death, to actively trust (have faith in) "the god" regarding that which cannot be proven.

> [Socrates] poses the question . . . : if there is an immortality . . . He stakes his whole life on this "if"; he dares to die, and with the passion of the infinite he has so ordered his life that it might be acceptable—if there is an immortality.[9]

Socrates' trust in the god, manifested in his courageous gamble on the soul's survival of the body, is demonstrated in his steadfast determination to live by the goodness of true wisdom even in the face of the death penalty. A Kierkegaardian reading of *Apology*, *Crito*, and *Phaedo* seems well justified, as there are no indubitable proofs for the soul's survival of death in Plato, and yet clearly Plato advocates a reckless, gambled concern for the true and eternal happiness of the soul and is not simply concerned with what we might now call deontological ethics.

This rejection of "human wisdom" and yet the tacit acceptance of divine wisdom that cannot be justified in merely human terms, can be seen more broadly throughout Plato's opus. In the so called early dialogues, no attempt to articulate a definitive justification of any belief is found to demonstrate an unassailable force of reason.[10] And this problematic comes up through all of Plato's works.[11] However, this does not relegate Plato to some exitless maze of fundamental ignorance.[12] Plato has a hum-

---

9. Kierkegaard, *Unscientific Postscript*, 201.

10. See Plato, *Complete Works*, trans. Cooper, xii–xviii, regarding the conjectural basis of a distinct periodized chronology attributable to Plato's works. I share Cooper's opinion that this conjecture is an unhelpful and potentially misleading interpretive map to Plato's thought.

11. The manner in which Plato de-constructively interrogates a simplistic "Platonist" understanding of forms in *Parmenides* does reveal the limits of 'earth bound' thinking, but it does not at all negate Plato's commitment to eternal metaphysical reality being the grounds of particular and contingent reality. Parmenides is a subtle and demanding dialogue and a close reading of it reveals that its apparent own goal in the famous third man argument is an important didactic tool in explaining what type of reality form is not.

12. If one reads the "early dialogues" through the eyes of Kierkegaard—whose methodological debt to Plato is very large—then what Kierkegaard calls "indirect communication" can be reasonably argued for in Plato. This method of communicating

Transcendence and Epistemology

ble trust (faith) in the god of divine wisdom whom he, like Socrates, seeks to serve. To believe in transcendent truths without justification does not make these truths arbitrary however, for the truths Plato believes in are necessary if Reason is real.

Plato has faith in Divine Reason and hence, the Divine Mind. This faith is a committed and specifically interested belief in transcendent meaning and this belief makes the highest praxiological demands on the believer. Plato's philosophy is thus essentially religious. Whilst, historically, Plato's faith in Reason is in no sense Christian, Christianity comes to find a deep sympathy with Plato from the outset of its theological formation, as can be seen in Saint John's faith in *Logos*. To early Christian theologians this sympathy was obvious, despite the equally obvious fact that Plato was a pagan.

Plato's beliefs are carefully reasoned out, and yet, they are held to with an interest, courage and passion that goes beyond what the best powers of human reasoning can finally tie down. Plato implies that no true belief stance can be held to without great existential courage. For this reason Plato despises manipulative sophistic illusions, rejects skeptical attempts at belief suspension, and boldly seeks to articulate transcendent myths. These myths reflect Plato's central, though unstated, belief in the validity, knowability and necessity of transcendent truth. Transcendent truth is knowable, yet, as it is the only grounds of what we can truly know, transcendent truth is not demonstrable via perception or any other 'merely natural' means.

If one does not start from this position of faith in reason, one cannot reason meaningfully at all. Without faith in reason, all perception and all language must seem to be meaningless self-generated chimeras. From here, however, the belief that language, perception and reason are chimeras cannot be held to as being true. For if one does not assume a knowable Meaning metaphysically prior to the flux and contingency of temporal natural existence in which human thought and language is

---

throws responsibility for the decision of belief on to the reader, but it is done with specific craft in order not only to encourage a commitment, but to provide an indirect opportunity for the reader to judge truly in her commitment of belief. Though it may appear so, the concealment of the author's beliefs is not a function of aimlessness or ignorance at all. Someone who intricately argues any cause for a price, under the conviction that truth cannot be known (a Sophist as Plato defines them) is very different to someone who believes truth can be known, but that the searcher must not rely on any human teacher to gain a false dogmatic certainty. In this manner, Plato and Kierkegaard seem very close. See Kierkegaard, *The Point of View*.

situated, there is no true and no false. Reason as sophistic manipulation cannot be true. If someone is not prepared to believe in knowable truth and meaningful reason, whatever the difficulties of understanding how we know truth may be, they can have no meaningful intellectual engagement with you that aims at a true knowledge of reality.

Consider these three beliefs:

1. If reason and meaning are true, one must have faith in them to reason meaningfully at all. (Hence, no philosopher is serious who uses reason and meaning to argue against reason, meaning and truth.)

2. For reason and meaning to be true, they must transcend the flux and contingency that is characteristic of what is apparent to a merely natural perspective (i.e., modern naturalism is a perspective that cannot sustain faith in reason).

3. For us to know reason and meaning the essence of our mind/being must be embedded in transcendent reason in a manner that excludes the very idea of the merely natural.

These three beliefs underlie Plato's theological and ontological epistemology. This is an approach to knowing transcendent truth that, though not demonstrable, is arguably the only way to have meaningful reason at all.

We will now try and tie in Plato's faith in Reason with a Christian understanding of the relationship between faith and knowledge.

THE EPISTEMOLOGY OF FAITH AND THE EPISTEMOLOGY OF SIN

In the opening section of *Ethics*, Bonhoeffer explores the two trees of Eden and notes that polarized moral categories—good and evil—are only known after sin and are, in an important sense, called forth by the false knowledge, the bad faith and the pretentious autonomy that is sin. Bonhoeffer notes:

> Already in the possibility of the knowledge of good and evil Christian ethics discerns a falling away from the origin. Man at his origin knows only one thing: God. It is only in the unity of his knowledge of God that he knows of other men, of things, and of himself. He knows all things only in God, and God in all things. The knowledge of good and evil shows he is no longer at one with his origin.[13]

---

13. Bonhoeffer, *Ethics*, 17.

Transcendence and Epistemology

Knowing God, and failing to know God, is at the heart of creation, fall, ontological upheaval, ethical tragedy and eschatological hope, which gives the Christian narrative of redemption its meaning. Hence, epistemology and transcendence is of pivotal concern to Christian theology.

Kierkegaard's central exploration of truth—his *Concluding Unscientific Postscript*—finds both sin and faith to be of inescapable epistemological significance.[14] Yet, Kierkegaard's quest to both know and appropriate truth frames the epistemological concerns of sin and faith in existential categories that are at once theological, ontological and ethical. To Kierkegaard sin and faith describe two fundamentally opposed knowing/being/doing relationships with transcendence (i.e., God).

What we could call the epistemology of faith encounters transcendence, within a relational context of trust in God, as the gift of Life. Here God who transcends created reality grasps us and illuminates us with life-giving truth.[15] Receiving this gift is not grasping a discrete gnostic illumination, for knowing, being in relation, and doing are here seamlessly integrated. What we could call the epistemology of sin, as the opposite of the epistemology of faith, grasps knowledge of the transcendent according to the natural lights of 'autonomous' human perception and reason alone. This is the obvious approach to transcendence for what Saint Paul calls "the natural man"[16] for, as Kierkegaard notes, "direct recognizability is paganism."[17] And where "the natural man" has, in Bonhoeffer's terms, "fall[en] away from the origin," then it makes sense to understand this "life" in Heideggerian categories, as inescapably existentially defined by Death.[18] Under the existential ontology of Death, Nietzsche also is right to see the "life" of "natural man" as a ceaseless struggle in which we create the endless tragedy of moral values as the stage on which we pursue, via the will to power, our own Homeric virtue.[19]

The temptation in Eden is constructed in deeply onto-epistemological terms. In Eden, pride, the essence of sin, is inextricably tied to both knowledge pursued in attempted autonomy from God and the state of being called death. This knowledge and way of being offers the freedom

---

14. Kierkegaard, *Unscientific Postscript*.
15. That is, with the life giving gift of Himself—note John 14:6; 8:31–32; and 6:53.
16. 1 Corinthians 2:14.
17. Kierkegaard, *Unscientific Postscript*, 600.
18. Genesis 2:17. Heidegger, *Being and Time*, 304–11.
19. Nietzsche, *Will to Power*, 449–50.

of autonomous will to the knower, gives us power to do both good and evil and presumptuously chooses death in order to be "as God." Epistemology and ontology are at the heart of the doctrine of the fall; and orthodox Christian doctrine insists that the fallen way of knowing and being is now 'natural' to us all. Yet, Christian dogma maintains that to simply go with what appears natural to us is to be sinfully blind to divine reality.[20]

From Eden we can surmise that the epistemology of faith rests in the relational attitude of love for God and in the practice of obedient trust in God and receives Life and lives in the real. To know God is to be at one with real Reality, and here, as in the Letters of John, there is only love and light and life, and here alone is true freedom—the harmony of our desire with the Creator's work so that we take joy in being the creatures that we really are. But this joy is deeply unnatural for us, for fallen creation is "subjected to futility"[21] and the real is hard for us to see—we see only the shadows of the real immediately now and we can only know what meaningfully causes those shadows if, as little children, we believe in what we cannot immediately see. On the basis of trust in He who is The Truth, Augustine advocates that we must believe in order to understand.[22] This is in harmony with the Biblical insight that true wisdom and true knowledge only come to us as gifts from God.[23]

Plato's faith in Reason can hence be seen to have much in common with the Christian epistemology of faith. Attempting to approach knowledge 'on our own' and by our 'natural' lights is doomed to failure, and the very categories of truth, meaning and reality dissolve the further along this trajectory one goes.

Having a view of how Plato's epistemology is grounded in transcendence, and a view of how Christian faith grounds true knowledge in devotional participation in God (true Being), we are ready to seek to trace the onto-epistemological movement from the Neoplatonist Christian realism of Augustine and Aquinas to the proto-modern naturalism of Ockham and Descartes.

---

20. Romans 14:23 (whatever does not proceed from faith is sin); 2 Corinthians 5:7 (walk by faith, not by sight); Hebrews 11:6 (without faith it is impossible to please God); John 3:3 (unless one is born anew one cannot see the Kingdom of God).

21. Romans 8:20.

22. Augustine, *The Teacher* 11.37—11.38.

23. Daniel 2:20-22.

A CAREFUL POSITIONING OF DIVERGENCE BETWEEN PLATO AND ARISTOTLE IN RELATION TO EPISTEMOLOGY AND TRANSCENDENCE

Modern realism—both of empirical and rationalist genres—is premised on the belief that the metaphysical and theological knowledge of Man, thinking and/or perceiving entirely within *natura pura*, can demonstrably yield a non-accidental grasp of truth. Whilst both modern anti-realism and post-modern irrealism know this belief to be false, they dismiss realism precisely because they believe there is no other way to truth than by the perceptions and thought structures of our exclusively natural epistemological powers. In this manner modern realism, positivism and anti-realism, and post-modern irrealism demonstrate themselves to be of the one onto-epistemological family.

As the divine—or at least the visible divinity of the heavenly bodies—is inherently natural in Aristotle, nominalist *natura pura* is totally foreign to Aristotle. And yet, it is the rise of natural science—a rise deeply indebted to Aristotle—that is the progenitor of the distinctly modern onto-epistemological approach. For Plato's epistemology is inherently dependent on a human participation in transcendent revelation whilst Aristotle's epistemology is more tacitly, more indirectly dependent on participatory revelation. This, over the passage of time and interpretation, is an important difference between Plato and Aristotle. Further, the material and natural nature of divinity in Aristotle makes the transcendence of divinity markedly less radical in Aristotle than it is in Plato. Hence Aristotle's epistemology permits a functional autonomy to human reason and perception from qualitatively transcendent revelation whilst such an autonomy is notably absent in Plato. Given the enormous influence of Aristotle over the high Middle Ages and Renaissance it seems that it is likely that we can trace the pathway to modern metaphysics as—by the eighteenth century—secular and naturalistic theology, in some measure to Aristotle. More to the point, Aristotle's science and natural theology is transformed by the nominalist transition to knowledge as representation and by the nominalist separation of nature from supernature, yet Aristotle's empirical, rational and theological approaches to natural knowledge are still recognizable in the onto-epistemological outlook of modernity.

I am here suggesting that whilst Aristotle is in no sense modern, modern naturalistic philosophy, theology, and science is, in important regards, Aristotle's offspring. Whilst not wishing to exaggerate the contrast between Plato and Aristotle, not wishing to diminish the genuine novelty of proto-modern empiricism, and not wishing to deny the revival of mathematical Platonism an important role in the formation of modern science in the Renaissance, yet a careful contrast between Aristotle and Plato does uncover important aspects of the story of the development of the distinctly modern onto-epistemological outlook.

Plato opens the Classical era of Greco-Roman thought by dealing such a powerful blow to pre-Socratic intellectual pluralism that the reverberations of that impact are still felt by us today. The idea of a knowable immutable reality, ontologically prior to the mutable uncertainties of appearance, gripped Classical culture. Belief in reason, as a divine, dependable and universally true exponent of this eternal reality, changed Western culture forever. As Burkert points out, Plato's emergence over the pre-Socratics hinges in large measure on his theological genius. Plato was able to provide an intellectually powerful mystical vision that could overcome the collapse of confidence in myth whilst maintaining continuity with the deeply religious rhythms of daily life in the Greek polis.[24]

---

24. The move from poetry and myth to mystical philosophy and religious science was a profoundly religious move, a move displaying Plato's theological genius. In fact, it seems reasonable to hold that Plato invented the conceptual shape of theology that is still powerfully alive in Western culture today. Burkert notes: "Since Plato there has been no theology which has not stood in his shadow . . . [hence] the aura of Late Antiquity and Christianity which thus attaches to Plato has become an embarrassment for many interpreters of classical antiquity" (*Greek Religion*, 321). Burkert maintains that: "The collapse of the authority of the poets and the myth administered by them did not bring an end to religion. It was too intimately interwoven with life. On the contrary, the upsetting of old patterns could actually have a liberating effect for the reflection on things divine: the concept of what is fitting for god had been established since Xenophanes, and with the new pleasure in radical thought one could draw consequences unimpeded by tradition" (ibid., 317). For, "Since Plato and through him, religion has been essentially different from what it had been before . . . through Plato reality is made unreal in favor of an incorporeal, unchangeable other world which is to be regarded as primary" (ibid., 322). And yet, in the *Laws*, Plato's interest in our sublunar situation re-asserts itself in a manner that has profound implications for the marriage of mystical philosophy with science. "Now natural science gained an intellectual, mathematical dimension. It thus enters a surprising alliance with piety. It becomes possible 'to come to the aid of ancient custom with *logos*' (Plato, *Laws* 890d)" (ibid., 326). And so, "astronomy becomes the foundation of religion" (ibid., 327), and "rigorous science and religious exaltation are the same" (ibid., 329). Thus Plato's integration of science and mystical philosophy, in the context where politics, religious piety and daily life were integral, shaped the Classical era in ways hard to comprehend after the advent of nominalism. Burkert sums the situation after Plato up like this: "[In Plato's *Laws*] the essential lines of the situation which was to hold for

Transcendence and Epistemology

Aristotle assumes the validity of this Platonic revolution, yet he puts his religious interests quite discretely into astronomy in a manner that has little interest in the more mystical and personal concerns opened up by Plato's powerful religious consciousness. In culturo-historical terms, Aristotle's religious outlook is out of step with the times as it is the mystical and soul concerned nature of philosophy that grips Classical culture. Such concern provides fertile grounds for Christianity to take root in the Greco-Roman world and by the second century AD "philosophy had come . . . increasingly to mean the search for God."[25] However, the Classical era was, as was Plato, far from dogmatic. Plato's humility in the face of the transcendent mysteries of reality is tacitly present in all of his dialogues. The Classical era, as the early Christian apologists well knew, was only a partial ally of dogmatic universal religion, such as Christianity. In some ways the tied down nature of Aristotle's observations and logic is more compatible with dogmatic certainty than Plato, though Plato's theological insights are certainly more suggestive of the basic tenets of Christian doctrine than are Aristotle's.

Aristotle, an academic fellow with Plato for twenty years, is obviously deeply influenced by Plato, though his intellectual scope and approach is markedly different to Plato's. Yet, Aristotle does not do as well as Plato during the Classical period. During the third century BC Aristotle's scientific philosophy waned in the face of epistemological concerns carried forward by the Skeptics, was displaced by the Stoic and Epicurean responses to skepticism, and was rendered somewhat obsolete by the increasing separation of science from philosophy. This period of philosophical divergence was more or less resolved back into Platonist directions by the second century AD. Yet, whilst important features of Aristotle's thought were absorbed into Neoplatonism, Aristotle did not regain a strong following in his own right until the eighth century in Byzantium. Via that revival, Aristotle found his way to the Islamic world from whence, in the thirteenth century, he conquered the West with great moment.[26]

Interestingly, Aristotle was more influential in the high Medieval era and after, than in the Classical era, and I think there were good reasons for this. The Medieval era was an age of religiously unified belief

---

the next 600 years becomes visible: the conflict between philosophical and traditional religion is denied" (ibid., 337).

25. Marrone quoting E. R. Dodds in *Medieval Philosophy*, 12.
26. See Brunschwig et al., *Greek Thought*, 554–75; 822–41.

with the intellectual certainty and tight rationality that flows from a single meta-narrative of truth. The Classical era was religiously pluralistic, and even in the first centuries of Imperial Christianity, no one ultimate belief frame gained unrivalled dominance.[27] The Classical era was less dogmatically anchored and more inclined towards both skepticism and philosophical mysticism than what followed in the wake of the collapse of its high culture by the sixth century AD. Thus, the Classical era favored Plato over Aristotle and read Aristotle through Plato. And yet, the prominence of Plato over Aristotle in the Classical era sat more naturally with the Greek head of the Roman eagle than with the Latin, more practical, more bureaucratically and politically centralized West. Patristic theological subtlety took a long time to develop in the West, finding its great Latin mind only at the end of the Classical era in Augustine. And whilst Augustine was the towering figure standing over Western Medieval theology, none-the-less, he had a distinctly Classical rather than Medieval mind.

Peter King notes that Augustine laid "the foundations for a new intellectual type of late antiquity: the committed non-dogmatic philosopher" and whilst "later generations [explored and developed] Augustine's account of knowledge, by then a new conception of dogmatic philosophy had arisen."[28] Here King points to one of the chief marks of distinction between late Classical and early Medieval approaches to truth. The old Medieval era was an age of dogmatic certainty where a powerful culturally shared, substantive understanding of meaning and truth, grounded in Christian faith, was more or less taken as given in what remained of its intellectual culture. By the twelfth century the unified cosmological certainties of this outlook in a new intellectual climate ready to take off welcomes a thinker like Aristotle and finds a less didactic and less demonstrable thinker like Plato more obscure.[29] And whilst Aristotle is a

---

27. See Marcus, *Christianity and the Secular* for a very interesting examination of what Marcus calls a secular civic space in which educated Christians and pagans of late antiquity could engage each other.

28. Peter King, from the introduction to Augustine's *Against the Academicians*, xix–xx.

29. Plato does not make his return to the West until substantially after Aristotle, yet the dominance of Aristotle over Plato in the Renaissance—see Schmitt, *Aristotle and the Renaissance*—indicates that whilst Aristotle is by no means insignificant to the Classical era, and Plato is by no means insignificant to the Renaissance, Plato's cultural dominance over the Classical world is as natural as Aristotle's cultural dominance over the Medieval and Renaissance worlds.

much harder fit for Christian doctrine than Plato,[30] yet, the rationality, demonstrability, and tangible/practical focus of Aristotle is far more akin to the rationalist tendencies of the Medieval mind than the more open and less demonstrable Platonist tendencies.

It seems to me that Aristotle takes the immediate apprehension of meaning, as embedded in nature and natural perception, as unproblematically given because Plato has defeated pluralistic irrationalism. Whilst Plato is not dogmatic, remains suspicious of flux in nature, and grounds truth directly in the divine, Aristotle taking—in a manner of speaking—Plato's faith as authoritative, finds natural revelation everywhere and reads nature with supreme confidence. Hence Plato suits a non-dogmatic age but interestingly, his very triumph fosters the kind of certainty that sits easily with dogmatism. And to an age underpinned by dogmatic certainty—such as the Middle Ages—Aristotle is perfectly suited.[31]

Yet, Lloyd Gerson is right: in important regards, Aristotle is a Platonist.[32] The first principles of science, morality, logic and metaphysics are taken as undemonstrable by Aristotle, after Plato's fashion, never as indubitable logical or empirical foundations. But there is nevertheless a difference of emphasis between Plato and Aristotle regarding epistemology and transcendence.

In Plato the Divine Mind illuminates our mind when, in contemplative love, we lay ourselves open to the uncreated light. We turn away from

---

30. This, and its interesting implications, are succinctly pointed out in Milbank's *Reason, Faith and Imagination*.

31. Marcus, *Christianity and the Secular*, notes that after Pope Gregory the Great, the high culture of Western Roman civilization experienced a dramatic collapse and the Church, as the only institution of Roman civilization to survive this collapse, takes on a far more dogmatic and culturally dominant role than was true in the late Classical era of Imperial Christianity. Intriguingly, this cultural dominance and dogmatic simplicity can only be judged as a fall into dark times from the stance of high academic culture. Newman, *The Idea of a University*, 15–17, points out that the new cultural era initiated by Gregory was also one of intense missionary zeal and religious expansion. It seems fair to see the early Middle Ages, maybe as a result of the collapse of high culture, as producing a new missionary zeal resulting in the eventual Christianization of 'barbaric' Europe, from the sixth to the eleventh centuries. In this "dark age" (dark in terms of the collapse of high culture and the disintegration of imperial 'peace') the Christian faith finally gains pervasive sway in Western Europe, and not through imperial power, but through a new age of martyrs, monks and missionaries, coming largely from the far West. By the twelfth century, Western Europe has a totally different culturo-religious landscape from Augustine's time. And its mind set and theology is, correspondingly, very different.

32. Gerson, *Aristotle and Other Platonists*.

the shadows and seek not only the real objects that cast the shadows of perception and human logic but the unseen divine light source of reality itself. The immediacy of divine illumination is more primary than perception and cannot be defined by the fluctuating perceptual manifold. In Aristotle, however, because we have divine illumination, through the divine faculty of reason, and because Nous is believed in and its attractive power is physically manifest in the translunar cosmos, an isomorphic relationship between reality (and there is no discretely spiritual or discretely material reality as such for Aristotle) and our faculties of perception is posited so we can see the true meaning of all that we perceive from the most common place aspects of daily life all the way up to the divine heavens themselves.

So we see that Plato has, arguably, a proto-Christian faith, and certainly has a deeply religious philosophical orientation. Yet, Aristotle is more clearly a pagan theist and is far more scientifically concerned with nature than Plato. Naturally, their approaches to the divine are very different.

What I am driving at is that Aristotle himself is open to being read with a Neoplatonist emphasis that is at least tacitly religiously situated, and equally open to being read with a nominalist emphasis that is primarily scientifically pre-occupied and only has a speculative and academic religious interest. Both of these readings are available and defensible to late Medieval Christians and Renaissance scientists.[33] So, for the purpose

---

33. Interestingly, the Enlightenment view of the emergence of modern science holds that in the late Middle Ages and the Renaissance, if one did not read Aristotle as an unquestionable authority, but rather sought to apply an observational and inductive openness to nature oneself, one was an antagonist of both Aristotle and the Church. This view is not convincing. Schmitt notes that there were, to start with, many Renaissance Aristotelianisms, and it is also clear that one could be an eminent Aristotelian, as Jacopo Zabarella was, and an upholder of Aristotle's own clear fallibilism (see, for example, Aristotle's *On The Soul* 403b 20–23: "For our study . . . it is necessary . . . to call into council the views of those of our predecessors who have declared an opinion on this subject, in order that we may profit by whatever is sound in their suggestions and avoid their errors"). In 1585 Zabarella explains: "I will never be satisfied with Aristotle's authority alone to establish something, but I will always rely upon reason; such a thing is truly both natural and philosophical for us, and I will also seem to imitate Aristotle in using reason, for in fact he seems to have never put forward a position without utilizing reason" (Schmitt, *Aristotle and the Renaissance*, 11). Charles Schmitt notes how William Harvey's "critical and positive approach to empirical knowledge" (ibid., 107) was an integral feature of his deep grounding in Aristotle. Schmitt also notes how the Jesuit school in which Descartes was taught was essentially Aristotelian, yet incorporating Platonistic mathematical advances (the Renaissance was an eclectic

of this chapter, there are two very distinct approaches to epistemology and transcendence that are both historically tied to Aristotle. This needs to be clarified because I recognize the depth and validity of a Christian Neoplatonist reading of Aristotle—as given powerful expression in the *via antiqua* of both Aquinas and Bonaventure—but for the rest of this chapter I am simply going to oppose Christian Platonism with secular naturalism, tracing the roots of that naturalism to the application of a non-Platonist and secularized Aristotelian reliance on observation and logic in science, and, eventually in metaphysics and theology too. For I see Ockham's secular naturalism as deeply influenced by the epistemological confidence of Aristotelian naturalism, and I see the later transformation of philosophy into secular theology as resulting from the background influence of Aristotle's natural theology (his metaphysics and astronomy). Neither of these trajectories towards modernity are, in themselves, fairly attributable to Aristotle—though the seeds of these trajectories are indeed in Aristotle—but it is these trajectories that I am here calling proto-modern Aristotelianism.

EPISTEMOLOGY AND TRANSCENDENCE: THE FAILURE OF PROTO-MODERN ARISTOTELIAN NATURALISM

Aristotle came back to the West in the twelfth century. Then, Jonathan Barnes points out, "for some four centuries Aristotle's philosophy and Aristotle's science ruled the West with virtually unchallenged sway."[34] It is not without significance that this period—the formative pre-modern period—sees the rise of nominalism, the decline of Augustinian Neoplatonist influence, the creation of the modern idea of the secular in Western culture, and the political, economic, artistic, intellectual, technological, social and theological developments that were to give rise to the modern world as we have come to know it. Further, Aristotle's sway, Barnes notes, did not actually diminish from the sixteenth century:

> Scientific empiricism—the idea that abstract argument must be subordinate to factual evidence . . . is largely [derived from]

---

and synthesizing era). Galileo himself despises the "paper philosophers" not because he holds "The Philosopher" in contempt, but because, unlike Aristotle, pedantic natural philosophers, such as Cesare Cremonini, refused to look up from their books and read the book of nature first hand.

34. Barnes, *Aristotle*, 86.

Aristotle. The point needs emphasizing, if only because Aristotle's most celebrated English critics, Francis Bacon and John Locke, were both staunch empiricists who thought they were thereby breaking with Aristotelian tradition.[35]

Barnes' comment is very interesting for it points out that whilst there are a number of strong tensions between late Medieval Aristotelianism and modern science, there is also, contra Bacon and Locke's own assessment of the matter, a direct continuity. Indeed, if the throwing off of Neoplatonism itself is at the heart of the shift towards a modern approach to truth and a more simply scientific Aristotelianism arises out of that shift, then this move starts very early. From the outset of the high Middle Ages old medieval realism—and hence a naive synthesis of dogmatic Christianity and the Neoplatonist realism native to the early Medieval era—had been largely abandoned. Furthermore, it is possible to argue that Aristotle's affinity with the nominalist *via moderna* is not overly forced. The Neoplatonist reading of Aristotle is, as Gerson points out, a highly defendable reading—yet it is still something of an imposition on Aristotle as it does not read Aristotle in his own right but always places his science and logic in a supplementary and derivative relationship to Plato's deeply religious orientation. If, unlike Plato, one finds no reason to hold reason within faith but grants a certain autonomy to reason and faith—as late Medieval Aristotelian theology often did—then a metaphysically Neoplatonist reading of Aristotle can seem merely traditionalist, intellectually regressive and absurdly complicated.

Given that scientific empiricism and philosophical rationalism—often seen as discrete from theology—grew in strength from the sixteenth century and are deeply formative of the modern world we live in, Aristotle as the great authority of logical and empirical thinking from the twelfth century can indeed be seen as having a big impact on Bacon and Locke. But, once reason and logic are treated as having autonomy from the revelation of scripture and church authority it is the impact of applying discretely empirical and logical truth seeking methodologies to theological and metaphysical questions—as distinct from embedding science and philosophy in theology after Augustine's more Classical fashion—that is of particular interest to this chapter. And here a proto-modern Aristotelian naturalism, as informed by the onto-epistemological assumptions of modern empiricism and rationalism, can be seen to underpin Enlightenment metaphysics, theology and science.

---

35. Ibid., 86.

Transcendence and Epistemology

Whilst Aristotle does see first philosophy as theology, and as the most intellectual, primary and highest form of human knowledge,[36] it is evident that Aristotle's theology is not, in any distinctive sense, religiously apprehended.[37] Further, it is arguable that Aristotle's theology/metaphysics is, in a proto-modern sense, scientific. Taylor's involved essay on Aristotle's epistemology argues that—when all is said and done—Aristotle "make[s] perception fundamental to all kinds of knowledge."[38] Where

36. Aristotle, *Metaphysics* 1026a 13–23; *Parts of Animals* 644b 32–645a 4.

37. By distinctly religious I mean involving ritual acts of exchange and communion where the devotee believes that the human and the divine interface in some manner with each other. Aristotle's visible gods—the heavenly bodies—are fit for human veneration, but, as befits their superiority to the mortal realm, they are not interested in us (Aristotle, *Fragments* 18; *Eudemian Ethics* 1238b 27; note also the Aristotelian *Magna Moralia* 1208b 24–35). Aristotle's supreme deity is neither visible (and thus cannot be meaningfully venerated or loved by us) nor concerned with us at all, being completely self-contained, though the object of devotion for the heavenly bodies (Aristotle, *Metaphysics* 1072a 19–1074b 14; note the skeptical 'if' of *Nicomachean Ethics* 1099b 11–17; *On the Heavens* 279a 11–279b 3). This "god of the philosophers" is not the God of Judeo-Christian religion but is an object of scientific speculation. No relational contact is possible between people and this god, and hence I consider this god to be outside of religion. Further, it is clear that to Aristotle, religious practices are sociologically important and thus to be upheld, but cannot be taken to contain or embody anything but the faintest remnants of truth (Aristotle, *Politics* 1314b 39–1315b 4; *Politics* 1335b 12–1 9; *Rhetoric* 1391a 30–1391b 3).

38. Taylor, "Aristotle's Epistemology," 116–42. From the same quote, Taylor, in a very brief fashion, summarizes the texts that most simply point in this direction thus: ". . . an adequate theory, whether theoretical or practical, proceeds from what is better known to us to what is better known (i.e., more explanatory) in itself (*Nicomachean Ethics* 1095 b 2–8, *Physics* 184a 16–18), what is better known to us is what is closer to perception (*Posterior Analytics*, 72 a 2–3), and the move from what is perceived to what is explanatory is carried out by induction (*Topics* 156 a 7–8)." That Aristotle can be credibly read in such a way as to give perception an epistemologically foundational role is crucial to the case I am seeking to make, so this chapter is very indebted to Taylor's carefully argued case in the notoriously difficult scholarly field of probing Aristotle's various musings on the nature of true knowledge. Aristotle's epistemology is difficult, it seems, for two reasons. Firstly, Aristotle is relatively disinterested in complex questions concerning how true knowledge works, as compared with simply getting on with applying careful observation and tight logic to the task of uncovering new knowledge in a vast array of investigative fields. Aristotle is a skilled practitioner of scientific knowledge and thus his understanding of how he does this is tacitly embedded in the craft he practices. Theory and practice are intertwined in Aristotle's epistemology, undergirded by his firm belief that knowledge as we actually experience it is inherently capable of being a non-accidental grasp of truth. So epistemological problems are noted by Aristotle but not seen as particularly important, and at times his stated epistemology is contradictory if one is looking for a unified and self-contained theory of scientific truth. Secondly, if one heeds Gerson's voice, it is highly credible to

knowledge is taken as grounded in perception then Aristotle's view of what little knowledge we can have of the divine can be understood as essentially perception derived, and the divine itself becomes, at least functionally for the purposes of limited human knowledge, naturalistic. The divine, through the mediation of great physical distance and abstract deduction, is here dimly known *about*. Such knowledge is metaphysically and cosmologically speculatively, inferential and naturally apprehended. Hence a non-Neoplatonist reading of Aristotelian natural theology—where one's paradigm for speculation is, after the modern fashion, "reductive, atomistic and [where possible] material"[39]—is an approach to cosmological speculation that is seductively inviting for Medieval and Renaissance scholars of natural philosophy. With Gerson, I do not think this is a justifiable reading of Aristotle, for the background influence of Plato remains strong on Aristotle, even though Aristotle is obviously a profound and original thinker of the first order. Yet, historically it seems that natural theology premised on the autonomy of reason from faith, tied either directly or indirectly to Aristotelian science and logic, leads easily to the separation of reason and faith, and this leads easily to their

---

hold that Aristotle takes an underlying Platonic stance for granted, even if he is often derisive of disembodied perfect Platonic Forms. For the mind/divine dependent notion of form itself, and the participation of our embodied minds in form, is assumed by Aristotle. Following on from this second observation concerning why Aristotle's epistemology is difficult for the modern mind to grasp, we can surmise why the internal difficulties with Aristotle's epistemology were often not so much of a problem for the Middle Ages. In the Middle Ages sensory knowledge is unproblematically believed to provide a non-accidental grasp of truth because human knowledge itself is ontologically situated within God. Here, the epistemological questions that so troubled the ancient Skeptics did not arise. However, skepticism returned to the West in the Renaissance because ontology had been removed from epistemology by theology, and then the beginnings of Cartesian doubt also emerged as inherent to naïve perception dependent epistemological foundationalism. For after Duns Scotus and William of Ockham, God becomes a being, not the grounds of being, so divine ontology is separated out from human knowing and we only have 'natural' epistemic resources to draw on when looking for truth. Thus, uncoupling human knowledge from ontic participation in the Divine grounds of being left the early modern scientific outlook very vulnerable to destructive fires of a new and dynamic skepticism, fueled by the recovery of ancient academic *epoche*.

39. This is King's description of Abelard's preferred approach to argument in "The Metaphysics of Peter Abelard," in Brower and Guilfoy, eds., *The Cambridge Companion to Abelard*, 65. Whilst, of course, Abelard and Roscelin before him only have Boethius' Aristotle to draw on, Rubenstein in *Aristotle's Children* is right to observe a new environment of intellectual exploration, contesting "Augustinian" realism, and tied in with Aristotle, harking back to the early twelfth century.

Transcendence and Epistemology

eventual opposition. Aquinas' role here, in the separation of faith and reason is complex, and whilst with Honnefelder[40] I believe Aquinas' influence does indeed open up the pathway for the instrumental rationality of secular modernity, with Milbank, I believe Aquinas' intentions in following a formal separation of faith and reason are inherently theological (i.e., there is no substantial separation of faith and reason in practice in Aquinas),[41] are valid, and did not of necessity lead to secular modernity. Yet historically, the high Medieval theological marriage between dogmatic faith and methodologically independent reason eventually resulted in an unholy and devastating divorce. Reason, as self-justifying, becomes unfaithful to faith, abandons her for faithless truth, and then attacks faith as rationally and scientifically unjustified. Thus free standing and scientific notions of reason give us nineteenth century Protestant Liberalism of Strauss' nature, and progressive atheism of Feuerbach's nature. Yet when autonomous reason has no ontological grounding in divine truth, then truth itself loses traction on the astonishing and the real. For to 'pure' (i.e., faith purged) reason the real itself can only be a speculative inference drawn, without guarantee, from the entirely transitory, meaningless and contingent manifold of that which is logically and sensationally apparent to 'pure' knowing and thinking. So the end result of this marriage and divorce is that reason kills faith and then reason itself dies. For if divine reality is not available to reason and arbitrary contingency is indeed the only reality we can know, what then is the point of reasoning?

I am here arguing that secularized natural theology, where reason is viewed as autonomous from faith and yet able to grasp ultimate truths all by itself, is the cause of our anti-realist metaphysical meltdown, for trying to ground justified true belief in empiricism/rationalism alone (i.e., in secular reason) is simply not doable. This being the case, I am also arguing that viewing reason as autonomous from faith cannot be reasonable. The opposition here is not between faith and reason but between two distinct faith/reason relations to truth. Rational and empirical evidentialism is a type of reason premised on faith in human naturalistically understood intellectual and epistemological powers, whereas rationality and observation seen as natural revelation is premised on faith in God to reveal Himself to us, through every truth. This latter way of thinking is well presented by Bonaventure:

---

40. Honnefelder, "Rationalization and Natural Law," 275–94.
41. Milbank, "Reason, Faith and Imagination," 11–12.

Faith's Knowledge

> All correct understanding proves and concludes to the truth of the divine being, because knowledge of the divine truth is impressed on every soul, and all knowledge comes about through the divine truth.[42]

Contrary to Bonaventure's intimate and primary understanding of the relationship between the Divine Giver of truth and the human knower and the knower's direct participation in Truth in order to know at all, the type of distant speculative appreciation of the divine consonant with Aristotle's distant and disinterested natural divinity is typical of what Pascal understands to be the abstract irreligion called forth by "the God of the Philosophers."[43] Pascal sees the God of the Philosophers as an idol created by, and in the image of, our own mind and experience.

In Aristotle's defense, it may well be a great intellectual failure to observe nature closely and not be taken in worshipful wonderment. Profound natural insight and self-evident reason may well infer the Unmoved Mover above the universe rotating the celestial spheres by the eternal attraction of pure intellectual love. Yet, the substantive content of Aristotle's basic metaphysical postulates about meaning, purpose, reason and value—the first and undemonstrable truths that underpin his whole system of philosophical science—become increasingly speculative as one seeks greater certainty within knowledge understood only in terms of human perception and formal logic. If you push the critical process of seeking certainty about the undemonstrable foundations of first philosophy to its logical end point then these foundations vanish altogether leaving naturalism itself completely ungrounded in truth.

Aristotle's natural theology, like all of his work, has an enduring profundity and simplicity to it. However, it is clearly theology without faith—that is, without a relational inherence of the devotee in the Divine—and it seeks no religious contact with the Divine but is content to postulate *about* the divine instead.[44] The difference between Plato's cave analogy, where the Sun is hungrily and spiritually sought, and Aristotle's contemplation of the humanly disinterested divine, naturally apprehended, is a

---

42. Bonaventure, *Commentary on the Sentences*, I, d. 8, pars 1, art. 2.

43. Pascal, *Pensées*, 309.

44. See Lubac, *Paradoxes of Faith*, 18. "Faith does not offer us a theory more beautiful than the philosophers': it raises us above theories. It has us breaking their circles. It makes us escape the limits of our own minds. It carries us past all sublime views on God to God himself. It establishes us in Being. Now this, which alone matters, only faith can do."

Transcendence and Epistemology

profound difference. And the spiritual concerns of Plato uncovered by his desire to probe into the human experience of death as seen in *Apology* and *Phaedo* is simply not there in Aristotle. The natural—ensouled matter beneath the orbit of the moon—is entirely enough for Aristotle when it comes to understanding the human lot. There is no religious hunger for God in Aristotle and nothing to be gained in contemplating the daemonic as it manifests in human affairs.[45] Death, love and religion are all entirely natural themes pointing to nothing beyond themselves for Aristotle. It is only astronomy—a distantly observing art, totally unconcerned with humanity—that fires Aristotle's being with religiously framed worship.

That is, having Aristotelian knowledge *about* God is to speculatively construct the idea of "God" to the best of our epistemological, theoretical and imaginative powers—and such a construct may well be not too far from the target of Heidegger's critique of onto-theology.[46] *Knowing* God, however, in the Judeo-Christian religious tradition, is a very different affair. To know God in the manner in which "a man speaks with his friend,"[47] in the direct and intimate terms of "our Father,"[48] is *not* dependent on our mental constructions of 'what' God is. For, to Judeo-Christian belief, God is a 'Who' rather than a 'what', and as *The* personal subject, He can only be actually known by us in the categories of interpersonal relation. Further, God's 'what'—if He does indeed transcend the universe itself—remains infinitely uncontainable by our finite minds.[49] To know God in this specifically religious and relational manner is to receive His self-revelation in the inter-personal terms of love in which He reveals Himself, rather than the terms of cognitive capture which are of metaphorical importance (and this is of real importance) but can simply

---

45. To speak of the daemonic here is to use the term with Aristotle's meaning; purely as a mysterious unintelligible psychic energy, found in all living things. See Aristotle, *On Divination in Sleep* 463b 12–14.

46. See Westphal's fascinating book *Overcoming Onto-Theology* for a wonderful re-claiming of the orthodox doctrines of creation and sin via counter-enlightenment philosophy.

47. Exodus 33:11.

48. Matthew 6:9.

49. An interesting tying together of revelation and apophaticism can be seen here. The 'Who' of God is knowable and even effable in the relational mystery of the self-giving *Logos* of God who is love. God, as Person, is no formal entity about which we can only assume apriori and empty knowledge. However, the 'What' of God, outside of specifically personal and revealed term, remains forever beyond our propositional knowledge. Yet, within the 'Who' revelation of divine love, God does reveal to us analogical 'whats' *about* 'who' He is.

not actually capture God as an object enclosed within our intellect. So the 'how' of 'who' knowledge is not essentially sensory information or rational comprehension but love. But because the 'who' of God and the 'how' of love (whom God also is) is the onto-epistemological grounds of created reality, there is no derivative 'what' knowledge given to us that is not embedded in God, who is love.[50] Hence, Origen insists, true knowledge is love, and any 'what' knowledge abstracted from that relational context is not knowledge at all.[51]

In Aristotle's theology, scientists distantly observe the realm of the divine via natural means (i.e., astronomy). There is a reverence, a humility, and an admiration for the divine here which seems much removed from the faithless and disinterested objectivist stance of modern secular reason. Yet, faith, as trusting, interpersonal responsiveness to the desire of God for us is no concern of Aristotle's, for whilst we desire the divine, Aristotle's God does not desire us. And besides, our existential context is always bounded by the sub-lunar (the realm of mortal nature, as differentiated from the realm of immortal nature) even though the human faculty of mind is divine and hence attune in harmonic resonance to the intellectual music of the Heavens. Aristotle's visible divinities are pagan, for these divinities do not transcend nature—but Aristotle's religious impulses are "above" paganism precisely because they are *not* religious but are discretely philosophical, dealing with divinity purely as a distant and discrete object of speculation for the admiring mind.

Nominalist individualism, the separation of faith from reason, and the emergence of discretely natural philosophy all developed in an intellectual culture nurtured by Aristotle's central role in European universities in the late Middle Ages and the Renaissance. And so a distinctly philosophical approach to the ultimate questions of metaphysics, discrete from religion, becomes embedded in the ground out of which Enlightenment philosophy sprang. Aristotle is thus taken out of a Christian and Neoplatonist interpretive framework and his approach to natural knowledge

---

50. See Pope Benedict XVI's Encyclical Letter, *Deus Caritas Est* for a clear statement of the centrality of "God is love" to the way the Christian encounters reality. Whilst Pope Benedict XVI does not specifically examine epistemology in this encyclical, his Augustinian emphasis on divine, desiring love as the foundation of all reality is both deeply non-foundationalist in a modern epistemological sense, and fully within the *via antiqua* of Bonaventure and Aquinas in relation to the primary place of lived religion, as true philosophy, as the grounds out of which the gift/revelation of all true reason and knowledge arises for human experience.

51. Crouzel, *Origen*, 99.

comes to undergird the emerging modern perspective that finally posits a discretely "rational" way of understanding ultimate reality—philosophy (i.e., ontotheology). From here, the "rational" ways of pure and practical reason are increasingly thrown against the "irrational" religious way of the substantive belief content of traditional Christian faith. The "rational" becomes the "natural" within its discrete sphere of secular knowledge and the "irrational" becomes the "supernatural" within its discrete sphere of authoritative (yet inherently suspect) religious postulates.

Taylor rightly observes that Aristotle's epistemology is grounded in his very naturalistic understanding of the human soul. From this grounding his empiricist epistemological foundationalism works well, within its limits, provided one does not push the question of how one knows the truth of the undemonstrable premises of knowledge. This truth and all teleological meaning is somehow infallibly inferred without demonstration from perception in Aristotle.

Aristotle's disinterest in skeptical epistemological concerns about perception and his disdain for Platonic spiritual notions of the human soul means he sees no reason to get tangled in the kind of problems of uncertainty and mystical revelation that Plato grappled with. Hence, it is possible to be Aristotelian and straightforwardly assume a valid equation between what perceptually and logically *is* with what morally *ought* to be and with what is inherently *meaningful*, and to find a more or less naïve empiricism the only sensible stance to take on truth. This integration sees knowledge analogically rather representationally—and so is not modern knowledge—and yet the self-contained naturalism of this stance translates easily into the science of *natura pura* and the development of representational knowledge common to nominalist science after Ockham. Whilst it is arguable that Aquinas' great genius was precisely in his ability to give Aristotle's appreciation for nature the theological grounding in the doctrine of creation that it needs in order to hold the connections between is, ought and reason in place, yet the nominalist separation of the natural from the supernatural is Aquinas' treatment of Aristotle in reverse. In both cases, Aristotle's natural philosophy exerts powerful influence and in both cases the transformation of the Stagirite is theologically motivated.[52]

Without a religious grounding any practical knowledge of primary truth Aristotle may seek—notably, knowledge of the *summum*

---

52. See Perrier, "Duns Scotus Facing Reality," 619–43, for a sensitive account of the theological concerns that motivated Scotus' philosophy.

bonum—is all derived naïvely from perception, from tight logic and from wise opinion even though the higher up and further away from sensory immediacy such knowledge moves the more speculative and less testable it gets and the more we must take on faith that such speculations are undemonstrably true.[53] This 'faith' is faith in our own mind. We must have faith in the perception and logic—the divine faculties of the human and embodied mind—that is the dependable natural grounds of the wise opinions of higher metaphysical speculation.

Pascal and Kierkegaard are withering in their dismissal of such faith.[54] Pascal notes that as the many incommensurable philosophical notions of the *summum bonum* indicate, there is no natural objectively empirical or unequivocally ration way of distinguishing between mere speculation and primary truth. Confidence in the natural powers of the human mind to truly grasp (let alone demonstrate) primary truth, let alone transcendent truth, is badly misplaced. But it is so seductive! We think our intellectual powers to be divine and so we attribute to our own nature (and the natural limits of human knowledge) a hubristic natural divinity. Unjustified confidence in the autonomous powers of the natural mind to grasp and contain the divine is a seductive possibility in Aristotelian approaches to metaphysics. As beautiful and noble minded as Aristotle's philosophy is, nevertheless, from the Judeo-Christian perspective, it risks the hubris of Babel: the attempt to climb to and seize Heaven, by sheer natural ingenuity.[55] The Biblical narrative sees such an endeavor as

---

53. Aristotle notes that "Of substances constituted by nature some are ungenerated, imperishable, and eternal, while others are subject to generation and decay. The former are excellent and divine, but less accessible to knowledge. The evidence that might throw light on them, and on the problems which we long to solve respecting them, is furnished but scantily by sensation; whereas respecting perishable plants and animals we have abundant information, living as we do in their midst . . ." (*Parts of Animals* 44 b 21–29). So whilst Aristotle finds the science of the divine to be the first philosophy, and the science of being *qua* being to be the highest, most abstract aspect of theology (*Metaphysics* 1026 a 21–33), yet, because human knowledge is dependent on sensation, more satisfaction for the mind can be readily gained by the study of perishable earthly things. Hence, what Aristotle regards as of primary importance in understanding the first causes of the whole natural cosmos, is also least accessible to mortal knowledge.

54. Pascal, *Pensées*; Kierkegaard, *Unscientific Postscript*.

55. "The Inklings" were very interested in this Tower of Babel pattern in the history of civilization. Their penetrating imaginative treatments of this theme rewards contemplation. See Lewis, *That Hideous Strength*; Williams, *The Greater Trumps*; Tolkien, *The Lord of the Rings*.

doomed to end in the fragmentation of meaning itself and the disintegration of civilization's unifying creative powers.

Yet before secular natural theology leads to the curse of Babel it leads to the abandonment of the knowability of transcendence itself. The comment famously attributed to Laplace, that he had no need of the hypothesis of God, is the natural outcome of finding perception to be the sole grounds of knowledge and of finding human logic to be self-sufficiently true. The transcendent becomes, at best, an extraneous hypothesis that those who so wish to can believe in. But, in reality, the mere idea of God has no relevance to knowledge and practice as autonomous modern Man actually thinks and lives. Tillich points out that our generally assumed naturalistic cosmological philosophy of religion makes "atheism not only possible, but almost unavoidable."[56] Further, as atheistic naturalism has matured in our intellectual culture, the collapse of belief grounded in the immediate and existentially committed knowledge of God ends up fatally wounding meaningful metaphysics, epistemology and theology. From that place of self-corrosive nihilism, naturalism itself, and the very idea of true belief, must fall.

In the final analysis, a secular, non-Platonist Aristotelian naturalistic approach to the knowledge of transcendence fails. And this failure takes down with it any confidence in a true knowledge of reality. This collapse is the end not only of metaphysics, epistemology and theology, but of philosophy, meaning and truth itself. Hypermodern irrealism—though inherently irrational—is the natural outcome of modern naturalistic onto-epistemological assumptions.[57]

THE VIABILITY OF THE PLATONISTIC APPROACH TO AN EPISTEMOLOGY OF TRANSCENDENT TRUTH NOW

Plato's stance on the need to have faith in reason, that is, on the essentially religious nature of philosophy, may be due for another revival. For now that ratio-empiricistic foundationalism has more or less destroyed

---

56. Tillich, *Theology of Culture*, 18.

57. See Frankfurt, *On Bullshit*. Professor Frankfurt wonders if bullshit (consumeristic irrealism) is more prevalent today than it has been in the past, and declines to answer this on the basis that it is an empirical question that is hard to answer. He does, however, note that bullshit is a pervasive feature of modern American life. I maintain that bullshit's pervasive presence is a natural corollary of the epistemological impossibilities of modern naturalism.

Western philosophy and theology, meaningful truth may yet again prove to be something we cannot do without.[58] Plato's rebuttals of both sophistry and dogmatism, grounded in the inherent contradiction of arguing against the transcendent reality of meaning and in an incisive critique of all forms of complacent belief naïvety, are as powerful and as needed today as they were when he first made them. Plato points us again towards the grounding of philosophy in theology, an outlook the so called "theological turn" has some interest in,[59] and that can indeed offer an alternative to postmodern ontological nihilism. But the type of theology Plato points towards—a distinctly religious theology—is very different to first philosophy about "the God of the Philosophers" that proto-modern Aristotelian epistemology and nominalist dualism finds of interest in speculations on the divine and on nature. And if we are to rise to our own Aquinian challenge in the transformative integration of secular reason and Christian faith—that is a baptism of modern science and logic in Christian theology that can give the natural meaning and purpose again, and that can construct a holistic vision of the cosmos that preserves a formal autonomy for doctrine and reason within a substantive unity of faith—then we will need to both discard our nominalist heritage and recover a more humble approach to Christian revelation and authority. We will need a theology of faith as the grounds of reason. As religious practice is, as Pierre Hadot points out, very much the original soil of Greek philosophy anyway, this call back to the grounds of faith for reason and civic practice is simply radical, not revolutionary.[60] Plato is a natural starting point in thinking about what such an approach may entail.

Living in a mythopoetic culture that was largely post-religious in its learned class and being fully unconvinced by the polytheism and degenerate religious anthropomorphism of his own religious heritage, Plato shows us a religious attitude that is yet bereft of a religion worthy of his devotion. That God is one, that God is entirely Good, that our souls (mind and distinct personhood) are derived from God, that God reveals Himself to us in our every true perception, thought, relation and act-these Plato tacitly believes and these ground his reasoning and questing to know and live truth. It is the Judeo-Christian religious heritage that recognizes so much of the God that Plato seeks (and Plato even seems to

---

58. See Kierkegaard, *The Sickness Unto Death*; Berger, *Facing up to Modernity*.
59. Janicaud, et al., *Phenomenology*.
60. See Hadot, *What Is Ancient Philosophy?*

know something of Christ as Christianity finds Him).[61] Plato's faith—unlike Aristotle's—is implicitly faith in God. And God, or at least the Forms in the Mind of God, is known to Plato via his immediate participation in the Mind beyond his own mind when he thinks truly. Yet Plato is, at least in terms of Abrahamic religion, a pre-religious devotee of God. For these reasons, Augustine, by providing a specifically religious fulfillment of Plato's vision of philosophy, develops the essence of Plato's outlook far beyond Plato. Augustine incorporates Plato's intellectual vision of the transcendent God into a specific historical revelation where God redemptively acts in "our" space and time. And so the barrier of heaven is sundered from above. The Divine is revealed in historical and human manifestation, and the Divine actively transforms us in Augustine. The grace of Theo-centric redemption and the notions of communion and communication with the Divine (comprehensible for all who believe, not just those very smart people with the liberty of contemplative leisure) are radical religious developments beyond Plato. But Plato's philosophy, as religious in form and aspiration, points to these specifically religious developments.

If the genealogy of modernity is as John Milbank describes it (and I think it is) then the breakdown of truth and meaning our culture is enmeshed in can be traced very closely to our secular and naturalistic epistemological foundationalism. At the logical end point of that philosophical tradition truth can no longer be believably grounded in anything more substantive than the inherent uncertainties of appearance, and meaning can no longer be grounded in anything more significant than the solipsistic semantic constructions of speculative imagination. Truth and meaning now break in our hands every time we seek to use them in any serious manner that is more than merely conventional. From here we can only have meaningful truth and true meaning if truth and meaning are understood in an entirely different way to the nominalist naturalistic trajectory of modern Western culture. There is now no viable belief possible in any equation of a true knowledge of the real with our secular epistemological modern heritage.

---

61. Consider the perfectly just man who is crucified in Plato's *Republic*, Book II, 361b–362c.

CONCLUSION

To be post-secular is to find secular reason not only unsatisfactory but unbelievable. If postmodern irrealism makes truth itself an impossible discourse, and if at least anti-realism must follow from any self containedly anthropocentric epistemological stance, then disbelief in *Logos* follows naturalistic secular reason as night follows day. That is, secular reason denies that reality is—as far as we can know—embedded in Reason. Such a stance makes reason itself unbelievable; but who can reasonably believe that reason is unbelievable? Surely this is a perverse inversion of Augustine; dogmatically dis-believing in order to not understand? Such anti-realism is also a fundamental affront to the orthodox Christian doctrine of *Logos*—a doctrine that great Christian mystics, ordinary humdrum Christian believers, and even your average modern pagan nature lover, all have persuasive grounds to trust.

Divinely given knowledge of transcendence is foundational to philosophy in the Platonist trajectory. In contrast, I have sought to show that a non-Platonist reading of the Aristotelian naturalistic trajectory falsely believes that transcendent knowledge can be attained by epistemologically anthropocentric natural means. This misplaced confidence leads eventually to the abandonment of the knowledge of transcendence itself. Without the knowledge of transcendence, philosophy falls into meaninglessness and language, reason and science have only an arbitrary and pragmatic coherence that can reveal no true knowledge of the real. This state of profound ontic meaninglessness and epistemological ignorance—which we are now in—can only be withdrawn from if we are prepared to ditch the very notion of modern nominalist secularity and take the turn to religion very seriously.

But this raises a question: how serious are contemporary philosophers and theologians about turning to religion? Do we still allow the intellectual norms of modernism to demarcate theology from philosophy? This chapter has sought to argue that the very idea of any strong demarcation between faith and reason is inherently fatal to both. Hence, if the line of reasoning I have sought to articulate has any significance, then theology should stop trying to be a non-faith speculative exercise after the model of secular naturalistic philosophy and philosophy should realize that without faith there is no reason.

2

Plato against Ontotheology

INTRODUCTION

FOR HEIDEGGER, WESTERN METAPHYSICS from Plato to Nietzsche epitomizes abstract intellectual hubris. Here, the Western metaphysical tradition is synonymous with ontotheology—an idealized and theoreticized false capture of Being and God by an "all too human" philosophy. This chapter will affirm the Heideggerian critique in so far as it applies to the philosophical hubris of the great currents of Western secular metaphysics and speculative theology from the fourteenth century to the twentieth century. However, I shall argue that Heidegger is far too sweeping in his dismissal of the history of Western metaphysical belief and Heidegger lacks sensitivity to the religious depth of Plato's metaphysical position.[1] Thus, this chapter seeks to bring a nuance to bear upon the totalizing tendency of the Heideggerian critique of ontotheology particularly in relation to the rejection of Western metaphysics *in toto* as ontotheologically infected "footnotes to Plato."

Two avenues of pitting Plato against ontotheology are pursued.

Firstly, Plato is viewed in sympathy with Heidegger's opposition to ontotheology. Because Plato never was modern he does not suffer from the epistemological foundationalism, the egocentric subjectivism and

---

1. To argue that Plato's metaphysics makes a pretentious and delusional religion out of philosophy (ie., Plato's metaphysics is ontotheology) is a very different thing from arguing that Plato's religious way and outlook implies a set of deeply held metaphysical beliefs (ie., Plato's "philosophy" is essentially doxological and praxiological and not philosophy at all in the modern and rigidly secular terms of speculative idealism, rationalism or empiricism etc.).

43

the nominalist sacred/secular divide that leans modern metaphysics and theology so easily towards ontotheology.

Secondly, and more profoundly, Plato is viewed in opposition to the anti-metaphysical stance of the counter-Enlightenment. Plato's "philosophy" is completely premised on a small family of allegorical, yet substantive, metaphysical beliefs—beliefs Plato finds necessary for reason, morality, craft and natural philosophy, but beliefs in no way established by human thought, morality, craft or observation. Hence, the rejection of metaphysical belief itself is mere sophistic babble to Plato. Given Plato's very strong grasp of the necessity of divinely given allegorical belief as the grounds of human reason, Plato rejects the totalizing scope of the critique of ontotheology and challenges metaphysical unbelief.

So Plato is of interest to us now if we seek to uphold the useful critique of modern reason brought forward by the counter-Enlightenment, and he is of interest to us now if, in a post-secular manner, we are a bit "over" the forceful dismantling of all metaphysical beliefs and are prepared to try tentative restorative moves towards meaningful beliefs concerning truth and reality.

However, in deference to the counter-Enlightenment, I wish to point out that I am making a limited claim in this chapter for Plato's antagonism towards ontotheology. I am not claiming that Plato cannot be read in an ontotheological manner, nor am I denying the general claim that the long Western traditions of metaphysics and theology have often demonstrated ontotheological tendencies. For I believe that ontotheology—as idolatry—is a perennial tendency in 'normal' human belief. But I am claiming that Plato can be read very convincingly as a pre-Christian advocate of spiritual humility and of the epistemology of revelation and faith as situated within the contemplative stance of worshipful devotion to God. Plato can be convincingly read within the tradition of "doxo-ontological"[2] belief—from Justin, Origen and Augustine through to Bonaventure and Aquinas—that has no truck with ontotheology. This is the tradition of contemplation as *worship* and it does "dance and sing." And this is a tradition of belief that I think it would now be profitable for us to carefully re-explore.

---

2. This is Michael Hanby's valuable term. See his *Augustine and Modernity*, 67.

A POST-SECULAR APPROPRIATION OF HEIDEGGER'S CRITIQUE OF ONTOTHEOLOGY

Before looking at Plato, I will seek to explain what I am and am not taking from Heidegger's notion of ontotheology.

Heidegger is, at least, a counter-Enlightenment aesthetic existentialist of the Void. Heidegger's opus grapples with a profound sense of crisis in the truth and reality belief traditions of nineteenth and twentieth century Europe. He tries to re-cast the lack in twentieth century Western epistemological, metaphysical and theological belief adequacy as a positive existential virtue and styles this re-casting as a recovery of pre-Socratic thought. Heidegger thus finds his own historical grounding in Western thought salvageable via a poetic pre-Classical restitutionism. This being the case, Heidegger has a very complex relationship with Classical thought.

Heidegger is a crisis thinker. The underlining profound inadequacy of all Western theological and metaphysical traditions from Plato to the present is upheld and yet a continuous interest in what went wrong with that heritage pre-occupies Heidegger. On the one hand, his crisis stance often makes his interpretation of Classical thought hermeneutically incredible;[3] on the other hand, his very philosophically deep speculative analysis of the Classical and pre-Classical worlds of thought, re-contextualized as a medium for his penetrating contribution to twentieth century thought, makes it impossible to simply dismiss his wild interpretive claims. This complexity is probably why so few serious critical studies of Heidegger's understanding of Plato have been undertaken.[4] Further, such studies are simply not that profitable for Heideggerian scholarship where his reading of Plato is primarily a window onto Heidegger's thought; and such studies are also more or less irrelevant to serious Classical schol-

---

3. Collingwood and Gadamer, for example, come to mind as far more careful interpreters of the meaning of Classical thought in its historical belief context than Heidegger.

4. In *Heidegger and Plato,* editors Catalin Partenie and Tom Rockmore note the obvious fact that "Heidegger's views of Plato are extremely complex" (p. xix). Further, Partenie and Rockmore note: "With rare exceptions, Plato scholars are not usually interested in discussing Heidegger's admittedly unorthodox views" (p. xxiv). Yet, there is some penetrating critical work in this area. See Gadamer, "Plato," in *Heidegger's Ways,* 81–94; Peperzak, "Did Heidegger Understand?" in *Platonic Transformations,* 57–112. In terms of the manner in which Heidegger misreads philosophy in the Middle Ages, and hence that era's theological and Christian appropriation of Plato, McGrath's *The Early Heidegger* is outstanding.

arship on Plato, which has no commitment to Heidegger's distinctive, somewhat a-historical interpretive stance.

For the above reasons this chapter does not enter into a serious engagement with Heidegger regarding his controversial reading of Plato, and does not explore the often fascinating and profound nuances of Heidegger's ontotheological critique; only one merit and one failure of Heidegger's ontotheological critique is taken up here. The merit of ontotheology is its insight into the delusional hubris of all reductively philosophical and distinctly modernist truth constructs. The failure of Heidegger's critique of ontotheology, however, is Heidegger's post/modernist blindness to the role of faith in non-reductively philosophical, non-post/modern, non-secular truth and reality beliefs. This is a critical failure in relation to Plato, for, as I hope to demonstrate, Plato is a deeply religious thinker and his thought is premised on faith. If this can be demonstrated then Plato is of far more interest to us when read in a post-secular context than he is read merely in a postmodern context. Following a post-secular line of interest then, this chapter draws what it finds of use from the concept of ontotheology not directly from Heidegger but from Westphal's distinctly faith concerned appropriation of Heidegger's critique of philosophical and theological hubris.

Merold Westphal's appropriation of Heidegger's ontotheological critique is sympathetic to Heidegger, based on strong scholarship, and—unlike Heidegger—very clear in its substantive belief implications. Most importantly for the post-secular stance of this chapter, Westphal's argument is grounded in religious faith. That is, it is an appropriation more able to understand Plato's thought as rising from proto-religious faith than our modern secular assumptions about philosophy typically allow.[5]

In *Overcoming Ontotheology* Westphal convincingly argues that the hermeneutics of human finitude and suspicion underpinning Heidegger's critique of ontotheology are philosophically very powerful and can be profitably aligned with the Christian doctrines of human createdness and

---

5. Westphal has no interest in Plato in *Overcoming Ontotheology*. Rather, Westphal is interested in showing where the critique of philosophical hubris aligns with Christian doctrine. Yet in his paper "The Use and Abuse of Metaphysics for the Life of Faith" (read at the University of Nottingham's Centre of Theology and Philosophy's second annual conference, Granada, September 2006) Westphal makes it clear that faith must have an aspect of substantive belief content that is metaphysical, though faith and ontotheology are anathema. Again, his Granada paper makes no reference to Plato but the stance, 'oppose philosophical hubris, embrace metaphysical belief by faith' is clear in Westphal and it is that stance that I apply to Plato in this chapter.

the fall. As creatures, we have no direct access to a God's eye view of reality; all aspiration to a knowledge of final truth, constructed in terms of purely human framing and limits, are hubristic. As fallen creatures our fellowship with the Divine Person who alone can give us truth is always to some extent incomplete—even where we are caught up in the redemptive and sanctifying grace of God—so any total vision of truth is pretentious and our fallen capacity for self-deception must be assumed to be at least partially active at all times. Yet, in the broader context of Christian belief, placing no confidence in human truth constructs does not imply that belief in God's powers of revelation are excluded when it comes to true beliefs—be those beliefs about physics or metaphysics. Whilst all human beliefs are indeed constructed in the terms of human history/language/culture and framed by the epistemological limits of our thinking perceptions, such constructs and limits need not imply the absence of truth, but—given Divine inspiration—can furnish the grounds for valid working metaphors of truths that are, indeed, in some measure, of Reality.

So the concept of ontotheology I am drawing from Westphal savagely attacks the pretensions of any notion of a divinely un-aided grasp of truth and limits any divinely aided grasp of truth to the realm of partial metaphor rather than total knowledge capture. This stance holds that the humility of faith is central to any view of truth and reason but rejects the self-defeating assertion that all views of truth and reason are false.

From here, then, we largely leave Heidegger behind and move towards Plato with Westphal's understanding of ontotheology in mind.

PLATO AND THE APOPHATIC AND PERSONALIST TRADITION OF THE GREEKS

In order to re-frame Plato outside of the belief limits of a secular counter-Enlightenment crisis stance, let us first see if we can think of Plato as a philosopher who is not, in any purely philosophical sense, an Idealist.

John Macmurray's fascinating work, *Persons in Relation*, links true knowledge to the mode of our existence, the personal mode. In this he is somewhat following the theological vision of Buber,[6] somewhat following Kierkegaard's analysis of the self and of knowledge as relational,[7] and

---

6. Buber, *I and Thou*.
7. Kierkegaard, *The Sickness Unto Death*; Kierkegaard, *Unscientific Postscript*.

is somewhat followed in the philosophy and sociology of science by Michael Polanyi.[8] Truth understood in the existential mode of personhood is rational, but rationality itself needs to be understood holistically here (i.e., including the logic of human emotion, physicality and spirituality and as always situated in language and community in space and time). In this line of thinking, to think of truth in terms of discretely objective empirical knowledge or of supposedly pure intellectual formulations is a hopeless reductionism and simply unreal. A Personalist line of thought thus seeks to recover truth in the mode of the person. Along these lines it is not difficult to argue that Plato was no abstract Idealist but was also very aware of the personal mode of human existence and knowledge. Yannaras finds apophatic Greek thought embedded in this personal and humble existential mode, so why should this mode not apply to Plato? Yannaras states:

> In the case of the Greek philosophical tradition, from Herakleitos up to Gregory Palamas, we may characterize apophaticism as the denial that we can exhaust truth in any formulation, the recourse, in other words, to the symbolic-iconological manner of expressing truth, as well as the adoption of the dynamics of *relatedness* (in the sense of the Herakleitean κοινωνειν, i.e., "being in communion") as the criterion for the verification of knowledge.[9]

If one reads Plato within this apophatic tradition,[10] then one sees both halves of Plato—his doubts and his beliefs—rather than finding hubristic Idealism to be what he is really on about and "Socratic ignorance" either an early phase of Plato's thought, or a mere ruse.[11] That is, it seems

8. Polanyi, *Personal Knowledge*.

9. Yannaras, *Absence and Unknowability*, 117.

10. In this work (Yannaras, *Absence and Unknowability*, 105) Yannaras finds Platonism to be guilty of the idealism Heidegger attributes to it. So Yannaras, it seems, does not situate Plato within this Greek apophaticism, even though he finds apophaticism common to much pre-Socratic and Classical Greek philosophy. Yet, Yannaras' reading of Plato's *eros* as idealism is, I think, debatable, even though Plato obviously has—from the perspective of Christian doctrine—a weak appreciation of matter and flesh as creation, and hence does indeed tend to disembody and intellectualize desire. Yannaras equates Plato's spiritual desire for Beauty with abstract, impersonal idealism based on a reading of *Symposium* 211b7-c9, even though Plato in 212a explains that this desire is the path of (*trans.* Jowett) "becom[ing] the friend of God." So I do not think it is fair of Yannaras to equate Plato's de-sensualized 'love of beauty for its own sake' with some passionless, impersonal, ideal "love" outside of relational participation in God.

11. With Cooper in his introduction to *Plato, Complete Works*, xii–xviii, I find

reasonable to hold that Plato's approach to truth—both his caution and his belief—can be more easily understood in terms of Greek symbolic-iconological and relational participatory modes of belief, than it can be understood in more recognizably modern, theoretical and reductively rationalistic modes of belief.

Whilst eternal Ideas and the capacity of the human mind to receive some vision of truth from beyond the flux and contingency of our spatiotemporal context *are* central to Plato's philosophy, his mode of belief concerning Ideas and Reality is not aligned with reductively philosophical or recognizably modern Idealism.[12]

We will now proceed from the general claim that it is reasonable to understand Plato's mode of belief as iconological, personalist and participatory to the specific question, is Plato an ontotheologian?

IS PLATO, IN WESTPHAL'S TERMS, AN ONTOTHEOLOGIAN?

Plato is, of course, no Christian. But for his work to escape Westphal's Christian critique of ontotheology it needs to demonstrate a proper appreciation of human finitude and be appropriately suspicious of the innate purity and goodness of human reason.

Plato and Human Finitude

In keeping with the mode of human existence, Plato pursues wisdom via a carefully calibrated integration of the transcendent with the immanent. This delicate and complex double move is characteristic of all of his dialogues. If one seeks to distil the transcendent kernel from the dramatic, immanent contextual husk in Plato, he appears to be the archetypal hubristic ontotheologian. And yet, if one only focuses on the immanent in Plato, his transcendent oracles appear as mere unsubstantiated fancy and the contingent specificity of context alone grounds his work. Both of

---

the interpretive device of a distinct chronology—early, middle and late Plato—to be fraught with difficulties. In reading the entire dialogues as one work I found a profound unity of approach underlying the often sharp differences in 'doctrine' that can be found between and within each dialogue. So no doctrinally discrete chronology, no Plato I, II & III, is assumed in this chapter.

12. See Gersh & Moran, *Eriugena*, for some refreshingly careful distinctions on a range of very different belief stances commonly lumped together under the heading "Idealist."

these views are one eyed. Plato writes synoptically and the vision of truth he offers has the outer eye grounded in the immanent and the inner eye probing the transcendent; the resultant combination of the inner and the outer, the visible and the invisible, the tangible and the intangible, is the "view" he seeks to communicate. The transcendent cannot be reduced to the immanent, and yet, we can only seek to grasp and articulate what the transcendent is in terms of our immanent context, a context not, in its own terms, suited to this aim. Plato sits with this uneasy tension and never tries to reductively resolve it. So whilst Plato does indeed favor the permanent reality of the transcendent over the transitory expressions of that reality in the immanent, he never tries to articulate the transcendent without reference to the limitations of the immanent.

After the cultural dominance of the totalizing and reductive metanarrative of rationalistic and objective scientific truth, grounded in epistemological subjectivism and authorized by modern secular philosophy, we have become accustomed to viewing Plato through our own reductive, egocentric and totalizing assumptions about truth. But this is our error, not Plato's. We have become so accustomed to reading Plato as a rigidly dogmatic Idealist that we miss the extent to which Plato couches all of his propositions in pseudonyms, in metaphors, in poetic myth, in the terms of humble and dependent religious devotion, in spiritual eroticism and hidden in "Socratic" irresolution. We do not even notice that Plato's voice only comes to us via the suggestive, specifically contextualized, personalized, temporally defined, open ended drama of the everyday.

The banquet in *Symposium*, for example, reveals Plato's literary genius. Plato revels in sensitive dramatic descriptions of the particular specificities of character, time and place. However this context is no mere back drop for the dialogue; rather delight in company and in the pleasures and desires of body and mind shared in the banquet reflect the themes of conviviality, passionate searching and inebriated disappointment that drives the religious love quest of philosophy itself through the dialogue. This synoptic mode of communication—immanently grounded and transcendently concerned—fails if one only sees the "philosophical" point of the dialogue or only revels in the literary genius of its particular culturo-historical construction.

In *Theaetetus* the mind grasps, by a mysterious power of her own, intellectual truth,[13] but the truth grasped is *not* a product of the human

---

13. Plato, *Theaetetus*, 185.

mind, and is not—remember the sun in the cave metaphor[14]—containable by the human mind in anything more than mere shadows or poor reflections, but is from *beyond* the human mind. In *Meno*, the human mind must have some affinity with divinity and have some derivative or pre-existent participatory association with *Nous* (Mind) in order to have the ability to grasp truth at all,[15] but this in no manner gives human *nous* the grasp of Truth that the divine *Nous* both has and generates. Epistemological humility, as in *Theaetetus*, is seen here in Plato expressly not being able to identify how the mind grasps genuinely intellectual truths and in truth itself not being a product of the human mind. Further—as diagrammatically demonstrated in *Meno*—whilst the human mind grasps universal mathematical truths, yet this truth is only expressible by the human mind in concrete examples tied to the realm of contingence, transience and flux in which we live. That is, the pure reality of eternal and unchanging truth is always only expressible by us via the terms of the imperfect realm in which we live. Truth itself is never fully revealed to us via those specific and temporal modes of conceptual mediation in which we must know "our" own thoughts. Truth itself remains essentially beyond conceptual grasp, essentially not egoistically ours, and our approach to its understanding—for we understand only as a result of the self-giving relationship divinely initiated between us and the divine—remains essentially unknowable in Plato.[16] Plato attempts to give us no humanly and temporally defined epistemological certainties and for this reason he totally escapes the critique of epistemologically foundationalist, egocentric, totalizing hubris assumed in secular scientific and philosophical reason that Lyotard finds—in my view validly—so profoundly inadequate. Plato has no ontotheological methodology in relation to how we know truth

14. Plato, *Republic*, 516, "Last of all, he will be able to see the sun . . ."

15. Plato, *Meno*, 82, ". . . there is no teaching, but only recollection"; 86, "And if the truth of all things always existed in the soul, then the soul is immortal."

16. Yet, this is, using Yannaras' terminology, a Greek "apophaticism of the person," not a Western rationalistic "apophaticism of essence" (Yannaras, *Absence and Unknowability*, 29). The interpersonal knowledge, the love of friends, is never a total knowledge about the person—the essence of any person is beyond human knowledge—but this knowledge through personal energies is the knowledge of love, and this is the deepest and truest knowledge. Plato, in worshipful contemplation, knows the divine Good as Mind (Person), in the terms of love, and this is not terms that can ever be conceptually sounded out—not even between ordinary people—by theoretical or rational or scientific knowledge. Henri Crouzel describes Origen's epistemology, fully within this Greek tradition, saying "knowledge is for him the same thing as union and love" (Crouzel, *Origen*, 99).

and makes no claims to have a humanly expressible complete and certain knowledge of truth.

Plato affirms that we need a symbolic-iconological vision of Reality cast beyond the necessary limits of our culturo-sensory knowledge in order to take belief seriously, but we cannot let go of the fact that our attempts to conceptually describe such a vision is not Reality. It constantly surprises me that Plato's clear grasp of both our need for a metaphorical vision of Reality and the fact that our metaphorical vision is not Reality, is not obvious to all his readers. The cave metaphor is, expressly, a metaphor.[17] It is Plato's feeble attempt to articulate his vision of Reality. Plato's Forms are allegorical. Does every tiny hair, Plato asks, have its perfect eternal Form?[18] In *Parmenides* Plato marshals powerful arguments that warn against taking Plato's own theory of forms too literally. Plato recognizes where his metaphors break down. This does not negate the appropriateness of metaphor itself for Plato's purposes but the difficulties that lead to the end of medieval Realism seem largely the result of mistakenly treating Plato's religious metaphors as if they were intended as doctrinal certainties or scientific theories or strict logical treatise. Seeing universals—after Abelard's logic—as mere manners of speaking is to reduce the spiritually suggestive metaphors of universality and unchangability beyond particularity and change, to a simple logical conundrum. It is to seek to define universality and unchangability within the terms of particularity and change, and to then think one has achieved something

---

17. Plato, *Republic*, Book VII, 517, trans. Jowett: "[I have expressed the meaning of] this entire allegory . . . according to my poor belief . . . whether rightly or wrongly God knows." The same passage translated by Lee, 1974: "[regarding] this simile . . . the truth of the matter is, after all, known only to god."

18. Plato, *Parmenides*, 130c,d, Cooper ed., Plato, *Complete Works*: [Parmenides asks] "And what about these, Socrates? Things that might seem absurd, like hair and mud and dirt, or anything else totally undignified and worthless? Are you doubtful or not whether you should say that a form is separate for each of these too, which in turn is other than anything we touch with our hands?" "Not at all," Socrates answered. "On the contrary, these things are in fact just what we see. Surely it is too outlandish to think there is a form for them. Not that the thought that the same thing might hold in all cases hasn't troubled me from time to time." Plato goes on to chide Socrates through Parmenides that in distinguishing between the dignified and the undignified the young Socrates is influenced not by philosophy but by the opinions of others. Even so, it seems clear that the spiritually upward drawing and unchangeable intellectual nature of divine form itself is not meant by Plato to give us a detailed explanation of empirical observations. His interest in form is more religious than scientific.

profound by showing that such things are impossible. Such reductionism misses Plato's point about eternal forms entirely.[19]

Plato and Human Fallenness

Plato's metaphysical analogies are deeply religiously premised and deeply skeptical of human nature, as exemplified in the *Apology*. Socrates is in trouble with the Athenians because he finds human wisdom worthless. Yet Socrates is always seeking to serve Divine wisdom.[20] The terms of human wisdom look solid and concretely grounded on first contact but Plato's Socrates finds they are in fact delusional and so generally accepted human authority, morality and dignity are harmless veneers in humble and charitable people but the masks of oppression and evil in the proud, the ruthless and the self-interested. However, Socrates does not abandon wisdom because of this but serves the god of wisdom in all the difficult to grasp, socially embarrassing, morally troubling and politically confronting pathways down which a devotion to Divine truth leads one. It is the call to humility before divinity and the subversive suspicion of all human knowledge and power constructs that an admiring Plato rightly discerns positions Socrates as a dangerous opponent of the Athenian status quo.

So, if we understand ontotheology through the lens of the Christian doctrines of creation and the fall as the presumption of a total grasp of

---

19. See King, "The Metaphysics of Peter Abelard," 65–125. In no manner do I mean to suggest that Abelard is anything other than one of the most innovative and brilliant thinkers of Western culture. However, the unhooking of Aristotelian logic from Platonistic participation, and the unhooking of language from participation in reality (and the resultant reduction of language to self-contained logical and conceptual games) can be traced, in the West, to Abelard's highly sophisticated nominalist irrealism. This move totally re-defines Classical and Augustinian logic in such a manner to make that logic look stupid. But it is the redefinition of Augustinian participation to operate within a non-Platonist, non-participatory view of Aristotelian logic that makes Medieval Realism look stupid, not Augustinian participation itself.

20. Plato, *Apology*, 23 a, b, "But the truth of the matter, gentlemen, is pretty certainly this: that real wisdom is the property of God, and . . . that human wisdom has little or no value. . . . when I think that any person is not wise, I try to help the cause of God by proving that he is not . . . [thus] my service to God has reduced me to extreme poverty [and public odium]"; 29d: "Gentlemen, I am your very grateful and devoted servant, but I owe a greater obedience to God than to you."; 39b: "When I leave this court I shall go away condemned by you to death, but they will go away convicted by Truth herself of depravity and wickedness."

truth by human knowledge and as the assumption of the intrinsic intellectual goodness of humanity, then Plato is no ontotheologian.

If the case for Plato and his metaphysics being opposed to ontotheology is strong then it has some interesting implications for us in our typically post-counter-Enlightenment metaphysical unbelief context. I would like to touch on these implications below.

A SKELETAL CHRISTIAN AND PLATONISTIC CRITIQUE OF THE CRITIQUE OF ONTOTHEOLOGY

Westphal points out that the hermeneutics of finitude and suspicion characteristic of Heidegger's critique of ontotheology are powerful and much needed negative tools that echo the negative side—the humble appreciation of human limitations—of the theologies of creation and fall. However, unlike these Christian theologies, the modern and secular hermeneutics of finitude and suspicion have no positive side—no view of Divine unlimitedness or human redemption—and therein is their fatal weakness. If all one has is finitude and suspicion, then all limited truth claims within the bounds of finitude and suspicion are mere assertions that must be undercut by their own hermeneutic. And indeed, the complex aesthetic linguistic games of the postmodern masters of textual manipulation revel in this double undercutting of not only their epistemologically naïve totalizing opponents, but of themselves as critics too. Maybe the Sophists are back. But if this is indeed the case, then Plato, slayer of sophistic impiety towards truth, may yet prove to have some of the best positive responses to the vacuum of serious belief generated by post/modernism that we are likely to find.

On the negative side, Plato believes that we can have no conceptual truth in any final or total sense, but on the positive side, Plato equally believes that unless we *believe* that the Person of Divine Truth (*Nous*) can grasp us, we should abandon the very idea of reason.[21] For this reason

21. See *Phaedo* 65-6 in conjunction with *Phaedo* 97-100. 65-6 describes how the senses can give no truth, so the soul must rely on the mind alone for truth when seeking knowledge of those transcendent glories such as absolute beauty and absolute good. Our earth bound epistemological powers cannot be believed in relation to truth, and hence truth cannot be proven in terms of our natural epistemological powers. In 97-100 Socrates explores Anaxagoras' conception of the ontic and cosmological primacy of Mind with great and hungry interest, but is disappointed by Anaxagoras' inability to give persuasive accounts of the goodness and meaning of why all things—as the product of purposeful, good, rational Mind—are. That is, Anaxagoras cannot

Plato against Ontotheology

Plato finds that the Sophists are in the end just not serious thinkers. They are linguistic game players.[22] Plato does not answer a fool according to his folly so whilst he can be as playful as the most able dialectician (and indulges in showing this facility off from time to time) his advice is let the players play and let those who take reason seriously have faith.[23] If we tried answering the positive belief void of secular post/modernism

---

make good on his claim to demonstrate the rational, moral and aesthetic meaning of everything that is created by Mind. But, as Plato sees mind as the essence of the soul (personhood), Plato seeks this Person beyond all appearance whose intelligence is distantly communicated in all Plato experiences. Putting the two cited passages together we may say that Plato believes that Someone akin to Anaxagoras' Mind must indeed be the source of all that is—and this gives our minds whatever powers of reason we do have, and links reason deeply to personhood—but there can be no proof for this belief that is constructed in terms demonstrable to the senses or contained by merely human conceptual logic. Hence, Greek apophaticism is present here; true essence is inexpressible in human speech, only iconic symbols of truth can be communicated by human language. Yet, unless one assumes that truth beyond the transitory, contingent and often meaningless world revealed via normal perception exists, reason (logos)— the human minds derivative intellectual kinship with Mind—is mere illusion too. A tacit participation of our mind in Mind, that cannot be proven or even expressed in the terms of the perceptual manifold and spatiotemporal existence, is everywhere assumed in Plato. Plato assumes that truth beyond our mind, in some measure, grasps our mind directly. This assumption is more explicit in the Neoplatonists and then Augustine—where the Christian terms of faith, belief and God easily take over from intellectual apprehension, reason and Mind—but the commonality between these different sets of terminology is in no manner forced.

22. Plato, *Sophist*, trans. Cooper, 231d: "[The sophist is] an athlete in verbal combat, distinguished in his expertise in debating." 233d: "the sophist has now appeared as having a kind of belief knowledge about everything, but not truth." Plato, *Sophist*, trans. Jowett, 268c,d: "He, then, who traces the pedigree of his art as follows—who belonging to the conscious or dissembling section of the art of causing self-contradiction, is an imitator of appearance, and is separated from the class of phantastic which is a branch of image making into that further division of creation, the juggling of words, a creation human, and not divine—anyone who affirms the real Sophist to be of this blood and lineage will say the very truth."

23. For example, when Plato argues like this: (*Phaedo*, 100b, trans. Jowett) "assume that there is an absolute beauty and goodness and greatness, and the like: grant me this, and I hope to be able to show you the nature of the cause, and to prove the immortality of the soul"—his "proof" relies entirely on the willingness of his interlocutor to have the passionate existential personal interestedness in that which cannot be scientifically or logically demonstrated; this Kierkegaard calls faith (see Kierkegaard, *Unscientific Postscript*). There is an existential leap of trust involved in serious belief formation that cannot be avoided and it is the failure of the Sophists to have that existential belief courage that renders them unable to take any belief, or truth itself, seriously. Reason— as anything other than a sophistic and political manipulative game—depends on faith so understood.

in this manner today we would find humble religious metaphysics may indeed give us a philosophical renaissance that could make serious belief itself worth doing again. And since it is very unlikely that consumerist irrealism will give people anything worth believing,[24] and since it is very unlikely that people can, in the long run, get on without serious belief,[25] such a renaissance may be sorely needed.

So ontotheology as the tacit absolutizing of finitude and a totalizing of suspicion to the exclusion of belief (relational adherence) in the divine Person of Truth, beyond human conceptual grasping, stands in direct opposition to reason itself for Plato. Plato's balance between skepticism towards human reason and participatory trust in divine revelation is necessary for any meaningful belief in truth itself, and it is this balance that makes Plato so easy to appropriate in Christian Classical and Medieval contemplation. Historically, we are now enough out of the shadow of the Enlightenment to understand the nature of our loss of this Christian Platonist tradition quite clearly. A post-secular understanding of how viable this lost tradition still is, is now emerging.

A VERY QUICK SKETCH OF THE FAITHLESS GENEALOGY OF METAPHYSICAL UNBELIEF

Paul Tillich notes a profound historical shift—started with Abelard and locked down with William of Ockham—in the philosophy of religion underpinning Western culture.[26] It is the shift away from an ontological participatory understanding of religious belief and towards a cosmological and nominalistic understanding of religious belief. The return of Aristotle to the West at the same time that medieval realism was fading gave self-contained human logic and perception dependent observation unprecedented belief formation powers. It is here that the "idea" of God first becomes a play thing of secular philosophical speculation, of secular scientific models, and of rationalistic and systematic theology. Here is where modern religious unbelief and the inevitable collapse of any meaningful metaphysical vision starts. Milbank makes a parallel argument in finding secular Western reason to be a nominalist Christian heresy that

---

24. See Frankfurt, *On Bullshit*.

25. See Berger, *Facing Up To Modernity*.

26. Paul Tillich, *Theology of Culture*, "The Two Types of Philosophy of Religion," 10–29.

cannot fail to produce the collapse of both faith and reason in Western culture.[27] Thus the origin of truth shifts away from God and comes to reside in the mind of Man.

It is strange how we tend to think of the end of Ptolemaic astronomy as replacing an anthropocentric cosmology with a radically decentred cosmology when in fact it is the replacement of a theocentric cosmology with a profoundly anthropocentric, nay, egocentric, cosmology that this cosmological belief shift to modernity signifies. Descartes' only solid foundation of belief is the existence of his own ego and hence the explicitly human faculties of thought and perception, referenced to nothing outside of one's own ego's knowledge limitations,[28] becomes the horizon of human meaning within which Kant must work. The West has never been more anthropocentric and it is this modern egocentricism that makes the pragmatic consumer irrealism of hypermodernism work for us. Self-worship, self-indulgence, self-constructed and commodified identities—these are the natural cultural outcomes of our modern egocentric cosmology.[29]

Before this nominalist egoism, Plato's faith in Divine Mind as the transcendent source of all meaning and truth that human minds can—iconologically—apprehend, gives rise to Aristotle's natural science and universal logic. Because Plato's faith in timelessly true, yet temporally and metaphorically revealing *Nous* has defeated the endlessly non-valent imaginative games of pre-Socratic sophistry, serious human reason is able to take off. Ironically, it seems that the great successes of nominalistic Aristotelian[30] reason and observation since William of Ockham, have led to hubris and a cutting off of reason from the essentially religious grounds in which it sits, and this returns us quite neatly to a sophistic frivolity towards reason and reality itself. So, far from science and faith or religion and reason being polar opposites, the real opposition is between faith, reason and science on the one hand, and dogmatic doubt, secular Man, and sheer meaningless irreason on the other hand. It is only the strange desire to either separate or integrate nominalist Christian

---

27. See Milbank, *Theology and Social Theory*.

28. Yannaras, *Absence and Unknowability*, 24: "Descartes . . . instituted the subject as the absolute determinative source of all knowledge and being, and subjected God to absolutized man . . ."

29. See Lasch, *The Culture of Narcissism*.

30. See Gerson, *Aristotle and Other Platonists*, for a persuasive case that a non-Platonist (i.e. nominalistic) reading of Aristotle is a faulty reading.

supernaturalism with secular scientific naturalism that makes faith and reason look opposed. Metaphysics, after Plato's model, as a humbly held, religiously received belief framework in which both the transcendent and the immanent are synoptically united, alone seems to give human belief any true reason and meaning. Plato's metaphysical attitude may be well suited to the most pressing needs for meaningful belief in our times.

CONCLUSION

In this chapter I have sought to demonstrate two things: firstly, that Plato can be validly read in sympathy with an ontotheological critique of modernist secular truth; secondly, that Plato's proto-religious metaphysical stance is not touched by the critique of truth and reality that falls out of the counter-Enlightenment "disenchantment of reason."[31]

If this case is strong, it has some striking implications for the importance of the contemporary study of Plato in our post-secular context, and for a renewed level of interest in the metaphysical tradition of the doxo-ontological appropriation of Plato by Christian Classical and Medieval thinkers. Maybe—via Plato's humble, iconological and participatory belief mode—we can still have meaningful beliefs about truth and reality; and maybe—as Plato suggests—we need to believe in divinely revealed meaningful reality in order to be distinctly human and, at least aspirationally, reasonable.[32]

---

31. I have borrowed this evocative phrase from the title of Paul Harrison's fascinating work on the nineteenth century treatment of Socrates by Hegel, Kierkegaard and Nietzsche. See Harrison, *The Disenchantment of Reason*.

32. Plato, *Phaedo*, trans. Jowett, 90e: "Let us . . . be careful of admitting into our souls the notion that there is no truth or health or soundness in any argument at all; but let us rather say that there is as yet no health in us . . ."

3

Faith in Plato and John

INTRODUCTION

THIS CHAPTER EXPLORES THE ways in which Plato and John share understandings of what faith is and does as well as the ways in which their understandings of faith differ. This chapter hopes to demonstrate that Plato and John have notions of faith that are intimately, even surprisingly related, even though they also have crucial areas of delineation. It also becomes apparent that whilst there are intimate ties between faith and reason in both Plato and John, and whilst what they each understand by reason has some striking metaphysical continuities, yet their stance on reason is epistemologically discontinuous precisely in relation to the different ways they evaluate faith. Thus this chapter seeks to explore the ways in which Platonic and Johannine faith are related and delineated and the findings of this relationship indicate something of how Platonic and Johannine notions of reason are also related and delineated.

These concerns may be of interest to contemporary theology for two reasons. Firstly, theologians working in Patristics and metaphysics may be interested to see to what extent John's outlook on faith has continuity with elements of Plato's philosophy. This chapter maintains that whilst Plato's high rationalistic epistemology is dogmatically problematic to Christian orthodoxy, yet because Plato's outlook is presuppositional and participatory and not foundationalist and objectivist, and because Plato's theological assumptions believe in an intangible divinity which is genuinely transcendence, elements of Plato's metaphysical idealism can be validly appropriated by Christian theology. Thus, John and the early church fathers often negotiate a dogmatically discriminating approach to the assimilation of Plato's heritage in the creation of high Christian theology. Plato is hence a serious formative influence on early Christian theology. Secondly, theologians interested in hermeneutic and postmodern philosophy may find this chapter of interest. John has an emphatically low epistemological approach, where divine revelation is inextricably embodied in word, flesh, history, community, and miraculous singularity. Hence John's approach to faith can be creatively engaged with the explorations of recent theologians sensitive to the crucial role of historical particularity in Christian faith.

However, gaining a workable handle on the term faith itself, establishing that faith is a legitimate word to use in relation to Plato, and establishing that one can reasonably speak of faith in John's gospel are all matters that must come prior to examining faith in Plato and John.

CAN WE SPEAK OF "FAITH" IN CHRISTIANITY?

From the outset it is important to note that there is no simple or single way of understanding what *the* Christian understanding of faith is. This observation does not imply that there are no meaningful Christian understandings of what faith is but rather it emphasizes the richness and complexity of what the word faith can mean in the context of the Christian religion.

In modern translations of the Christian scriptures πίστις is often rendered in English as the noun "faith" and πιστεύω is often rendered in English as the verb "believe." Words broadly meaning faith and belief using the stem πιστ- play an important role in the Christian scriptures where they are used extensively and with no small range of meaning.[1]

---

1. According to Kohlenberger et al., *Greek English Concordance*, different forms of the word πίστις occur 243 times, different forms of the word πιστός occur 67 times, different forms of the word πιστεύω occur 241 times, and various negative words (such as ἀπιστέω, ἀπιστία, ὀλιγόπιστος) occur 48 times in the New Testament. Altogether there are 599 uses of belief/faith words with the stem πιστ- in the Christian scriptures. The New International Version translates these words into variants of believe, belief, believe in, believe on, faithful, faith, proof, pledge, trusted, trustworthy, reliable, relying on, committed, sure, etc. According to Metzger, *Lexical Aids*, 1, there are 137,490 words in the twenty-first edition of the Nestle Greek New Testament. Excluding definite articles etc., Metzger's most frequent category of New Testament words are those used over 500 times, most of which are common words used in Greek. The next category of high frequency words is those of over 200 usages. Here significant theological words such as λόγος and πνεῦμα are found, and in this frequency πιστεύω and πίστις

Faith in Plato and John

Because this word family is so important to the living Christian religion and because these words have complex meanings in their original scriptural settings, these words now carry elaborate and diverse histories of interpretive, praxiological and doctrinal development which have been in continuous motion for the past 2,000 years.

However there are at least three broad ways in which the notion of faith has been understood in different Christian traditions. Firstly, faith—the noun—is the propositional content of divinely revealed orthodox dogma, which is believed—the verb—and so faith is the highest species of objective truth. Here, a central feature of valid belief in the true faith is acceptance of the authority of the Church as guardian of the divine deposit of faith for Roman Catholics, or acceptance of the authority of the Scriptures as inspired/inerrant revealed truth for Protestants. Secondly, faith is seen as a saving trust in the Person of Christ and is essentially relational. Here faith is not strictly a verb or a noun, but is encounter and experientially grounded. Thirdly, faith is an avenue for the release of spiritual and miraculous power. These three approaches can be mutually exclusive or they can mingle, and they can mingle with different emphasis, and they can be labeled under different theological headings.

The point of what has been sketched thus far is simply to illustrate that it is not at all easy to say what the Christian understanding of "faith" is, and that "faith," whatever it is, is not an easy thing to tie down. In this chapter I plan to side step this problem by deriving a definition of faith from one primary Christian source—John's gospel. If I can adequately describe what John means by "faith,"[2] then I will have a definition of Christian faith to work with that is genuinely Christian. This is as much as can be expected of one short chapter.

However, given the broadly Christian context of the many Western uses of the word "faith," can one meaningfully talk about "faith" in relation to the pre-Christian, non-Judaic and philosophical writings of Plato?

---

appear. (In John's gospel alone πιστεύω appears 98 times—a very high frequency.) In general the frequency of these πιστ- words is very high and the role that faith/belief plays in the Christian religion is correspondingly very important.

2. The question of whether it is valid to speak of "faith" in relation to John's Gospel is one that will be taken up shortly in this chapter. Yet here it can be simply noted that the New International Version of the Bible does tend to translate John's ἐπίστευσαν εἰς as "faith in"; see John 2:11; 7:31; 8:30; 14:12, etc.

Faith's Knowledge

CAN WE SPEAK OF "FAITH" IN PLATO?

Commenting on Plato's *Republic* 511e, Paul Shorey claims that:

> πίστις is of course not "faith" in Plato, but Neoplatonists, Christians and commentators have confused the two ideas hopelessly.[3]

The first difficulty with Shorey's comment is that he appears to imply that there is a single and clear meaning for the word "faith" which not only all Christians agree on, but which all Neoplatonists and all confused commentators accept too. This implication is untenable. Yet, leaving that to one side, Shorey can be understood to be making quite a narrow and technical point. Historically, "faith," as different Christians influenced by Neoplatonism came to understand and use this term, simply did not exist at the time and place in which Plato was writing. Further, in *Republic* 511e, πίστις is positioned in the low division of the divided line analogy. So it seems that δόξα, the low belief realm of opinion, where one's beliefs are derived from a naïve trust in shadowy images (εἰκασία) and uncertain convictions (πίστις), is distinct from ἐπιστήμη, the high realm of genuine knowledge, where one attains true understanding (διάνοια) and true intellection (νόησις). Shorey is thus asserting that it is not exegetically legitimate to translate πίστις in Plato by any word explicitly concerned with the divine. Further, historically, it is anachronistic to relate Plato's conception of πίστις to later Christian and Neoplatonist notions of "faith."

So, there are apparently simple and solid reasons why Shorey does not want anyone to translate the word πίστις as "faith" in *Republic* 511e. However, these reasons look untenably reductive the closer one looks at the divided line analogy and the more seriously one thinks about why Christians and Neoplatonists *did* find something related to their own conception of "faith" in Plato's use of the word πίστις. As Johannes Van Ophuijsen has decisively dealt with Shorey's failure to recognize the natural links between Christian and Neoplatonist conceptions of faith and Plato,[4] we shall look briefly at Shorey's approach to πίστις in the divided line analogy in order to see if, at least there, Shorey's caution is valid.

Firstly, it is by no means self-evident that Plato's low epistemological categories—of which πίστις is one—have no connection with the divine truths accessed in his high categories. In the famous divided line analogy it is clearly possible to argue that Plato's use of the idea of a ratio may well

---

3. Shorey, Loeb Classics Library, Plato, *Republic*, Books 6–10, 117.
4. Van Ophuijsen, "Making Room for Faith," 119–34.

imply a relationship between the lower and immediate perceptions of the temporal human animal with the higher and abstract thoughts of divine and eternal intelligence. Indeed, some relationship between the tangible and the intangible and common opinions and truth is implicit in Plato's dialectical methodology. Typically, Plato starts an enquiry with an examination of things that appear beautiful, true and good in the common and shadowy belief manifestations of δόξα and seeks to proceed by rationally addressing the contradictions and uncertainties of what is merely taken to be true until the point is reached where one can leap into the higher spiritual revelations of ἐπιστήμη. That is, Plato's thought is, in general terms, seeking to use the low realm of δόξα as a sort of gestalt doorway to the higher truths of ἐπιστήμη. Plato's dialogical technique seems to imply that there is some incomplete yet inherent dependence of the common impressions and convictions of δόξα on the ontic spiritual realities only clearly graspable via ἐπιστήμη. In general terms, Plato's approach to the illumination and grasping of divine things has—as we shall see—strong parallels to the manner in which the writer of John's gospel uses the term πιστεύω. If John's word can be translated as "faith"—and John's word is also clearly connected with the realm of the tangibly manifest[5] (Plato's low epistemological categories)—then why should John not be seen as using a term in some ways continuous with Plato's prior use? What seems to be going on here is not, so much, the imposing of a Christian idea of "faith" on Plato, as of Christianity taking up, though modifying, a recognizably Platonic conception of faith. Here the primacy of the unseen over the seen, the gestalt passageway to participation in the spiritual via the low avenue of the realm of the tangibly immediate, and a belief orientation seeking revelatory truth from beyond mere immediacy, seem to be basic onto-epistemological outlooks shared by both Plato and John. If that is indeed what is happening and if Plato's divided line analogy supports an epistemological outlook that has elements of commonality with John's use, then it is invalid to merely assert that Plato's conception of πίστις and John's undoubtedly Christian conceptions of faith should be kept entirely distinct from each other.[6] Πίστις in Plato and πιστεύω in

---

5. Note John 1:14; 2:11; and, in Johannine literature, 1 John 1:1. John places the revelation of God in concrete, tangible terms.

6. Van Ophuijsen notes: "In one important sense Shorey is clearly right. That *pistis* in Plato is 'of course' not "faith" is true, indeed a trivial truth, if all that it means is that Plato's conception of *pistis* is quite different from Hebrew or Christian ones; that, for instance, it does not involve belief in the divine nature of a particular individual,

John are, indeed, not equivalent, yet, considering the deep impact of the Greco-Roman world on first century Judea, it would be odd if they were not related; and it is certainly possible that they might be deeply related.

Further, whilst some key well known passages of Plato's corpus do indeed contrast mere δόξα with ἐπιστήμη in a manner derisive of mere δόξα, Van Ophuijsen points out that Plato does *not* have an undifferentiated stance on whether his low belief categories—impression, faith, belief, doctrine, opinion—are good or bad.[7] In general terms Plato's dialogues function on the premises that low belief categories are appropriate to their proper place, good as possible doorways to higher truth, foolish if relied on too literally by those who should know better, and dangerous and thoroughly erroneous if the merely tangible and merely culturally given are taken as either concretely real and absolutely true in their own right, or are approached in the attitude of irrealist skepticism. In the *Apology*, the *Sophist* and *Gorgias*, Plato exposes the falsity of naively absolutized conventional opinion, he attacks the believability of clever skeptical irrealism and he unpacks the dangers of the rhetorical arts of mere persuasion. This polemic passion—against mere opinion and mere argument where there is no serious and deep interest in truth—can be detected throughout Plato's corpus. An unphilosophical disinterest in transcendently referenced reason exploits the inconclusive and malleable nature of what is immediately accessible to perception and culturally formed beliefs, but such disinterest and instrumental manipulation is entirely shameful in Plato's eyes. Plato's opposition to mere δόξα is targeted at Sophists who have no belief in truth, and this attack is not intended as an assault on religious piety and is certainly not seen by Plato as an assault on the committed belief in the reality of transcendent truth, a conviction basic to Christian faith.

It is now possible to do word searches on Plato's corpus very easily, so I looked at all the words starting with the stem πίστ- in the Plato corpus and it is evident that Plato uses the same words the New Testament uses for "faith" and "belief" in a wide variety of ways, some of which are

---

or conceiving of this belief in terms of grace, or of an infused virtue that is necessary for salvation. But . . . it seems fair to point out that Plato has exposed himself to being read in ways that suited the diverse agendas of these overlapping sets of readers . . ." Van Ophuijsen, "Making Room for Faith," 132–33.

7. The formation of children and non-philosophers in both good opinions and good habits, where they must trust their betters, is crucial, for example, to the educative life of the good state outlined in Plato's *Republic* and in his *Laws*. See Van Ophuijsen's chapter cited above.

Faith in Plato and John

clearly religiously friendly and easily and fairly appropriable by Christians and religious Neoplatonists.[8] We will explore this territory later in the chapter. But more profoundly, the very outlook of faith—understood as belief in an unseen divine transcendent Mind which is the grounds of all human perception and conception—is essential to Plato's thought. This, and explicitly religious belief outlooks in Plato, Shorey accepts, even though he has an insistent aversion to using the word "faith" in translating Plato.[9] Shorey's aversion seems shaped by his determination to view Plato's religious outlook as strictly philosophical in contrast to all Christian, Neoplatonist and confused understandings of faith. But this seriously limits Shorey's understanding of Plato's theology and reveals a rather inadequate grasp of Plato's theological impact on the ancient

---

8. Using the word search tools in the CD-ROM *Perseus* 2.0 I was able to examine the 108 uses of words beginning in πιστ- found in Plato's corpus. This search is by no means an exhaustive survey of all the uses of the πιστ- stem in Plato's corpus, however, it is a reasonable general survey, big enough to give a fair sense of the range of meanings Plato applies to this stem in his corpus. Here is a reasonably large sample of the broad range of use categorizations that I noted: Loyal warrior (*Laws* 1.630a); confidence (*Republic* 5.450d; *Phaedo* 107b); pragmatic reliance (*Laws* 7.824a; 12.947e; *Laws* 3.682c); relational reliance (*Timaeus* 20b; *Phaedrus* 256d); reliable argument (*Philebus* 13a); reliance on a believable authority (*Philebus* 57d); trust (*Laches* 186d); pious trust (*Laws* 3.701c; 5.730c); trustworthiness integrating legal, religious and mathematical warrants (*Laws* 6.771c); financial trust (*Laws* 5.742c; 8.849e; 11.915e); trust that what is said is true (*Apology* 17c; 19b); trust in an intellectual insight (*Philebus* 22e); trusting truth (*Meno* 81e); belief grounded in tradition and likely to be true (*Laws* 6.782b; 6.782d; 8.850b); stable belief about true goodness and that which most intimately concerns the soul (*Republic* 6.505e); belief of religious doctrines (*Laws* 11.927a); belief in the immortal soul (*Phaedo* 70b; 87e); belief of the soul—high epistemological category (*Phaedo* 83a); ironic distaste for the beliefs of religious authority (*Timaeus* 40e); assent based on respect for authority (*Laws* 12.965c); faith in the gods (*Laws* 12.996c; 12.996d); faith in inspiration (*Cratylus* 339a); belief on the edge of human knowledge, respecting the limits of understanding—a reverence for mystery (*Cratylus* 425b); high epistemological belief (*Republic* 7.534a; *Phaedrus* 245c; *Republic* 10.603a); belief/faith/conviction as a low epistemological category (*Republic* 6.511e; 10.601e; *Gorgias* 454d—455a; *Timaeus* 29c; 52b); convincing (*Philebus* 50c; *Charmides* 161a); plausible (*Critias* 111a).

9. In Shorey's introductions to the Loeb Classical Library's *Republic*, Shorey speaks of Plato's faith not a few times and sometimes in ways that are directly compatible with some Christian doctrines. See Plato, *Republic*, lxiv: "Plato's belief in immortality was a conviction of the psychological and moral impossibility of sheer materialism, and a broad faith in the unseen, the spiritual, the ideal." Even so, and possibly because he wished to his preserve Plato's metaphysical faith from the negative connotations he saw tangled up in Plato's epistemologically low use of πίστις, he consistently refuses to translate πίστις as "faith" in Plato. Note Shorey's comment on *Republic* 534a: "Always avoid 'faith' in translating Plato," Plato, *Republic*, 205.

world. On these matters, Burkert's understanding that Plato essentially invented Western theology and grounded the West's religious consciousness in this view of transcendent divine goodness that is yet analogically and participationally comprehensible by the human mind, is well borne-out by the depth and power of Burkert's scholarship.[10] Cornford points out that there are rich lines of developmental continuity between the religion and philosophy of the Greeks, and along that track, Dodds notes that Plato is very concerned with right belief, practice and religion in the Greek city.[11] Further, as the impact of Plato on the Greco-Roman world deepened into the early Christian era, not a few scholars have noted how profoundly concerned Greek philosophy became with God, and how deeply Hellenism and Judaism interacted in the formative period of the Christian faith.[12]

So far it seems reasonable to proceed on the premise that particular understandings of what "faith" means within different Christian traditions can be meaningfully described and it is reasonable to use the term "faith" in relation to many Christian scriptural uses of the πιστ- stem and to at least some of Plato's uses of the πιστ- stem. But, can we speak of "faith" in regard to Saint John's use of the word πιστεύω?

---

10. See Burkert, *Greek Religion*, 305–38. "Since Plato, there has been no theology which has not stood in his shadow. For many centuries Platonism was simply the way in which god was thought of and spoken about, in the West as in the Islamic East. The aura of Late Antiquity and Christianity which thus attaches to Plato has become an embarrassment for many interpreters of classical antiquity . . . Since Plato and through him, religion has been essentially different from what it had been before," ibid., 321–22.

11. See Cornford, *From Religion to Philosophy*; also Cornford, *Principium Sapientiae*. See Dodds, *The Greeks and the Irrational*, particularly chapter VII.

12. See Dodds, *Age of Anxiety*. Dodds notes the profound significance of "the new importance attached in Middle-Platonist speculation to the personal quest for God," ibid., 91. See Niehoff, "Did the *Timaeus* create a textual community?" 161–91. Here Niehoff examines the ways in which pagan philosophers of the second and third centuries CE sought to de-appropriate Plato from Christian apologists. This struggle is firmly set within the context of the engagement between Alexandrian Jewish thinkers and Plato from the first century, who also became increasingly under stress from Christian appropriations of both Judaism and Plato. The point to note here in terms of this chapter is the degree to which Judaism itself was, at the time of the writing of the Christian scriptures, deeply engaged in the thought world of Greek philosophy.

CAN WE SPEAK OF "FAITH" IN JOHN?

The question of whether it is legitimate to speak of faith in John hinges on whether it is fair to sharply delineate faith from belief, or not. For John does not use the word πίστις (faith) at all, but he uses the word πιστεύω (believe) extensively. If these two words are different grammatical forms of the one 'thing', and John is emphasizing 'faith/belief' as a verb, whereas other New Testament writers also describe 'faith/belief' as a noun, then I can see no objection to speaking of John's understanding of 'faith' (a fuzzy English word that can be used as a noun or a verb) whilst recognizing that John has a particularly active, existential and spiritually dynamic understanding of what faith is. But if faith and belief really are distinct 'things' and the active personal/relational/existential attitude of belief must be sharply delineated from the objective/propositional/authoritative and received dogmatic content of faith, then we cannot speak of 'faith' in John.

Latin theology has a long tradition of distinguishing that which is unique to faith from that which is unique to belief. Put simplistically, the Latin tradition seems to distinguish between the objective dogmatic authority of faith and the subjective personal surrender of belief, although faith and belief cannot be meaningfully understood without reference to each other in the Christian religion.

Interestingly, this Latin approach to faith and belief seems absent from Greek theology.[13] There may be quite a simple linguistic component to this. In Latin, as in English, *fides* (faith) and *credo* (believe) are etymologically distinct from each other, whereas in Greek 'faith' (πίστις) and 'believe' (πιστεύω) are built on the same word stem. That is, in Greek, someone examining πίστις and πιστεύω has a natural sense that one is working with different grammatical forms of the same root 'thing', whereas someone examining *fides* and *credo* in Latin, or 'faith' and 'belief' in English, gets the sense that one is working with linguistically

---

13. In Yannaras' *Elements of Faith*, the English translation of chapter 3 (pp. 11–14), titled "Faith," moves without explanation, between the word 'faith' and 'belief' simply assuming—as in Greek—that these two words are grammatically distinct but conceptually identical. Further, in this chapter Yannaras specifically rejects a Western notion of 'faith' which he characterizes as 'objective' and tied to an authority that one simply 'believes'. The Orthodox tradition as he describes it understands faith/belief in inherently interpersonal terms and rejects what he characterizes as an ideological and authoritarian conceptual delineation between 'objective' institutionally authoritative faith and 'subjective' submissive personal belief.

distinct units that may well be conceptually inter-related but which still imply some sharp definitional delineation.

If the issue at stake is simply to do with which language you read the New Testament in, then clearly, the Greeks have it over the Latins (and the English) on this one. Yet, no less a Latin than Joseph Ratzinger treats belief and faith so integrally in his famous *Introduction to Christianity* that it is clear that contemporary Roman Catholic scholarship on the nature of faith and belief is as intimately engaged with the Greek New Testament sources as it is with the Roman tradition of doctrinal development.[14]

There may indeed be serious conceptual and political concerns involved in the question of whether one can separate out Christian faith from Christian belief, and these are not simply linguistic concerns. Yet, clearly there are good linguistic grounds for holding that there is a profound inter-relatedness between faith and belief in the Greek New Testament. Hence, resting on linguistic terms alone, this chapter does not find John's use of the word πιστεύω to prohibit us from seeking to understand what his Christian conception of faith is.

So, all preliminaries aside, what are Plato and John's understandings of faith?

OVERVIEW OF THE RELATIONSHIP BETWEEN PLATO AND CHRISTIANITY ON FAITH

If one looks at the range of meanings given to verbs and nouns with the stem πίστ- in the Christian scriptures, one is struck by the extent to which Christian understandings of faith are on the one hand at odds with Plato, and on the other hand, strikingly indebted to Plato. In general terms, the role of belief/faith in the Christian scriptures seems to positively revel in the high spiritual role it gives to Plato's low epistemological belief categories. And yet, the underlying commonality in broad metaphysical beliefs, in spiritually focused moral seriousness and in revelation dependent

---

14. See Ratzinger, *Introduction to Christianity*. The introductory section of this rich and pastorally attuned work of theology (39–100) delves into the nature of Christian belief, and, somewhat like Yannaras, swaps without explanation between the terms faith and belief. I am not accusing this great theologian of sloppiness here, but am rather pointing out his deep scholarly embeddedness in the Greek New Testament in relation to the way he uses the terms faith and belief in this text. It should also be noted that this text was written in German where *Glaube* (faith) and *glauben* (believe) seem to provide a linguistic environment strikingly similar to Greek in relation to these two words.

conversion between Plato and the Christian scriptures is often striking. Theologically, epistemologically and metaphysically there seem to be clear areas of divergence and sympathy between Plato and Christianity on faith. Drawing on how both Plato and John use πιστ- stem terms, we will now seek to clarify where these two approaches are incompatible and where they overlap.

PLATO ON FAITH

It is important to realize that 'faith' in Plato's day was not a distinctly religious or dogmatic notion. Rather, 'faith' has a range of work-a-day meanings that can also be applied to religious, dogmatic and philosophical contexts. In Plato, πιστ- stem words are typically situated in the contexts of business, friendship, war, deep existential commitments, reasonable hearsay, and mundane daily life.[15] Where πιστ- words connate propositional belief concerning the 'supernatural' (such as what legislation one should make to protect a murderer from the distraught and malevolent soul of the man he has killed—*Laws* 865d–e) and religious faith (that is, relating to proper respect in cultic practice—see *Laws* 701c) there is no change of mood from ordinary language to specialized religious or theological language in Plato. It should be noted here that spirits, cultic practice and the deeply ingrained role of religion in civic life are all normal features of Plato's reality assumptions, and they are not bracketed out from his philosophy. This is not to say that Plato accepts whatever myths and superstitions are normal to the common folk of his cultural context—far from it—but he never thinks to de-mythologize the spiritual and the religious themselves. His philosophy is intimately concerned with the theological and the moral, and further, if he has no persuasive reason to find a religious practice or a common belief about spirits unbelievable, he will believe it. In fact, as Burkert points out, particularly in the *Laws*, Plato is very concerned to make philosophy and religion align and considers impiety as unfavorably as he considers sophistry.[16]

---

15. See note 8.

16. See Burkert, *Greek Religion,* 337: ". . . so much of Plato's experience and sense of reality went into [the *Laws,* hence they give to us] the most differentiated and most intensive image of polis religion. At the same time the essential lines of the situation which was to hold for the next 600 years became visible: the conflict between philosophical and traditional religion is denied. In respect of the traditional religion, conscious conservatism is espoused . . . Philosophy recognizes gods. The atheists remain

The freshness, respect and naturalness with which Plato describes cultic piety in the full range of his dialogues demonstrates that this natural religiosity is no mere conservative political pragmatism emerging out of the crustiness of old age in Plato, but is simply part of Plato's world view. Further, this naturalness of a religious and spiritually attuned outlook on reality in Plato is one shared by first century Christians in the Judeo-Greco-Roman milieu. Yet, in striking contrast to Saint Paul, Plato did not call this outlook 'faith.'[17]

Before looking more closely at Plato's specifically epistemological usage of πίστις it is worth touching briefly on the way in which, despite the terminology, Plato's influence can be clearly seen in the New Testament outlook on faith.

It was obvious to both Plato and Aristotle that what is self-evident depends, at least in the first instance, on who you are, what your assumptions are, and where your core value loyalties already lie. So in both Plato and Aristotle the notion of the interpretive openness of the 'obvious', and the assumption that many people will not see what is really true, is intimately tied up with the comprehension of and belief in the undemonstrable ground premises of philosophy, theology and science.[18] Thus, what James K. A. Smith calls the presuppositional outlook of Christian faith shares much common ground with Plato's philosophical outlook.[19]

For example, after the cave analogy in *The Republic* Plato establishes that blindness to truth, which is darkness in the soul, is of two kinds—that

---

a negligible minority; there are no longer trials of atheists. Thus the customs of the ancestors allow all social functions of cults to be played out."

17. See 2 Corinthians 5:7. Here Paul affirms πίστεως and mistrusts εἴδους.

18. See Aristotle, *Posterior Analytics* 72b: "Now some think that because one must understand the primitives there is no understanding at all; others that there is, but that there are demonstrations of everything. Neither of these views is either true or necessary." See Plato, *Laws* 966c–68b. Here Plato explains why guardians of the law must show theological aptitude (theology is here interchangeable with astronomy) in order to demonstrate the qualities of intelligence and character that cannot be expected in those with no understanding of divine matters.

19. See Smith, *Who's Afraid of Postmodernism?*, 15–58. Here Smith links Derrida's recognition that we always bring interpretive and communally formed presuppositions to every belief context, with Christian orthodoxy. I am here arguing that Plato and the Christian gospel both claim to apprehend truth, but, both also recognize that some will simply not 'see' the truth. Hence, both Plato and Christianity do not seek truth justifications that can be foundationally demonstrated in the reductive modern terms of 'objective', scientific or merely logical necessity. In this regard, Plato, orthodox Christian belief and Derrida share some common ground.

produced by the absence of light, and that produced by too much light (*Republic* 518–19). That is, ignorance makes us blind yet revelation can equally blind us if it is too intense. So, in thinking about what radiant magnitude of truth is suited to the delicate eyes of our soul, Plato turns to education. Astronomy, it is agreed, is a science well suited to the enlightenment of the soul. Yet Plato well understands that many people will see no use for this devotional study. Note how Shorey translates *Republic* 527d–e:

> 527d "I am amused," said I, "at your apparent fear lest the multitude may suppose you to recommend useless studies [astronomy]. It is indeed no trifling task, but very difficult to realize[20] that there is in every soul an organ or an instrument 527e of knowledge that is purified and kindled afresh by such studies when it has been destroyed and blinded by our ordinary pursuits, a faculty whose preservation outweighs ten thousand eyes; for by it only is reality beheld. Those who share this faith will think your words superlatively true.[21] But those who have and have had no inkling of it will naturally think them all moonshine . . ."

Saint Paul's understanding of spiritual discernment and his understanding of why some people lack the ability to understand the truth revealed in the Christian gospel is strikingly similar in tenor to Plato's profound sense of the gulf between a mundane and overly sensual understanding of reality and a philosophically and spiritually attuned sense of reality.[22]

---

20. Here Shorey renders ἀλλὰ χαλεπὸν πιστεῦσαι as "difficult to realize." Jowett renders this, without any translational nervousness as "difficulty in believing" *Dialogues*. Grube and Reeve translate this more in line with Shorey's cautious approach to πίστ- stem words in Plato, as "it's very difficult to realize," Cooper, ed., *Plato Complete Works*.

21. This is Shorey's rendering of οἷς μέν οὖν ταῦτα ξυνδοκεῖ, ἀμηχάνως ὡς εὖ δόξεις λέγειν· Interestingly, where Shorey boldly uses the word "faith" here, Grube and Reeve also step into the realm of religious illumination and use the word "belief." Jowett, however, does not use either "faith" or "belief" in translating *Republic* 527e and it seems to me that his meaning is more in keeping with the text than Shorey, Grube and Reeve's renderings, who seem to want to make sure we understand how faith and belief must be properly applied and not applied to Plato, whatever the text may say. Even so, the use of "faith" by Shorey here in a positive manner in relation to what are obviously high epistemological insights has translational validity. Shorey seems artificially concerned to make sure faith and belief as low epistemological categories are never confused with high epistemological insights, whereas this passage illustrates that Plato does not share Shorey's concern with rigid definitional purity in his use of πίστ- stem words.

22. 1 Corinthians 2:14; Romans 1:18–25

Faith's Knowledge

In broad terms then, it seems evident that a Christian conception of faith, as a responsive apprehension of divine revelation given to us from the realm of transcendent non-material truth, is quite straightforwardly Platonic. The lines separating Plato's philosophy from Christian faith seem, on this front, non-existent.

So, it is clear that Plato is a pious pagan, he—like the first century followers of Jesus—is deeply embedded in an enchanted cosmos where religious and spiritual assumptions are foundational cultural outlooks, he is profoundly theologically concerned in his metaphysical/moral/political thinking, and he is writing in a culture and an era when πίστις had no particular theological meaning. Bearing all this in mind, let us now turn to what Plato meant by designating πίστις as a low epistemological category.

When Plato speaks of πίστις as an epistemological category, Shorey is, I think, right to insist that this does not illuminate Plato's theological outlook one way or another. That is, one should not draw inferences that later Christian conceptions of faith are being either denigrated or advanced by Plato's epistemology. This is not to say that there is no connection between Plato's epistemology and the Christian understanding of faith. Far from it, for I hope to demonstrate that Plato's epistemology and the Christian understanding of faith found in John have intimate ties. But terminologically, πίστις in Plato's epistemology and πιστεύω in John's soteriology convey almost opposite evaluations. We shall explore that point carefully when looking at John. But here, all that need be said about Plato's epistemological understanding of πίστις is that things tied to perception and hearsay cannot be relied on in themselves and lead only to mere opinion if not processed by higher reflection. Only by rational reflection do we feebly grasp true reality, which lies beyond appearance, beyond untested opinion and above the mundane temporal and transitory realm of becoming. In this sense 'belief,' as the placing of high confidence in low epistemological categories, is beneath philosophy. Indeed, the role given to πιστεύω in Christian faith—and belief here is tied to the categories of hearsay and the rationally impossible—is precisely what philosophical pagans in the early years of Christianity found so common, so superstitious and so intellectually degrading about the Christian religion.

To sum up. Plato uses πιστ- stem words in many ways, some of which are inherently religio-friendly, and Plato powerfully shapes the theological outlook of the ancient Greco-Roman world. Plato's theological outlook undoubtedly influenced Christian cosmological understandings and metaphysical beliefs and this shapes the Christian understanding of what faith itself is. The outlook which believes in the existence of a transcendent spiritual reality, beyond mere appearance, and the conviction that the spiritually receptive person can understand some analogical truths about divine reason, is basic to Plato's philosophy, and something remarkably similar to this outlook is assumed in the Christian faith. In this sense, Plato's theological outlook is profoundly formative of the Christian theological outlook. And yet, Plato also sows the seeds for conflict between Christian faith and philosophical reason—particularly in the manner in which his epistemological mistrust of tangible reality leans Plato's outlook towards dualistic rationalism. Intelligent Greco-Roman pagans from the second century were often deeply frustrated by the refusal of Christians to ground their doctrines in the arguments of objective and epistemologically high universal reason. Often the "offence of the gospel" was indeed the Christian insistence on what seemed to the pagans to be *mere* belief.[23] So the question of the relationship between Plato's philosophy and Christian faith is not a simple one. It is a question that requires not only an understanding of Plato's theological convictions but a good understanding of specifically Christian conceptions of faith and reason. And so we turn to John.

---

23. Note this important passage from Dodds, *Age of Anxiety*, 120–21: "Had any cultivated pagan of the second century been asked to put in a few words the difference between his own view of life and the Christian one, he might have replied that it was the difference between *logismos* and *pistis*, between reasoned conviction and blind faith. To any one brought up on classical Greek philosophy, *pistis* meant the lowest grade of cognition: it was a state of mind of the uneducated, who believed things on hearsay without being able to give reasons for their belief. St Paul, on the other hand, following Jewish tradition, had represented *pistis* as the very foundation of the Christian life. And what astonished all the early pagan observers, Lucian and Galen, Celsus and Marcus Aurelius, was the Christians' total reliance on unproved assertion—their willingness to die for the indemonstrable. For Galen, a relatively sympathetic observer, the Christian possessed three of the four cardinal virtues: they exhibit courage, self-control and justice; what they lack is *phronesis*, intellectual insight, the rational basis of the other three. For Celsus they are the enemies of science: they are like quacks who warn people against the doctor, saying that knowledge is bad for the health of the soul. Later on Porphyry seems to have repeated the same protest against 'an irrational and un-examined *pistis*'; Julian exclaims, 'There is nothing in your philosophy beyond the one word "Believe!"'"

JOHN ON FAITH

Having carefully examined each of the 98 usages of πίστ- stem words in John's Gospel, it is clear to me that John uses this word πιστεύω in a very specific and consistent manner. For, as Beasley-Murray notes, John's gospel, in all its parts is written "that you may believe."[24] So there is no need to carefully delineate the different senses and uses of πίστ- stem words in John as we have done in this chapter for Plato.

The structure of Christian belief in John runs as follows. God speaks His Word—which created and sustains the world—right *into* the world in the person of Jesus of Nazareth (John 1:1–18). Jesus is the incarnate revelation of God, the very personhood of God, made directly relationally comprehensible to the human situation (John 10:30; 14:9). This revelation apprehends people as a radically inter-personal encounter with divinity and always has the effect of fundamental confrontation on the hearer. The Word of God inevitably generates a spiritual crisis in the hearer demanding an inescapably interpersonal response of either love and surrender, or hatred and rejection. This crisis effect is played out most clearly in the crucifixion.

The Word of God is the seed of God seeking to germinate the human soul and bring it into a totally new order of life (John 1:4; 3:3; Luke 8:11). And yet, the Word of God can be deflected by the hearer from the life giving intention of the Divine Sower (John 1:10–12) and then the effect of the Word is one of judgment rather than salvation (John 3:18–21). For whilst the Word of God is given in such a manner that preserves responsive human freedom, this Word is unstoppable in its effect; either to salvation or judgment. Thus the Hebrew trope "the word of the Lord" (Jeremiah 1:4) with its inexorable efficacy (Isaiah 55:10–11) is very influential on John.

John's use of Greek λόγος is read through a prior Hebraic understanding of God's creatively powerful speech (Genesis 1) and the immanent prophetic in-breaking of the Word of the Lord into the mundane realm of historical space and time. In response to the prophetic in-breaking Word of the Lord, the existential reception of the revelation of God is belief, and so faith leads to ontological and spiritual transformation which is manifest in a spiritually enabled practice of life characterized by truth and freedom (John 8:31–32) and a radical inversion of ethical normality (Matthew 5:1–10). Further, the rejection of the Word of God is unbelief;

---

24. Beasley-Murray, *John*, lii. Here citing John 20:30–31.

Faith in Plato and John

yet unbelief here is no propositional judgment but is firstly an epistemological, relational, praxiological and ontological act of autonomy and pride (sin) of the creature raised against the Creator.

Thus divine λόγος and human πιστεύω are intimately tied together at the very heart of the Johannine understanding of both salvation and judgment. To the Christian, faith, reason, truth and life are inseparable.[25]

An interesting epistemological feature of how the Word comes to us in John is tied up with the completely different evaluation of δόξα in John when compared with Plato. The Word of God is *manifest*, made apparent, in the humdrum ordinary world of becoming, of flesh, of historical particularity, in John. This makes the sub-lunar realm a medium for God's Word and so God's *glory* is manifest right inside the ordinary, temporal, material world. Thus the word δόξα no longer signifies unreliable opinions about the distracting realm of the merely *apparent* that it often does in Plato, but in John δόξα refers to the glorious tangible *disclosure* of God's presence in our space and time. Thus, John's gospel powerfully affirms the essential goodness of sensually experienced creation. So the humble, the common, the low, is glorified by God who condescends to enter into the very realm of our transitory and inherently fragile existence. Hence the word δόξα, as in the Septuagint, means glory in John, for we have seen God in the tangible realm of the flesh (though God is not flesh, John 4:24), and the response of faith is one of amazed worship at this manifestation of unfathomable divine condescension and beauty.[26]

This vision of the divine gifting of the lowly comes with an entirely new theo-political imaginary where the King of Glory is humble and seated on a donkey, where the outcasts of society are the especially favored of God and where the powerful, the wealthy and the learned are

---

25. Copleston rightly observed that ". . . it is difficult to separate Plato's epistemology from his ontology." *A History of Philosophy,* 142. In this regard John and Plato are of one accord. Issues of knowledge are essentially ontologically and existentially charged in John. Thus, Kierkegaard's epistemological center piece—*Unscientific Postscript*—is deeply Johannine in the manner in which it understands epistemological issues in terms of faith and unbelief which then connects the relational knowledge of these spiritual orientations with truth and falsity regarding different ways of living (existential truth) such that true propositional knowledge is derived from existential truth hinging on the right spiritual choice, rather than propositional truth being in some sense neutrally accessible. Christopher Simpson's beautiful text on Kierkegaard, *The Truth is the Way*, is a highly valuable read on the integration of faith, truth and praxis in Kierkegaard.

26. This line of thinking both connecting and contrasting Plato's approach to δόξα with John's is presented in passing by Prince in his *Rediscovering God's Church*, 419–20.

judged and found wanting (Luke 6:20–26; 1 Corinthians 1:18–20).[27] The Kingdom of God that Jesus embodies is a radical inversion of the norms of power, knowledge and privilege embedded in the status quo of the Greco-Roman world of first century Palestine.

The low nature of the Christian Messiah, of Christians and of Christian doctrine is essential to the Christian faith. Jesus was not a member of the aristocracy, the intelligencia, the priesthood, or the wealthy merchant class. On those fronts he indeed had "no beauty that we should desire him" (Isaiah 53:2). The Messiah of the Christian religion was a rural tradesman, yet he was obviously a man full of raw crowd drawing charisma and a man aware of his powers. The pious, respected and politically experienced leaders of this Yeshua's day appear to have seen him as someone who sought to entice the people away from legitimate religious and political authority, someone who exploited the volatilities so delicately held together at that time and place, and someone who led the people away from God. The Talmud describes this Nazarene as someone who disturbed the good order of society with his magic and his populist false teachings, and thus, he was a justly executed criminal.[28] Yet, the magnificat in Luke's gospel (Luke 1:46–55) depicts the Christian faith as the hope of the poor, the powerless, and the down trodden of Israel, and the hope of the non-citizens of the Roman Empire. Indeed, the Promised One Mary anticipates is to be the terror of the rich, the powerful and those invested in the reality structures of the prevailing status quo. Certainly the appeal of the Jesus movement firstly to rural peasants in Northern Judea, and then to the great unwashed under-classes of the mega-cities of the ancient world, bears out the inherently non-elite nature of early Christianity.[29]

---

27. See Yoder, *The Politics of Jesus*; Brueggemann, *The Prophetic Imagination*; Cavanaugh, *Theopolitical Imagination*.

28. See Beasley-Murray, *John*, 107–8: "The allegation that Jesus sought to lead the people astray . . . is preserved in a famous passage of the Talmud: 'It was taught: On the eve of the Passover they hanged Yeshua. And an announcer went out in front of him for forty days saying: 'He is going to be stoned, because he practiced magic and enticed and led Israel astray. Anyone who knows anything in his favor, let him come and plead in his behalf.' But not having found anything in his favor, they hanged him on the eve of the Passover.' (*Sanh.* 43a; there are further references to this in *Sanh.* 107a and *Sota* 47a, see Str-B 1:1023–24)."

29. Nietzsche, as Simone Weil well grasped, was right: ". . . the conviction was suddenly borne in upon me that Christianity is pre-eminently the religion of slaves [and] that slaves cannot help belonging to it . . ." Weil, *Waiting for God*, 67.

John's understandings of both divine λόγος and human πιστεύω embraces the Platonically low metaphysical and epistemological categories of flesh, time, particularity and becoming, and entrusts the message of the cosmic salvation event to a very human, unlearned, and non-ideal community which then transmits this message through hearsay, and, it is asserted, the power of the Spirit of God confirming the message of the gospel by miraculous signs (John 20:30–31; Mark 16:15–20). And as Brueggemann points out, such a prophetic and miraculous message, with its entirely subversive reality imaginary, is inherently mistrusted by those accustomed to making sense of the world and gaining some realistic control over the world. In the prophetic tradition in which Jesus stands, the "Word of the Lord" is typically only accepted by "those ill-schooled in explanation and understandings. It comes to those who will settle for amazements they can neither explain nor understand."[30] As Matthew's gospel puts it, a certain child-like trust and child-like openness to the incomprehensible is necessary to enter into the Kingdom of God that Jesus proclaimed (Matthew 19:14). And yet, John 1 clearly shows, high contemplative thought is not excluded by John.

The consistent manner in which John uses belief/faith implies a conscious and coherent epistemological outlook, and it seems reasonable to hold that he knows he is using classically low terms for his onto-epistemological vision, and he does so purposefully. Most remarkably, John holds to the Platonist metaphysical vision of transcendence at the same time that he affirms the goodness and importance of the common, the lowly, the experiential/material, and the validity of knowledge gained via the senses and hearsay.[31] This insistence on the importance of the epistemologically low signals that the empirical trajectory within the West—advanced by theologians such as Robert Grosseteste and Albert Magnus—is a fully Christian outlook, at the same time that John's obvious commitment to Platonic transcendence affirms the importance of the Western idealist trajectory. A Johannine outlook on reality is one in

---

30. Brueggemann, *The Prophetic Imagination*, 104.

31. Indeed, with Aristotle, John has a higher opinion of observable nature and its divine revelatory capacity than Plato does. Thus Aquinas—for example—is well able to use Aristotle in exploring the manner in which God reveals Himself in immanence and in the structures of ordinary thought and experience, whilst holding fast to his Augustinian Neoplatonist metaphysics. Even so, Aristotle, with his instrumental distaste for common religion (*Politics* 1314 b39—1315 b4; *Rhetoric* 1391 a30—1391 b3), and Plato, with his commitment to high rational theology, are carefully re-configured by Aquinas in order to be made amenable to Christian doctrine.

which empiricism and idealism are dialectically engaged, and held in constructive tension. Even so, faith is no academic matter in John and he resists, as does Paul, esoteric intellectualism and cultural elitism firmly.

So faith in John is the human response of surrender to the divine offer of redemption; it is a response of believing, of receptively hearing the divine Word of God spoken in the crisis of the call to total surrender and spiritual re-birth. And it all happens in the very tangible historical realm of temporal, concrete, daily reality. This being the case, John obviously has a strange and profound agreement with Plato's understanding of πίστις as a low epistemological category. However, the valuation given by Plato to that which is epistemologically low could not be more strikingly contrasted than with John's valuation. Let us now turn to the relationship between Plato and John on faith and reason.

PLATO AND JOHN ON FAITH AND REASON

John shares Plato's faith in the sense that Shorey is happy to use that word in relation to Plato. That is, Plato's belief in divinity that transcends the tangible shadow lands of our becoming, immediately experienced, and transitory mundane "reality" is mirrored in John's Hellenized Hebraic conception of the Creator God who transcends His creation totally. Even so, John's evaluation of the tangible created work of God lacks the tendency towards denigrating the spatiotemporal that Greek dualism was prone to.[32] John also shares Plato's faith (understood as existentially committed conviction) in the ultimate rationality of this transcendent God and in the human capacity to analogically understand the Word of God which is revealed to us. Yet, in John the Word of God is spoken to us in an ordinary human language and via a particular interpersonal encounter. Plato and Christianity also share similar conceptions of conversion connected to what one existentially believes about truth and the

32. A degree of Platonic Hellenistic dualism can be seen in John, and more clearly, in Paul, where bondage to the flesh is equated with the life of sin, darkness and futility. Yet the situation is more nuanced than it at first appears. There is a distinctive Hebraic influence on John and Paul with its more concrete understanding of the sacredness of the human heart/mind/body unity (somewhat akin to Aristotle's *On the Soul*), and so Humanity's creation in the image of God sacralizes the body as much as the heart and the mind and does not abstract the elements of the human condition out from each other. Hence the importance, in the Pharisaic tradition out of which Christianity springs, of the bodily resurrection of the dead and the Christian understanding of the body as the temple of God's Spirit.

Faith in Plato and John

transformative effect that truth so grasped must have on the soul of the believer. Thus, reason, truth, conversion and faith go together in John in a manner that has strong continuities with Plato. In particular, John's use of λόγος in reference to divinity is embedded in both the Hebrew understanding of the creative Word of God sustaining all reality, and in the influence of Greek philosophical conceptions of λόγος. Thus far, faith and reason in Plato and John are showing large areas of commonality. But we can go one step further. Epistemologically, both Plato and John agree that faith is a mode of knowing tied to classically low epistemological categories. But it is in the understanding of how the knowledge medium of faith is to be evaluated in the quest for truth that demonstrates the most surprising innovation of John, if one considers John's world view to be deeply embedded in some of Plato's central theological premises.

Crucially, John's valuing of the epistemologically low means that salvation is not dependent on how smart or educated you are. In contrast to Plato, salvation is not an elitist enterprise that can be discovered only by higher intellectual knowledge. This is vital to the appeal of Christianity to the lowly people of the Greco-Roman world whom Jesus and His church embraced. This also sheds light on why the esoteric and sophisticated gnostic teachings of the second century were considered so un-Christian by those who eventually won the battle to define Christian orthodoxy.

Dodds looks closely at the central role that πίστις plays in the early years of Christianity in ensuring that Christianity did not become indistinguishable from the many forms of philosophical religion that flowered in the twilight of Greco-Roman paganism.[33] The first centuries of the Christian religion are a fascinating story of the slow intellectualization of Christian theology and apologetics, at the same time as a concerted effort was made to ensure that the core of Christian belief itself was preserved from elitist intellectual capture. The great minds of Patristic theology that secured their place in the development of Christian orthodoxy were very careful to preserve a non-academic understanding of the core of Christian belief. This core is located in a public and particular historical narrative, which makes politically uncompromising claims for the universal Lordship of Christ, and is embedded in public signs of miraculous power confirming the ongoing realities of that historical narrative and divine Lordship. This outlook is not epistemologically grounded in the timeless proofs of higher reason or the elite knowledge of esoteric cults.

---

33. Dodds, *Age of Anxiety*, 102–38.

Thus the propositional teachings of the Christian faith are both accessible and confronting to the simple and the learned alike. In this sense the Christian religion is not a philosophy and distinguished itself from the philosophical religions and their easy synthesis with civic cultus so characteristic of pagan late antiquity.[34]

Most significantly, as Christian thought developed, Patristic theologians took belief in orthodox doctrine as the starting point for valid reasoning rather than as premises which could be established independently by some objectively impartial and inherently necessary reason. This defined the Christian approach to orthodox belief and the distinctly Christian understanding of reason thereafter.[35]

John maintains that it is divine Reason that brings us into a place of primary crisis and calls us to respond with a relational, transformative belief in the Lordship of the incarnate Word of God (that is, we are called to believe *in* Jesus), and so Christian faith is the essence of rationality, though its reasonableness is not the product of human insight but it is a transformative gift of divine revelation. And this revelation so surpasses the wisest intellections of the learned as to make the gospel of salvation radically accessible to both the intellectually wise and the intellectually foolish (1 Corinthians 1:25). Yet practically, it is harder for the high, the pious and the educated to receive the Word of God than the lowly, the sinner and the simple. John makes much of the refusal of those who are invested in the prevailing religious, intellectual and moral status quo to be open to the radical judgment of the Word of God about the futility of

---

34. Newbigin, *The Open Secret*, 16–17, notes how the *ecclesia theou*, the public assembly called by God and promoting the universal claims of "Jesus is Lord" for all humanity, could not avoid clashing with the *cultus publicus* of the Roman Empire. The Empire had no problem with a large variety of cults of personal salvation—*cultus privatus*—and philosophical cults that offering secret knowledge and spiritual salvation abounded; but Christianity was never one of those.

35. This outlook is alive and well in some of the finest minds of recent Western theology such as Henri de Lubac. "When, through excess of zeal, there is a tendency to confuse dogma and theology, far less is it an undue magnification of theology that results from it, than a misappreciation, a sacrilegious minimization of dogma, which thereby becomes reduced to a system of more or less clear ideas . . . Though Dogma and theology are always intimately related and can never be separated, yet they are never entirely of the same stuff. Dogma is a vast domain which theology will never wholly exploit. There is always infinitely more in Dogma, considered in its concrete totality, that is to say in the very Object of divine revelation, than in this "human science of revelation," in this product of analysis which theology always is." De Lubac, *Paradoxes of Faith*, 227–28.

Faith in Plato and John

human wisdom, morality and religion. Only the humble and the radically surrendered receive the gift of God to eternal life—be they wise or foolish. This type of radical crisis and confrontation is on every page of John's gospel.

Making matters even more difficult for Greek rationality, the core of Christian dogma is inherently and particularly miraculous—the claims of the deity of Jesus of Nazareth and His physical resurrection from the dead. Not only is the doctrinal core of Christian belief inherently miraculous, but New Testament teaching maintains that God Himself provides the ongoing warrants for the truth of what Tertullian calls these impossible Christian beliefs[36] with miraculous signs (Acts 4:23–31; Romans 15:18–19; 1 Corinthians 2:4–5).[37] The sign structure of John's gospel is its basic organizational schema and the inherently miraculous nature of the Christian gospel is demonstrated in the pattern of Christian proclamation and apologetics sketched in the New Testament. And so rather than the universal and rationally demonstrable being the grounds of believing in the truth of the Christian gospel, it is the particular and the unrepeatably singular which provides the truth warrants of Christian doctrine. This is very un-Platonic.

---

36. Tertullian mocks Marcion's high distaste for the idea that Christ had a real body with the famous phrase "certum est, quia impossibile" i.e., "it is certain because it is impossible" (*De Carne Christi* V); see *Ante-Nicene Fathers*, Roberts & Donaldson ed., vol. 3:525. Yet Tertullian is no irrationalist. Note this passage from *De Paenitentia*, I: "For reason is a property of God's, since there is nothing which God, the creator of all things, has not foreseen, arranged and determined by reason; moreover, there is nothing He does not wish to be investigated and understood by reason," ibid., 657. Yet, as Kierkegaard also discovered, if one rejects the discourse of reason assumed by the prevailing intellectual elites, one is readily labeled as an irrationalist, however hard the dominant stance might be to believe.

37. Jenkins (*The Next Christendom* and *The New Face of Christianity*) points out that today it is in the global South, that is the global underclass, that the Christian gospel is again proving powerful, and its method of evangelism is somewhat akin to the New Testament reliance on the miraculous power of God. The spirit of Saint Gregory Thaumaturgus seems to be abroad again. Malins (*Prepare the Way for Revival*) emphasizes the role of the manifest presence of God seen as normal in the miraculously dynamic form of Christianity at home in the South Pacific. See Burnett, a Fellow of the Royal Anthropological Institute, in *World of the Spirits*, for an astute insight into the living forms of non-Western spiritism in the Third World, and the 'super-natural' reality frame simply accepted by these people. As Brueggemann implies, such an approach of openness to the miraculous is simply unbelievable to an educated First World perspective.

CONCLUSION

Plato and John both believe that reality transcends appearance. However, there is an important difference between them. To Plato, appearance points to, but does not finally enter into, the true Insights of intellection; for John, God's glorious appearance as a common man makes concrete tangibility itself the medium via which the eternal is revealed to us. That is, whilst Plato and John both understand πίστις to be a classically low epistemological category, Plato finds truth beyond this epistemological realm whereas John finds it within this epistemological realm.[38] And here, the gospel can easily be, as Saint Paul well understood, an offence to the truth conception pursued by high Greek intellection. For in John's gospel, God seeks πιστεύω from us in response to being confronted by His incarnate, crucified and resurrected Λόγος. Such a schema could be little other than a profoundly impious and irrational affront to Plato. Yet, to finally side with John against Plato, this offensively low outlook may in fact be far more epistemologically realistic than high Greek intellection. After the counter-Enlightenment, after hermeneutic philosophy, after the insights of the sociology of knowledge, the conviction that truth could be grasped by high, rationally necessary and universal epistemological endeavors seems, at the very least, hard to believe.[39] But in John, divine Reason embeds Himself in the fuzzy woof and warp of a particular, enfleshed, en-timed, spatially, linguistically, culturally situated, concrete and even shameful historical existence. And, as we too exist in such fuzzy and tangled places, maybe what Saint Paul calls the foolishness of God—that is, His saving addressing of Himself to us in such an ineradicably low manner—is entirely reasonable.

---

38. See Yoder's "But we do see Jesus: the particularity of incarnation and the universality of truth," *The Priestly Kingdom*, 46–62, for a powerful exposition of the essential role that the classically low categories of historical particularity play in the Christian approach to being apprehended by divine truth.

39. Smith, *Who's Afraid of Postmodernism?*, 27, notes that the Christian, too, has dogmatic reasons for being suspicious of the notion that the human mind is capable, within its own resources, of apprehending truth. What Reformed theologians call the noetic effects of sin makes the apprehension of truth only possible after the grace of God has acted on the human mind via the convicting work of the Holy Spirit.

PART TWO

Application

What Is Applied Theological Epistemology?

THE THEORY SECTION OF this book uses conceptual, historical, and textual analysis in order to sketch some broad outlines charting developments in Western intellectual history that concern the relationship between faith and truth. Thus, conceptions about what theologically premised epistemology is—expressed in both Platonist and Christian terms—emerge from the preceding three chapters. As sweeping as much of the theoretical component of this book is, its genre is recognizable within the prevailing discourse of scholarly rigor. However, the applied section of this book engages in a type of personally interested social critique of some specific contemporary institutions and policies. I am very aware that whilst the applied chapters that follow are all thoroughly researched, the genre employed may make these chapters look more like journalistic advocacy than precise and solid scholarship. And indeed, some of these chapters were written as works of journalistic advocacy. Yet, if my theoretical section works then one is led to the conclusion that some of the dominant modern assumptions about what constitutes solid scholarship may be invalid and hence this applied section should still be taken seriously.

Dominant assumptions of modern scholarship typically include the separation of faith from reason (to the exclusion of faith), the separation of nature from divinity (to the exclusion of divinity), the isolation of facts from values (to the relativization of all values), the objectivity of research[1] and the autonomy of discrete spheres of scholarly expertise.

---

1. I do not mean to suggest that objectivity is invalid, only that it is not metaphysically neutral. That is, where objectivity means an openness to truth beyond what

Within this mode of discourse it is expected that scholars must (and can) shelve their metaphysical perspectives, their personal interests and their moral and religious commitments when they are doing proper academic work. Yet if the theological approach to epistemology outlined in part one of this book can be taken seriously then many of these normal academic assumptions must actually restrict what truth can be known rather than facilitate the knowledge of truth.

For if truth has this metaphysical and divinely gifted dimension to it that is presupposed by both the Platonist philosophical tradition and the Christian theological tradition, and if our knowledge of truth is—as Bonaventure maintains—always most deeply a knowledge of God,[2] then modern solid scholarship, as immense and dazzling as its multifaceted shards of specialized research are, constructs a kaleidoscope of knowledge that is oblivious to the grounds and meaning of true reality itself. Through this kaleidoscope we see only the shifting fragments of our own knowledge constructions (even though this sight is only possible because

---

reality conception I poetically construct, this is itself a very strong (and highly admirable) value commitment in the epistemological process. On this, see Michael Polanyi's epistemological approach to objectivity in science. Yet, where 'objectivity' implies the achievement of rationalistic and/or empiricistic purity because the knower's epistemic framework is defined by reductive naturalism and the interpretive assumptions of a nominalist conception of the ontological autonomy of human subjectivity, this is not a 'pure' objectivity at all. To the contrary, such so-called objectivity is a deeply and unavoidably metaphysically and theologically committed stance that excludes certain truth possibilities in the interpretive process. Being a metaphysically and theologically 'loaded' knower is not problematic, for it is unavoidable, but the unavoidably belief situated context of the knower mitigates the notion of 'objectivity' as any form of 'pure' openness to truth. In this sense we have no pure knowledge of the true though this in no way necessarily implies that we cannot participate—'impurely'—in true knowledge. It all depends on how you understand the relationship between some finally real Reality that is beyond complete capture by human knowledge and the immanent apprehensive capabilities of the human condition. David C. Schindler outlines the Platonist stance I am trying to hold on this matter very well: ". . . the transcendence of goodness [in Plato] nevertheless necessarily *includes* (without reducing to) immanence: thus metaphysics includes without reducing to ontology, and "exteriority" includes but does not reduce to interiority. Therefore while goodness (i.e., justice) for Levinas ultimately does violence to reason, we will argue that [the transcendence of goodness] is the necessary *ground* of reason, and thus that the reversal its transcendence entails fulfils rather than destroys reason," Schindler, *Plato's Critique*, 7 n. 12. Here also it can be seen that in Plato the mind's grasp of truth is understood to be an inherently moral, aesthetic and religious process as much as it is an intellectual process and (at least for Aristotle) a scientific process.

2. Bonaventure, *The Journey*.

What Is Applied Theological Epistemology?

of light from beyond). Within this prism chamber we *cannot* see anything beyond the fascinating and endlessly variegated mobile constellations of discrete facts and constructed meanings, situated—as knowledge—entirely within the epistemic boundaries of immediate perception, manipulative use and abstract (be it formal, linguistic or probabilistic) logic.[3]

Presupposing God and our essential relation to the divine and recognizing the integrative manner in which we know anything, the theological epistemology I have sketched in part one departs quite frighteningly from the familiar methodologies of modern, kaleidoscopically valid knowledge. For a Christian theological approach to epistemology presupposes some directly interested and divine Personal intervention from beyond our "all too human" knowledge in all human knowledge. And a Christian theological approach to epistemology also presupposes a personal response to this intervention, the response either of faith or of sin, in all knowledge. In this essentially Personalist epistemic framework, observation, love, moral sensibility, reason, illumination, what Kierkegaard calls passion and what Simone Weil calls attention[4] are presumed to all function together—within our historical, embodied, enacted and communitied context—to form knowledge. And here, in this complex

---

3. The analogy of the kaleidoscope is here to be contrasted with the analogy of the window. On this, George Orwell notes that: "Good prose is like a window pane," Orwell, *Why I Write*, 10. As a critique of political propaganda it is clear that Orwell holds that good prose does not hinder a vision of truth and good prose, merely as prose, is secondary to that which it points to. Here rhetorical effect is secondary and substantive qualitative vision gives form its meaning and style its beauty. Here, there is a tacit faith that 'objective value' exists such that authentic qualitative truths can be known. Thus, specific political states of affairs are truly good or bad. Yet in our knowledge institutions we seem to have lost philosophical faith in the existence of true meaning and value beyond the internal epistemological perimeters of human perception, language and behavior, and thus knowledge itself has not so much lost its way as now has no way to truth to find. We seem unable to pursue the high life of thought from the premise of confidence in that life that most Classical and Medieval thinkers held. Our very consciousness is locked inside the kaleidoscope. But maybe it is we rather than the ancients who are wrong about knowledge. Arendt, *Between Friends*, 25, still finds that "Truth . . . is the condition for the possibility of thought." In The Abolition of Man, 50, C. S. Lewis takes up Orwell's analogy thus: "The whole point of seeing through something is to see something through it. It is good that a window should be transparent, because the street or garden beyond it is opaque. How if you saw through the garden too? It is no use trying to 'see through' first principles. If you see through everything, then everything is transparent. But a wholly transparent world is an invisible world. To 'see through' all things is the same as not to see." Thus, in The View from the Bridge, 9, Ryckmans notes that "he who believes in nothing, sees nothing."

4. Weil, *Gravity and Grace*, 116–22; Kierkegaard, *Unscientific Postscript*, 29–34.

interactive web of factors, it is presumed that our knowledge is still grounded in the transcendent, thus it can still be, in some measure, true. In a modern knowledge environment characterized by the reductive, quantifiable atomization of 'purely natural' knowledge, such an epistemological approach seems far too chaotic, uncertain and fictive to be knowledge at all.

Yet the applied section of this book quite consciously departs from the presumptions of metaphysical and theological neutrality, of naturalistic objectivity, of value/fact disintegration, of personal disinterest and of objectivist abstraction from the spatiotemporal and community context of the knower. And it is this very departure which defines the application of the theological epistemology outlined in part one of this book.

But before launching into the application of theological epistemology, let us first recapitulate on the theory.

If a commitment to reason as a pathway to true knowing is an act of faith in the divine gifting of truth to the human knower—as I claim Plato implies—then all knowledge that participates to some extent in truth is theologically premised. Truth seeking that is not explicitly embedded in an outlook of religious faith suffers from trying to justify its basic epistemological assumptions as if unmediated perception and mere logic gave us some sort of sure and immediate access to Reality. Such endeavors are notoriously difficult to sustain. On the other hand, explicitly theologically premised approaches to knowledge escape the counter-Enlightenment critiques of modern epistemological foundationalism, for unlike naturalistic modernism, the warrants of truth are not produced by the perceptive, linguistic and rational powers of the human knower, rather the powers of the human knower participate in a limited manner in transcendence. Thus this Classical theological conception of truth—particularly as Plato articulates it—is not a stance grounded in proofs constructed in the terms of the knowledge powers of 'purely natural' humanity.

Further, this Platonic stance recognizes the radical openness of all knowledge so that whether one is open to receive truth or not is a complex matter that concerns not only right perception and logic, but the right attitude of receptivity to that which ontologically grounds and spiritually transcends the perceptive, linguistic and logical powers of humanity. Thus the correct outlook of good faith in the divinely gifted premises of human reason itself is necessary for any lover of wisdom to know truth. Proper piety is hence basic to the love of truth. Here reasoning rests not only on right perception and valid argument but on the disposition of trust in the divine giver of insight which provide us with our limited ability to have accurate perceptions, valid arguments, correct interpretations, true values and right relationships.

Yet, so the final chapter of my theoretical section argues, John maintains that the human knower is profoundly dependent on the particularistic and free initiative of divinity towards the human knower in the apprehension of truth. John also maintains that the human knower is also free to reject divinely offered truth on the grounds of the vain pursuit of ontological autonomy from God (sin). John's outlook paints a radical picture of the dependence of true knowledge on the particular, historical, contingent and open features of the relationship between God and the human knower, which is markedly distinct from high Greek epistemology in general. That is, the Greek desire to transcend the ordinary horizons of human knowledge's humble situation via abstract and universal knowledge, by encyclopedic factual knowledge, and by poetically idealizing the contingent and temporal as if they were the necessary and eternal, is not finally compatible with a Christian understanding of what truth is and how it is known. Hence, a Christian understanding of truth easily finds itself situated against what it sees as the philosophical pretensions of high Greek epistemology. Conversely, high Greek knowledge finds Christian faith to be superstitiously embedded in mere opinion, contingency, impossible miracles, particularity and unjustified belief. As Saint Paul clearly saw, Christian truth is too low, too foolish, for the wisdom of the Greeks.

So the theoretical component of this book finds the modern dismissal of metaphysical knowledge ill grounded and self-defeating, and yet finds high Greek thought too pretentious in its assumed God's eye viewpoint. In contrast to both these outlooks, the Christian stance maintains confidence in the transcendent origins of all meaning and truth that the human situation can apprehend, and yet never seeks to extract the divine kernel from the human husk in the apprehension of truth. Classical high Greek thought—though profoundly different to modern instrumental and disenchanted knowledge—does not escape the counter-Enlightenment critique of the pretensions of all high Western knowledge, even though the glib dismissals of ancient knowledge by many a counter-Enlightenment and postmodern thinker falsely equates pre-fourteenth century theologically premised knowledge with post-sixteenth century naturalistic and purely 'philosophically' premised knowledge. That is, whilst the situation before the separation of faith from reason is profoundly different to the situation after that extraordinary shift in the premises of the West's philosophy of religion, yet the inability of human knowledge to transcend its very non-divine, finite and contingent limitations is now very well grasped by postmodern and hermeneutic philosophy.[5]

In our postmodern epistemological context the Christian confidence in divine truth, yet its commitment to the very non-divine context in which all human knowledge is constructed, offers a distinctive alternative to the unattainably high aspirations of Classical and Enlightenment truth, *and* to the scientific reduction of truth to the 'mere' facticity of the 'purely' material, *and* to the hypermodern pragmatic irrealist rejection of the West's high truth heritage altogether.[6]

---

5. Of course many of the ancient Sophists and Classical Skeptics were as aware of the difficulty—even impossibility—of distinguishing between Platonic piety and delusional hubris as any postmodern epistemological nihilist. Yet, history was not kind to them. In *What is Ancient Philosophy?* Pierre Hadot links this historical failure with the unsuitability of the skeptical way of life and thought to the religious tenor of the Classical age. As Walter Burkert in *Greek Religion* points out, Plato's pious and civic understanding of philosophy, and the cultural victory of his theological vision over skepticism and the Sophists, had a remarkable impact on the assumed truth outlook of the ancient world. Thus the question of why skepticism has achieved such a widespread cultural victory in our intellectual culture today, though it did not succeed in antiquity, even though the greatest apologists of skepticism come from antiquity, reflects very interestingly on our culture's distinctive assumed conceptual canvas concerning truth and religion. With John Milbank, I think nominalist theological developments in the late Middle Ages are central to the development of the modern Western mind. Thus, combining Milbank's work concerning the theological origins of the modern sundering of faith/God from reason/nature with good historical scholarship on the reception of ancient skepticism by the proto-modern milieu—such as Popkin & Schmitt eds., *Skepticism from the Renaissance to the Enlightenment*—makes for fascinating reading.

6. This commitment to both transcendence and immanence makes a Christian truth perspective subject to attack from both idealists and pragmatists, and both pantheists and materialists. Yet, oddly enough, some sociological thinkers seem comfortable with the integration of the transcendent with the immanent and show a keen awareness of how hard any sort of commitment to transcendence has been after nineteenth century idealism. In Facing up to Modernity, 247, Peter Berger notes: "Transcendence has been, shall we say, declared 'inoperative' by the major agencies that 'officially' define reality—the universities, the school system, the medical system, the communications media, and to some extent even the courts. Those who may be described as the official 'reality definers'—loosely speaking, the intellectuals and would be intellectuals—are, throughout the Western world at least, overwhelmingly attached to that 'modern scientific world view' which proscribes transcendence. In our society, as in others, these agencies together constitute what I like to call a 'reality police'. The 'reality police-men'—teachers, psychiatrists, commentators and so on—watch over the cognitive boundaries of the culture. In their perspective transcendence in *any* of its

What Is Applied Theological Epistemology?

Stated in slightly different terms, the faith of Classical and Enlightenment truth in the divine capabilities of the human knower is not justified, but this does not require the abandonment of faith in divine truth itself. Though, where any claim to truth is made, this claim cannot be done outside of the context of faith as distinct from final proof. For truth as from and of transcendence can only ever be partially apprehended and can never be totally contained for it is always contingently expressed in the context of immanence. Thus any claimed knowledge of truth is faith's knowledge and any claim to knowledge that has no interest in truth fails as a serious knowledge claim.

If all this does indeed follow then a Christian understanding of truth is at least as valid as Classical and Enlightenment claims to truth and can counter skepticism towards truth itself in ways that escape the critical power of a postmodern disbelief in Classical and modern truth. And yet, this integrative contextual approach to transcendently sourced truth—committed to the openness of faith rather than the closedness of proof and situated at odds with pragmatic and skeptical truth methodologies—jars our knowledge culture. Our knowledge culture is not jarred by contextual information and interpretation without transcendence or by specialized knowledge without metaphysical truth horizons—these are comprehensible. But in the chapters that follow I am assuming that all knowledge is interested, personal, situated, communally shaped, historically engaged and interpretively open at the same time that I am assuming that this is the medium through which divine truth can analogically reach us. Indeed, all the things that modern approaches to truth like to abstract out of intellectual endeavor—personal interest, specific situations, values, ontological beliefs, religious convictions—are basic to the 'low' Christian understanding of the messy and never final truth revealing process that I argue is basic to a Christian theological epistemology in "Faith in Plato and John."

The chapters that follow seek to exemplify this messy, interested, contextualized and incomplete approach to divinely gifted truth. As such, they are modeled after what might be called the ad hoc social critiques of Jacques Ellul, John Howard Yoder, and Stanley Hauerwas.[7]

---

historical forms is viewed as contraband goods." Thus the philosophy of knowledge that is sociologically contextualized without necessarily being reduced to the cognitive boundaries of modernity's anti-transcendent reality assumptions—such as found in the works of Peter Berger, Christos Yannaras, Michael Polanyi, Talal Asad, Jacques Ellul and Michael Budde—is an important influence on the following chapters.

7. "Social critique"—whether it is done by Marxists, liberals, modern scientists,

Faith's Knowledge

Ellul, Yoder and Hauerwas—hereafter referred to as Ellul et al.[8]—are renowned for their prolific streams of ad hoc and inter-disciplinary topical essays. Whilst tough intellectual rigor, deep and broad learning and a consistency of stance is apparent, their writings as a whole defy formulation into any discrete intellectual system. Like Kierkegaard, they are committed to the fragmentary and open ended nature of all human knowledge and do simply not believe any human claim to indubitable or final or faithless true knowledge.[9] They are all very engaged in the

---

nihilists, or whoever—always draws on the value commitments and truth beliefs of the particular understanding of reality and goodness that the critic adheres to. Here "Christian social critique" is no different to any other form of critique. However, critique itself—even when done by progressive liberal humanists—is often seen as suspect in academia for two reasons. Firstly, the modern scientific aspiration of objectivity and facticity somewhat disdains the distorting lens of values and belief commitments—particularly religious beliefs and values. Secondly, values and belief commitments are not considered to be 'hard' knowledge and are somewhat outside of the proper scope of genuinely scholarly enterprises. Values and beliefs are a matter of (personal) opinion not of knowledge, of *doxa*, not *episteme*. However successful this scientistic disdain for moral, theological and metaphysically anchored critique may be, the three thinkers I am modeling this section of my book on all persuasively maintain that this disdain is itself anchored in moral, theological and metaphysical belief commitments, as is all human knowledge. Stanley Fish puts forward a succinct case for the presuppositional and committed basis of all knowledge in a New York Times article, dated 17 May, 2009, titled "God Talk, Part 2."

8. I am here locating Ellul, Yoder, and Hauerwas together in a methodological and teleological manner, rather than in a substantive or dogmatic manner. I do not mean to imply that these three highly independent thinkers form a recognizable school or movement. However, they do all approach knowledge in a situated and open manner at the same time as their conception of truth itself is not defined simply by the situated and open context in which they are totally embedded.

9. Skepticism and the type of faith Kierkegaard upholds share more in common with each other than either of them have with any dogmatic presumption of a certain, indubitable knowledge capture of truth—be that presumption grounded in a naturalistic scientific certainty or in a supernaturalistic religious or idealist certainty. Faith's approach to truth is as skeptical of indubitable certainty and necessary proof as is skepticism. Yet faith—as a positive belief stance that embraces uncertainty and accepts the limitations of human knowledge, yet trusts in God, without 'proof', for the gift of what F. H. Bradley calls a partial and incomplete apprehension of truth—does not struggle with the difficulty of fundamental self-contradiction in the manner in which skepticism does. For the difficulty of how one can be committed to skepticism itself in a skeptical manner is by no means easy to resolve. However, attempts at such a resolution are very serious and the impact of the negative and provisional belief stance towards apparent truth—the tentative approach to knowledge pursued under the methodology of reasonable doubt—deeply historically forms the modern scientific outlook. Important scholars in this field are Richard Popkin, Myles Burnyeat, Jonathan Barnes and Charles Schmitt.

public issues of their time and place and they are engaged as Christians guided by the truths of their faith which gives their work its polemic and prophetic edge. At the same time they powerfully resist what Heubner describes as "the idolatry of theoretical closure."[10] They have in common an appreciation that knowledge is historically and culturally situated, arises out of the habits, assumptions and practices of the life forms in which language and thought is inevitably situated, is formed by communities of interpretation, and cannot stand independently of concrete and interested personal specificity. Yet these contexts alone do not account for truth for these theologians believe that the heavenly music of the divine gift of truth is expressed in these very earthly contexts for those who "have ears to hear."

For Ellul et al., human existence is not defined merely by the intricacies of human artifice, nor do we ever have unmediated access to divine truth, but, as Saint Paul explains, we have divine treasure in earthen vessels. Thus, we can only touch a true knowledge of, say, education,[11] politics,[12] and technology[13] through our explicitly interested, embodied, committed, faith premised and relational involvement in specific instances of these lived realities. In that context the present action of the Holy Spirit reveals what light of truth is needed for the specific concerns of a given time and place.

That is, small 't' truths given by divinity through the provisional and immanent context of our embodied, communitied and temporal existence can be apprehended by those who are spiritually open, but big 'T' Truth remains always with God. And yet, small 't' truths participate in Truth in order to be truths rather than mere poetic or perceptional constructs. Inventions of the imagination (ποίησις) and observed facts (*factum*) are both 'made' by the human mind (in community), but truth is dis-covered (ἀποκαλύπτω), is found (*invenio*), and is given to us from beyond the human mind. Yet none of the small 't' truths we find can be presented to our minds outside of the medium of imagination, facts and community. Herein lies theological epistemology's commitment to the essential creative integration of the human and the divine in the art of human knowledge.

---

10. Heubner, *A Precarious Peace*, 91.
11. See Hauerwas, *The State of the University*.
12. See Yoder, *The Politics of Jesus*.
13. See Ellul, *The Technological Bluff*.

Trusting in this divine/human integrative approach to truth, the theological epistemologies of Ellul et al. cannot be separated from the particularity and contingency of their actual involvement in history. This is strongly in keeping with the final chapter of this book's theoretical section wherein the distinctly Christian understanding of the revelation of God is inextricably embedded in historical specificity.

In this outlook a distinctive relationship between truth and historical particularity can be observed. Revelation embedded in time, place, language and singularity, and spatiotemporally continued via distinctively situated and diversely imperfect communities of belief, practice, culture and power, is unable to rise above the concretely human in its apprehension of the divine. Unlike an approach to truth that seeks to extract eternal ideas and abstract universal laws from concrete particularity, and unlike the abandonment of truth itself out of an awareness of the flux and contingency in which all human knowledge is embedded, this stance sees divine revelation—only ever analogically and partially knowable to the human condition—in human history. So this position is metaphysically bold, for transcendent truth is presupposed, and our analogical knowledge of it, as gifts embedded in time and space, is believed in. And yet, the claims of true knowledge made are explicitly fleeting and partial, embedded, as they are, in the flux, contingency and incompleteness of historical specificity. This is the humility of faith's knowledge.

Ellul et al.'s epistemological outlook takes the opposite approach to truth to what is generally the case in modern secular knowledge. There, metaphysical agnosticism, if not total skepticism, is presupposed in relation to the grounds of all ontological, cosmological, teleological, religious and moral truth beliefs and the quantifiably particular is studied with an eye to formulating universal necessary laws of mechanistic or probabilistic behavior which can then be manipulated and controlled by various technologies. Thus the modern mind tends to think of truth in the terms of *scientia*, where quantifiable knowledge and universal natural laws unleash instrumental power. The modern mind has lost confidence—lost faith—in truth understood in the terms of ontological *sapientia*. To this outlook, the approach of Ellul et al. seems metaphysically presumptuous, without factual groundings and superstitiously restrictive of instrumental potency.

What one assumes about the nature of truth—is it a divine gift, or is it an exclusively natural power of human perception and reason?—makes a very big difference in how one evaluates the modern world.

What Is Applied Theological Epistemology?

Without finding instrumental *scientia* itself to be invalid—indeed, it is as equally a gift of God as *sapientia* to the Christian—the theological epistemology of Ellul et al. finds that where *scientia* is not understood as a divine gift, all manner of problems follow. For where knowledge as manipulative power is understood as being 'ours' without any accountability to divinity in how we use it, and without any reference to what the divinely gifted good, true and beautiful ends of our powers actually are, a most virile idolatry is embedded in modern technological power. And from this arrogation of the creature's autonomy from the ontic realities gifted to the cosmos by the Creator, we worship our own knowledge and enter a realm of profound spiritual alienation from our true natures. From this doxologically distorted epistemological fount—from this idolatry—great rivers of despair, sin and human evil flow.[14] Thus theologically premised beliefs about the underlying ontological, qualitative and aesthetic realities of human existence imply an unavoidable 'social critique' of the world that seeks to know and control 'reality' only in the terms of theologically gutted *scientia*.

So the outlook on truth defined by the Christian faith is incomplete if it is not situated in the messy cut and thrust of the explicitly interested, evaluative and worship concerned dynamics of the life situation of any given person's actual historically situated existence. For Christian truth in the present is found in the practice of Christian life, situated in the communally embodied (yet never fully adequate) continuation of the prophetic and redemptive work of Christ, and is lived under the hope of the eschaton. So this believed yet largely 'unseen' or 'hidden' horizon of ontological and doxological truth always informs the present context of concrete Christian practice and makes a Christian appreciation of truth always disruptive of the norms, beliefs and values of the modern Christian community, and of the broader cultural world in which that community lives.

Indeed, it seems reasonable to hold that a broad cultural lack of collective transcendently directed faith accounts for why the very notion of normative critique is now considered strangely out of place within secular Western academia. For surely if all that is is natural and quantifiable, and nothing that truly is is metaphysical and qualitative, then how

---

14. Generally speaking, this idolatry is as at home in the modern Western Church as it is in secular modernity. Indeed, in the final chapter of this book I argue that there is no manner in which the Church can live in the modern Western world and not participate in this idolatry, other than by the miraculous enabling of the Holy Spirit.

can anything that is—being natural—be wrong in any way other than conventionally? There is nothing unnatural about murder and rape and the exploitation of the weak by the strong, though there may be socio-evolutionary instinctive and conventional sanctions that shape the way in which society allows murder, rape and the exploitation of the weak by the strong to 'function'. The very notion of critique—so it seems to me—arises out of some trust in the validity of metaphysical truths that normatively judge whether something is good or bad beyond the scope of simply what 'naturally' and conventionally is. Such a stance can yet affirm the limited and incomplete categories of all our knowledge. The point being made here is that one's views about truth and about the true nature of reality very much shapes the terms and scope of normative judgments, and these judgments do in fact direct the social practices and qualitative goals of our very form of life.

So, the theoretical part of this book implies that the modern secular outlook on knowledge not only has theological roots but is reasonable and believable only to the extent that it is a stance upheld by a committed and undemonstrable confidence in its truth—it is a stance of faith. Yet, having faith in the autonomous validity of human reason underpinned by no transcendent ontological bearings, and having faith in the discretely natural nature of nature—to the exclusion of metaphysical, spiritual and intrinsically qualitative realities within and beyond the materially apparent—undercuts faith in truth itself. Thus modern secular scientific truth easily reduces to irrealist pragmatism, to 'reality' being meaningful only as manipulative potency within the kaleidoscope of 'purely' human knowledge. This outlook on truth in turn has profound implications for practices of power within the modern life form, and for that life form's values and beliefs. It is to these implications that we now turn.

So applied theological epistemology is the application of a theological understanding of truth in general to the particular context in which the theological epistemologist lives in a truth concerned manner. In what follows I have decided to risk trying to be a theological epistemologist (following the examples of Ellul et al.) and have selected four arenas of my own life experience—the university, the domestic atmosphere in Australia produced by the post-9/11 international relations context, the modern hospital and the modern church—in which to look for truth. As truth is here understood to be primarily concerned with what C. S. Lewis calls "objective value,"[15] this endeavor ends up looking like social critique.

15. Lewis, *The Abolition of Man*, 11–12.

What Is Applied Theological Epistemology?

And because the Christian understanding of truth requires a personal commitment to that which is genuinely true, good and beautiful, these chapters end up looking like polemic social critiques.

To claim to examine any given messy real life situation in order to "find truth," and worse still, in order to give a true evaluation of whether such a situation is "objectively" good or bad, cannot fail to sound remarkably pretentious. Yet, that it does sound pretentious is illustrative of two points I have been making all along. Firstly, our culture has lost faith in truth itself. Secondly, the idea that truth is embedded in faith—not proof—and that the contextual contingencies and incompleteness of all human knowledge contexts are not overcome by truth, is foreign to the assumed notion of truth that our skeptical academic and hyper-modern consumer cultures have rejected.

Yet perhaps we have lost faith in truth because our modern conception of truth—though reductive and materialistic—is yet too 'high', too divorced from the flux, incalculability, mystery and particularity of the contingent historical and communal context in which the human knower actually knows, and hence modern truth lacks both humanity and humility. And then the life forms of the ideologies of modern progress (nationalism, fascism, communism, economic liberalism, technologism, consumerism), particularly in the twentieth century, have imposed their proud truths and cosmic visions on the tiny world with unprecedented transformative and destructive impact. So there are significant ideological reasons why we now fear the very idea of truth. Yet, if the Christian understanding of truth is true, we fear a misapprehension of truth and not truth itself. The conception of truth that this book is premised on is a roughly Anabaptist conception where the highest revelation of truth we can receive is one not of abstract universal conceptual or political violence, but is one of particularist and redemptive suffering; it is the Lamb who was slain. But this Lamb, in all his historical and contingent particularity, is also the very Logos of God; hence the baffling highness and the shameful lowness of Christian truth. Hence, the confronting metaphysical and qualitative boldness and the uncertain particularist and contextual humility of faith's knowledge.

4

The Iron Cage Closes

INTRODUCTION

THIS CHAPTER IS HERE reproduced exactly as it was first published in the Australian Public Affairs quarterly magazine *Quadrant*, in early July of 2007. That article was published just before the Academic Board of my University voted to shut down its Bachelor of Arts degree and to terminate its "old" Humanities and Social Science offerings. The addendum also reproduced in this chapter was an unpublished article I wrote in late July of 2007, after the Academic Board's decision had been made.

Whilst the specific details of my own university's neoliberal rejection of its humanist roots is of no great significance in the history of twenty-first century Western culture, this chapter serves a couple of important functions in opening the applied section of this book. I have already argued that a specific context in place, culture, relationships, and time is the necessary carrier of human meaning, and that the existential dynamic of human interestedness is, in reality, inseparable from any human account of what matters. Yet, I have also sought to argue that this radical contextuality does not remove truth and transcendent value, but is the necessary media of the kind of higher meanings basic to our lives which, paradoxically, cannot be reduced simply to context and interest. Thus in this chapter I seek to incorporate specific contexts and explicit interests into an account of what is more than simply contingently wrong with the very *telos* and operational normality of the neoliberal university. This is an approach that Kierkegaard would have no difficulty recognizing as deeply tangled in the epistemology of faith. Even so, this approach flies in the face of the epistemic norms of Modernity: norms presented as dispassionate, objective, impartially 'reasoned', factual, quantitative, verifiable, and most of all, realistic.

The other three chapters that follow have more reflective content in them than this chapter, but this chapter plunges the reader into the more personally situated and explicitly interested approach to knowledge and meaning that the first section of this book has sought to give some justification for.

THE IRON CAGE CLOSES

It seems that I am a relic of an intellectual tradition that is now obsolete. Some years back I did a Bachelor of Arts in the Social Sciences and went on to do Honors in Philosophy. I'm now doing a doctorate in Sociology at the Carseldine Campus of the Queensland University of Technology (slogan, "A university for the real world®"). Being an intellectual product of the "old" Social Sciences and Humanities I understand that my Vice Chancellor, Professor Pete Coaldrake, sees my type of study as likely to have poor employment outcomes and my research as likely to have little industry linked funding possibilities. So I am somewhat irrelevant to QUT's real world®, and hence, likely to be a cause of statistical embarrassment to my university's proud branding in vocational outcomes once I graduate.

This may all be true. But is this a valid reason for QUT to now seriously consider abandoning its traditional offerings in the Humanities and Social Sciences? As a hypothetical, let us assume we are not CEOs in the education industry but are just interested in ideas and truth, and let us ask what a sociological perspective can say to this question.

The brilliant Classical sociologist Max Weber points out that one of the defining features of our modern way of life is the creation of large controlling bureaucracies. These institutions are governed by an impersonal instrumental logic—"formal rationality"—which neatly coalesces with the absence of "substantive rationality" (intrinsic and transcendent values) in the economic dynamics of our consumer society. The final effect is an all pervasive, de-humanizing institutional control—Weber's "iron cage"—quarantining human dignity and transcendent vision out of daily life.

Weber does not claim that modern bureaucracies are by definition oppressive, for no bureaucracy (as yet) is formally pure. Yet, Weber notes that where the operational logic of instrumental efficiency and institutional control becomes overly pure, institutional power loses contact with intrinsic human values and then the human conditions on which our society depends are placed in serious jeopardy.

George Ritzer has taken up Weber's insights in a wonderful little book titled *The McDonaldization of Society*. Ritzer notes that modern management values are all "formal"—efficiency, calculability, predictability and control. These values and their organizational structures may be well suited to some types of business—say, international fast food chains—but are typically very bad for us when applied to "managing" people or envisioning intrinsic organizational aims. For example, another sociologist, Zygmunt Bauman, persuasively analyzes the Nazi Holocaust as a pristine case study in the political topography of formal institutional rationality. The impartial and purely formal implementation of directives from above, however dehumanizing and barbaric those directives may be, constitutes, ironically, the integrity of the bureaucrat's professionalism. Thus administrative professors may destroy the intrinsic values of university education with a clear conscience—they are merely implementing directives from above or responding to market and administrative necessities outside of their control.

Weber, Ritzer, and Bauman give us good reasons to be cautious when our institutions are run by a highly remunerated executive class whose professional world view is entirely contained within the values, logic, goals and political realism of institutional pragmatism. Such an environment attracts executives who are pure careerists, good linear processors of a legalistic bent, and who, in exercising their professional integrity, can sacrifice all substantive loyalties to the formal systems logic that furthers their own advancement. Weber describes them as "specialists without spirit, sensualists without heart."

Further, formal bureaucratic structures, being inherently pragmatic, are deeply invested in positional subordination. Effective executive power here relies on command and obedience and preserves executive decision making as an enclosed process only for like-minded responsible elites. People who know how to climb these structures respect the laws of total subordination to their superiors and executive secrecy and expect the same treatment when they reach high office. No insubordination or brand disloyalty will be tolerated. Formal bureaucratic logic is hence entirely opposed to collegiate organizational structures based on substantive values (such as traditional universities).

If Weber is right then it can be no surprise if QUT's executive sincerely believes that modern universities are essentially businesses and the "old" Humanities and Social Sciences are irrelevant to universities for the real world®. QUT's executive must be forward looking in its restless search for the right branding of its product in the higher education market. Thus the executive believes it must turn away from its traditional offerings in the "old humanities" and towards the "new humanities"—the Creative Industries Faculty (CIF). Here the executive can reasonably expect to find a sexy new brand of media linked scholarship at one with its market driven pragmatic values. This might look "philistine," notes our Vice Chancellor, but really, he is rather proud of being so cutting edge in the real world® educational market place.

The executive also seems to assume that enterprise in the "new humanities" should be as unconcerned with a serious critical analysis of the power structures and human concerns of the real world® as the executive is. This expectation is well evidenced by the treatment of academic members of the CIF who have been so brazen and disloyal as to publicly critique the ethics, humanity and intellectual validity of brand approved projects deemed a marketable scholarly enterprise by QUT. CIF lecturers Gary MacLennan and John Hookham have been suspended without pay for 6 months after they critiqued the reality TV, industry linked CIF doctoral project, "Laughing at the Disabled" earlier this year.

Does QUT's disciplinary tribunal here function as an inquisition style punishment mechanism for QUT staff who publicly speak out against ethical, humanitarian or intellectual failures endorsed by QUT? Do these staff speak out, even though they know they are going to get in big trouble with the approved brand upheld by the executive, because they are still tainted by "old" university values now obsolete in the education industry? The "formalism" of our executive refuses to even consider that substantive moral issues are at stake here as it brutalizes any of its own academics who stand against the degradation of human values in our universities. Self-censoring and timid compliance—described well in Hamilton and Maddison's *Silencing Dissent*—seem now normalized amongst the socio-culturally critical organs of our tertiary system.

Understanding and combating the dehumanizing risk that Weber identifies in modern life has exercised many serious thinkers. Jürgen Habermas finds that the dominance of our daily lives by monolithic bureaucratic power structures is only half our problem. At a personal level, relational fragmentation and atomism typically characterize the cultural ethos of late modern consumerism. Hence, there is a great absence of mediating political structures between individuals and large bureaucracies. Put another way, we are either part of the impersonal bureaucratic structures of instrumental power that control our lives, or we are marginalized from the political context of our own life.

So we can have power and corporate identity at the loss of intrinsic human values or we are politically marginalized if we refuse to be subsumed into the various corporate machines that control our lives. Building a constructive tension between collective identity and personal freedom whilst upholding substantive human values is very hard for us modern people to do. This task becomes more difficult the more unaccountably powerful and pragmatically inhumane the institutional structures that we live in become.

The logic of executive power at QUT, as demonstrated in the proposed dissolution of the School of Humanities and Human Services, is neatly illustrative of Weber's insights. Executive power at QUT is remarkably unfettered, showing signs of being rather advanced, in Weber's terms, as a formally efficient bureaucracy. For there appear to be no intrinsically *intellectual* values upheld by the executive, only branding, financial and business values really® matter. Without malice, then, but as a kind of managerial birth right, the executive does not seem to see its role as facilitating the intellectual work of serious and independent academics for an inherent civic value, rather it seems to see academics as an addendum to the institution's market image and profitability. The whole institution, apparently, serves exclusively "formal" ends. This is what a university for the real world® looks like, though this no longer looks like a *real* university where intellectual quality and academic independence flourish for the common good.

At QUT our executive, governed by its own pragmatic rationality and often in pursuit of undisclosed agendas, controls all serious power. This is because we have a business (in confidence) model of executive power at QUT. The executive finds that dedicated academic staff in the Humanities and Social Sciences are problematic to the real world® brand identification of QUT, so our Vice Chancellor then proposes that the School of Humanities and Human Services (SHHS) be dissolved (20 April 2007). From here, formal dehumanization leaps into action. The

The Iron Cage Closes

executive "consults" the relevant stake holders and advisory bodies about what options can be pursued in the wake of this proposal.

Given this power situation, let us be explicit about what "consultation" here means. The primary stake holders—staff and students in the SHHS—are not consulted about whether the "proposal" to dissolve us is academically, inherently, or even financially justified (each year QUT is many millions of dollars in surplus). The SHHS carefully critiqued the executive's stated rationale for dissolving us and demonstrated powerfully that this rationale was vacuous and biased. The School's critique found, in effect, that the executive selectively interpreted data in order to ostensibly demonstrate what it ideologically presupposed. As any Social Scientist can tell you, this is a very old trick but still the main stay of public relations and political manipulation for many large corporations. Even so, the "change management" process set in motion by the "proposal" moves ahead unabated.

So, isn't it nice to be consulted? Well, stake holders, how would you like to be cooked? Roasted, deep fried or barbequed, or, for the lucky and compliant ones, moved sideways into the salad bar? Put your order in now before we decide for you. This is "consultation." Various advisory boards, like the University Academic Board, have no executive power and the process of status advancement and tribal loyalty tacit in environments of power assures that bodies to whom the executive is in theory accountable are typically populated by like-minded powerful people. This is the political reality in which "stake holders" (i.e. people holding their own stake as they climb the lonely hill of Golgotha) can "negotiate" with the executive.

Negotiation. This brings us to the campaigns run by our National Tertiary Education Union aligned staff spokesperson and the Student Guild in response to the executive's proposition to dissolve the School. Because of the way executive power works in our university, academic staff have no real power, and because of the atomization of individual students and the failure of effective mediating structures between students and the university executive, students have no collective voice, no genuine representation, and no power. All the power chips are in the hands of the executive so what is effectively happening is that managerial political realism and the logic of instrumental pragmatism is tacitly accepted by the official staff and student opposition as it seeks to work within political reality. This type of negotiation from a position of powerlessness can only have one outcome. Total failure.

This is the same tired story of union power since Hawke. In *The Hawke-Keating Hijack*, Dean Jaensch examines the way in which the ALP of the 1980s became iconic in its instrumental pragmatism and its acceptance of the logic of modern bureaucratic and financial power. The NTEU, the Student Guild and Professor Coaldrake, with his deep personal links with the ALP, are all part of the same political machinery of bureaucratic alienation. (Not that the "other side" of politics is any different.) Students protesting cry "don't close our school" but institutional power will not respond to this plea, so none of "our" official campaign organizers have any serious chance of getting what students and staff actually want through the formal channels open to them.

So, is QUT a cultivator of humanity aspiring towards inherently good civic goals, or is it a Weberian iron maiden that crushes the humanity and transcendence from its staff and students in its contracting embrace?

Like probably all Australian universities, QUT has both contrary forces acting within it at the same time. However, it seems worth asking what is the proportional balance of those forces and where are the proportions of those forces located within the institutional structure? As a post-graduate student at a close knit campus with wonderful, intelligent student friends, a great library, and a caring collegiate environment of scholars of high quality intellect, I have experienced the humanizing cultivation of deep and rich learning at QUT in abundance. It is for this reason that I am so shocked, so anxiety ridden, so angry at the manner in which the executive elites of my university seem bent on destroying the delicate flower of humane civilization that is seeking the sun at QUT Carseldine. Should not my university's administration be nurturing, facilitating, even improving the intellectual life at Carseldine?

It seems that I and the university's executive have very different beliefs about what the "core business" of a real university should be. The "old" view is that a university's "core business" is to facilitating the pursuit of true knowledge, and in so doing, to cultivate the human soul. Formation in *sapientia* (wisdom) is necessary for those who wish to gain the responsibility and power of *scientia* (knowledge) or else the powerful will have no understanding of truly good and inherently humane ends and will perpetrate stupidity and evil with their powerful knowledge. Indeed, the smarter and more powerful the unwise are, the more evil and stupidity they will inflict.

Does our QUT executive know that Western universities historically arise from the church and find their substantive values from theology? If they haven't read Weber, Honnefelder, and Dupré, they probably have no idea that their "modern" disinterest in traditional university values also arises from the theological degradation that produced formal rationality. But why would our executive want to know about that when the industry linked possibilities of scholarship with, say, reality TV is such a great opportunity for QUT's distinctive brand of excellence? The "philistine and proud of it" real world® brand.

If the Vice Chancellors of Australia are now looking at QUT to see how we go in getting rid of traditional offerings in the Humanities and Social Sciences so that they too can be more effective providers of "new" industry-linked scholarship, then I'm leaving. I will have to go overseas to finish my studies and I will have to stay there to find academic work of any core value to me.

But, what do you think the "core business" of Australian universities should be?

ADDENDUM TO "THE IRON CAGE CLOSES"

Humanities at QUT: A View from the Watch House

On the eighteenth of July 2007, the QUT Council met to vote on the Academic Board's recommendations that the School of Humanities and Human Services (SHHS) be dissolved at the end of 2007 and that consideration for some new liberal arts degree program be explored for implementation in 2009. I am a doctoral student in sociology and a sessional lecturer at the SHHS so I was at the protest outside the council meeting. Usually these meetings drag on for some hours so I wasn't planning on staying for long. However, there were about twenty or so police there when I arrived, and probably about forty or fifty protestors. One QUT student, Lauren, a remarkably intelligent and politically passionate young woman, had already been locked up in a vacant office by police. About ten minutes later I was arrested myself, so I ended up spending four hours in the watch house being processed and charged for obstructing a police officer in the course of his duties. The police were after Lauren, for she had returned to the campus after being instructed to leave. As I was standing next to her, this put me in the middle of the scrum that developed when the police officers moved in. So I was an obstruction, hence I literally copped it in the neck.

Before I went back to study I had been a chaplain and had also done voluntary work in half way housing for street kids and at watch houses. I've had quite a bit to do with youth who have been in trouble with the law and so I was fully aware of the difficult nature of police work. I have never verbally or physically abused a police officer and I have always believed in non-violent protest. The reason why I was one of the three lucky protestors to be singled out for arrest seems to be that I had the misfortune of falling on top of the officer who grabbed me from behind and forced the back of his hand into my wind pipe (sorry about that Adam). Once I was on top of a police officer and we were both on the ground, I was history. Three or four officers swooped in, I was hand cuffed in no time flat and chooffed off to the watch house.

The next day our Deputy Vice Chancellor, Professor David Gardiner, came to the SHHS to tell us that Council had accepted the Academic Board's recommendations to dissolve our school. I find David to be a man who is very thorough in the performance of his duties and he is certainly an intelligent man. Yet, there was a strange confluence of synergies between my 4 hour stint in the watch house and the hour and a half spent with my colleagues listening to David explain to us what the Council had decided.

In the watch house I wanted to ring my wife to let her know where I was. I'm tapping on the unbreakable glass but no-body will even look at me let alone respond to my request. I will be dealt with when it suits them and in the manner that suits them. What is important to me is of no particular concern to them. I have no right to demand anything. This eerily recalled to me the "consultation" process my university's administration had conducted with us academics. Professor Gardiner made it explicit: consultation is not a commitment to agreement between the management and the staff and students, it is simply a part of the required change management process that provides information to the administration.

Students and staff have only really wanted two things: a commitment to no forced redundancies and an assurance that, in whatever form, serious scholarship in the traditional Humanities and Social Sciences be at least maintained at QUT. We only have 21 academic staff, so it is hardly a big ask. Yet the administration has flatly refused to give us these assurances. We will be dealt with in the way that they see fit, when and how it suits them. If we are compliant we are not treated like law breakers, but

The Iron Cage Closes

we are Human Resources that the administration can shift and process as they see fit. Professor Gardiner informed us that in the contemporary work place environment, this is "the real world."

This comment gave me a flash back to the occasion when I was hit by a truck on my bicycle (I owe my life to the helmet). Sure, in "the real world" if you are big and powerful, you get your way. What, after all, was I expecting being small and powerless on the open road, mixing it with massive, busy and important players who hardly even noticed my existence? Yes, that is the "real world"—but is it a humane and reasonable world, and is it the only possible reality?

In this example of institutional re-structuring, all that QUT staff and students can do is protest impotently and get thrown in the slammer if we cause any trouble. I don't like protesting, I'd much rather be reading Plato and Newman (eerily, I'm reading "Apology" and "The idea of a university" at the moment). And I certainly don't like getting thrown in the slammer. I was in a cell with a TV I could not turn off, and no books for four hours—I know this is a totally trivial inconvenience compared with what people at Villawood get, but for an academic who detests popular culture and does not own a TV, this was pretty hard core! Even so, I'd rather make a bit of noise on the way down than just roll over and watch what I value at QUT be restructured into oblivion.

But who cares? I submitted this article complete with dramatic pictures of myself being mugged by three policemen to The Higher Education supplement of *The Australian* newspaper for their next edition after July 18. They didn't publish it. Instead, they published a short media release from Peter Coaldrake assuring readers that everything is fine at QUT because the SHHS has been shut down via a careful process of consultation. Nothing to worry about. With the VC talking up riots on the 4BC radio station at 6am on July 18th, and someone from the university administration calling the police in before any students even arrived, and with *The Australian* having read my side of the story, it does indeed seem as if both fairness and humanity are irrelevant to "the real world."*

I think it is time we took a long hard look at the type of reality we have created. I think the administration should be held accountable for the strong arm treatment of its own students at the hands of police when there was nothing our ordinary security team could not have handled. This is an administration that relies on force rather than reason, with no heart for humanity, no interest in genuine negotiation for stake holders in its restructures, and no interest in ongoing scholarship in traditional

Humanities and Social Science offerings. In this reality, Barbarians rule—bow down or be crushed. Is this the reality we want or a reality we must simply accept? Or is it a reality beneath the dignity of scholarship, a reality in violation of the heritage of Western universities, a reality brutally at odds with ordinary human decency? If so, then this is a reality we are morally, intellectually and humanly obliged to contest.

5

Australian Universities in Transition

Moral, Pragmatic, or Religious Drivers?

INTRODUCTION

IN VERY BROAD TERMS, Australian universities have undergone two radical changes in cultural ethos in the twentieth century. The first of these transitions, finally flowering in the late 1960s, was from a conservative, classical, and at least tacitly Christian ethos to a progressive, liberal, secular, and humanist ethos.[1] The second transition, in the late 1980s, was from a progressive liberal humanist ethos to a conservative neoliberal pragmatic ethos.[2]

Using a geological analogy, contemporary Australian universities rest on three strata of incommensurable value frames, laid in rapid succession. Australian universities when I was born (1965) had an entirely different institutional ethos to the university of my undergraduate studies (1985), which, in turn, had an entirely different institutional ethos to the university in which I did my doctoral studies (2005). This rapid succession of teleological outlooks and operational norms means that a riot of shallowly submerged incongruities about the aims, values, practices

---

1. Franklin, *Corrupting the Youth*; Collingwood, *An Autobiography*.

2. Dawkins, *Higher Education*; Pelikan, *The Idea of a University*; Readings, *The University in Ruins*; Coaldrake & Stedman, *On the Brink*; Coady, *Why Universities Matter*; Norton, *The Unchained University*; Hayes & Wynyard, *The McDonaldization of Higher Education*; Cooper et al., *Scholarship and Entrepreneurs*; Bok, *Universities in the Marketplace*; Cain & Hewitt, *Off Course*.

and nature of higher education now under-girds your average Australian university. Yet these incongruities are carefully concealed by the forceful fiscal cultivation of specific ground covers. Under the fiscal governance of neoliberal institutional management the old intellectual foliage that thrived in classical soils is now almost extinct, but increasingly liberal humanist foliage is suffering major depletion too and can see itself going the same way as the classical foliage. Neoliberal foliage is, of course verdant, being carefully cultivated by our university executives.

What drives these transitions, and are the transformed universities that we now see improving, degrading or just aimlessly changing?

It has become increasingly common for culturally reflexive Australian academics to feel that the transitions they are caught up in are for the worse.[3] This is also true for many Australian academics working in the sciences as well.[4]

In 2007 the executive of the Queensland University of Technology[5] (the university where I was then studying) seriously considered not offering an Arts degree. In its "change management" process, the executive wondered out loud if our university could justify the ongoing existence of traditional humanities and social science offerings at all.[6] This question arises in the administration's executive consciousness not just because of periodic dips in Arts degree enrollments, but as a response to the long term financial need to niche market itself as an institution, thus product branding is now all important. QUT decided it would strongly market the "new humanities"—media studies, fashion studies and other exciting industry linked and vocationally relevant offerings in its Creative Industries Faculty—and so it did not want brand confusion for prospective clients (students). The administration was worried that if QUT still has a School of Humanities where we teach and research in enterprise and vocationally irrelevant subjects such as sociology and history, this would tarnishes our innovative and practical corporate image. So the School of Humanities and Human Services (SHHS) was dissolved on 31 December 2007. Through most of 2008 the tiny body of existing academic staff in dedicated humanities and social science scholarship employed by QUT

3. Connell, "Core Activity"; Davies, "The impossibility of Intellectual Work"; Winefield et al., "Occupational Stress in Australian Universities."; Hil, *Whackademia*.

4. Davies et al., "The Rise and Fall of the Neo-liberal University"; Woolcock, *Within the Hollowed Halls of Learning*.

5. QUT hereafter.

6. Gardiner, "Change proposal."

were told that some liberal arts program was being considered for possible implementation in 2009, but come the end of 2008 the administration finally came clean informing us that there would be no new degree.

In the process of this shut down the administration not only strung us all along but was also very heavy handed. Some of us—including myself—were arrested and locked up in the city watch house whilst non-violently protesting outside the Academic Board meeting that decided to close the SHHS down. As the Administration appointed and controlled the Academic Board, there was never any doubt that the Board would approve the Administration's will, so we knew that when the Board met to discuss the closure of the School, closure was a foregone conclusion. In preparation for the student protests at that fated meeting of the Academic Board the Administration had thumped the drums of pending trouble that morning on local radio and had called the police on to the campus before any students arrived. The protest body was only about fifty students, but as QUT's standing security officers were only authorized to protect QUT property and staff, and not to violently man handle QUT students, it seemed this was inadequate force and thus the police were needed. The Queensland government's draconian Police Powers and Responsibilities Act of 2000 gave the police sweeping rights in the discretionary use of force towards any 'trouble makers', and this is the force that the university used against its own students and staff who were upset about the executive's decision to close their school.

Leaving administrative brutality to one side, there can be no doubt that the direction of these broad cultural transitions are bad for academics in fields of learning tied to a liberal humanist or (worse still) classical vision of what a university ought to be. Yet, moral and teleological judgments can only be reasonably adjudicated from within a single evaluative frame. Trying to work out who is pursuing good ends by reasonable methods, and who is pursuing bad ends by unreasonable methods where the contesting aspirants to virtue and reason operate out of different evaluative frames and teleological assumptions, is futile.

The argument put forward in this chapter holds that morality and reason are not culturally basic enough to judge between neoliberal, liberal and classical conceptions of what a good university is. Each outlook has its own morality, its own rationality and its own set of tacit teleological and cosmological assumptions. Yet religion, as the basic cultural ground out of which morality and rationality arise, is deep enough to provide credible grounds of adjudication between these otherwise incommensurable morality and rationality frames.

This approach seems strongly prejudiced towards favoring a Newmanesque classical stance over the distinctly secular conceptions of liberal and neo-liberal university teleology, for of the three, only the classical stance has a tacitly religious teleology of what a university is.[7] However, this chapter does not find that a classical stance is better than a liberal or a neoliberal stance merely because it is tacitly religious, for this chapter finds all three stances to be profoundly religious. Thinking religiously, the dynamics of ritual, cosmological and teleological belief and worship in each stance, and the consequences of the competing understandings of reality embedded in the varying practices of power and knowledge, opens up a much deeper evaluative frame than mere morality and rationality. So this chapter finds that it is religious drivers that shape the passage of transition in our culture at large, and hence in universities, and so it is from thinking with religious categories that we are likely to get the best understanding of whether these transitions are good or bad.

But before we apply a theological approach to sociology in order to try and evaluate institutional morality and instrumental rationality in Australian universities, let us look a bit more closely at why both morality and rationality are not adequate conceptual frames for this task.

FROM LIBERALISM TO NEO-LIBERALISM: THE FAILURE OF WESTERN MORAL THEORY

Since Kant, moral theory—and metaphysics—has been in a peculiar crisis in the West.[8] Put simply, Kant demonstrates that the only valid grounds of approaching truth available to the modern Western mind allows us no substantive contact with transcendence. This creates the distinctly Western, distinctly modern problem of meaninglessness that we have yet to conquer, fueling our morality depleted political discourse of instrumental rationality.[9] Substantive moral and metaphysical truths can no longer be anchored to qualitatively intrinsic, teleologically inherent or religiously transcendent absolutes that have a broad cultural acceptability. After Kant we have tried as hard as we can to produce moral certainty from non-transcendentally referenced evaluative constructs. The second half of the nineteenth century was the high water mark of a scientific

---

7. Newman, *The Idea of a University*; Pelikan, *The Idea of a University*.
8. Harrison, *The Disenchantment of Reason*.
9. Casey, *Meaninglessness*.

'realism' of a post-metaphysical and post-religious nature. This realism signaled the triumph of the truth discourse of modern secular reason. The cultural success of this realism launched secular liberal humanism as a progressive intellectual force that steadily eroded its traditional more transcendently referenced competition in Western high culture. However, this progressive nineteenth-century stance takes off well but has a natural bent towards self-destruction once it is in the air. The hermeneutic of suspicion works like a charm unmasking the exploitative self-interests that were the *real* (i.e., material) realities behind the convenient self-delusions of so called traditional moral truth.[10] Thus, religiously referenced absolutes were exposed as self-deceptions furthering the economic, political, ego and sexual interests of the patriarchal ruling class at the expense of the masses on whom their power and privilege depended. But here the dog of suspicion bites twice. For if material self-interest is indeed the only reality, then what can make any human power—be it regressive or progressive—fair and just? Progressive 'critique' becomes a stance only of destructive value, for if one holds that power itself is an inherently self-interested business, and if one cannot construct or maintain a fair society without power, then what grounds can be found to justify any political revolution that aspires to create and sustain a politico-economic utopia? Callinicos ably locates the birth of French post-structuralism in a profound disappointment with revolutionary socialism in the aftermath of the brutality of Stalin and in the failure of 1968 to produce a genuinely socialist polity in France.[11] However, this disillusionment with progressive revolution itself, and hence, with classical Marxism, may be not nearly as ill-founded as Callinicos maintains. Progressivism only works as a political ideology if its destructive power is premised on the moral appeal of liberation for the oppressed. But, given a dogmatic commitment to materialism and given the hermeneutic of suspicion, why should we not wonder if revolutionary liberation itself is not merely an ideological ruse? It seems we have produced an inherently self-defeating progressive liberal humanism.

Critique—an essential revolutionary component of nineteenth-century progressivism—explicitly maintains that transcendently referenced value beliefs are inherently false, hence oppressive and regressive, and must be overthrown. Critique also tacitly assumes that there are such

---

10. Ricœur, *Freud and Philosophy*.
11. Callinicos, *Against Postmodernism*.

things as substantive progressive moral values (i.e., equality and liberation) that should replace the old values. However, both of these beliefs cannot be sustained by the post-Kantian onto-epistemological assumptions that underpin them.

Kantian anti-realism in epistemology provokes the Hegelian idealistic ontology of spirit in a bold attempt to recover transcendent and substantive absolutes, yet Idealism's failure to be concretely grounded produced the Marxist shift to a functional and pragmatic ontology of materialism (truth as historical and material praxis). From this materialist realism, atheism and scientific anti-idealism arise as the necessary prerequisites for genuinely progressive nineteenth-century thought and politics. Yet, when there are no knowable transcendent absolutes, when all values are constructs, then the value constructs of modern secular realism are no better and no more objectively demonstrable than the constructs of traditional transcendently referenced moral beliefs. So the self-defeating grounds of nineteenth-century positivistic progressivism produced the nineteenth-century counter-Enlightenment tendency seen in both Kierkegaard and Nietzsche.

Kantian epistemology, Hegelian idealism, and positivistic materialism are all decisively rejected by Kierkegaard.[12] Armed with these unfashionable disbeliefs, Kierkegaard rejects the entire modern secular outlook on reality that was emerging in his times. Kierkegaard is a non-secularist, not, as Milbank and Dupré are, on the grounds of a powerful critique of secular modernity stemming from late medieval nominalism and the theology of Duns Scotus and William of Ockham.[13] Rather, being in various ways in agreement with Hamann and Jacobi, Kierkegaard never found Kant and Hegel's epistemological arguments and existential consequences at all convincing.[14] So Kierkegaard gets a name for being an irrationalist because he ridicules the whole belief frame of modern secular reality. And yet, in doing so, Kierkegaard is firmly established within the inherently religious genealogy of truth underpinning Western thought since Plato. Unlike Kant, Kierkegaard does not abandon knowable transcendent truth; yet truth is only accessed via faith. Christian theology becomes the basis of Kierkegaard's epistemology, his ethics, his aesthetics, his psychology and his sociology. Kierkegaard never accepted

---

12. Kierkegaard, *Unscientific Postscript*.
13. Milbank, *Theology and Social Theory*; Dupré, *Passage to Modernity*.
14. Surber, *Metacritique*.

a secular view of reality as being either credible or possible. This insight is shared by the post-secular thinkers of our day and is a necessary starting point for a philosophically serious critique of the materialist and pragmatic reality frame in which neo-liberalism is situated.[15]

In Nietzsche, however, materialism itself is mytho-ritualistically radicalized. Now morality is inherently and jubilantly exploitative and is better than Christian morality because it is honest about the materialist and agonistic nature of all moral construction.[16] So, Nietzsche advocates, the West can be redeemed only by recovering the pagan myth of power as a struggle for conquest amongst outstanding elites. This is a rejection of progressive revolutionary values premised on the incipient Christian slave mentality of equality and the inherent resentment of the mighty by the masses. Marx (though possibly not Stalin or Hitler) is too Christian for Nietzsche.

Given the absence of knowable transcendent truth and the philosophically unconvincing reductively materialist reality outlook of nineteenth-century positivism, the credibility of progressive and revolutionary liberal humanism as an improvement on the West's old transcendently referenced truths, looks, given the passage of time, increasingly like a massive confidence trick. Further, to swing in a more Durkheimean direction, where there can be no valuable reality bigger than "all too human" cultural construction, and where individual economic freedom, as the underlying material praxiology of our industrialized consumer society is the tacit political value, there can be *no* culturally unifying substantive value beliefs of any solidity.[17]

Liberal humanism as a ground of critique undermining the 'old' transcendently referenced order, and as a basis for constructing a 'new' scientific and humane order, falls over and is devoured by its postmodern philosophical progeny and its neoliberal political progeny.

Neo-liberalism is the praxis of conformity to existing political and economic status, and hence it involves the 'post-ideological' advocacy of the current ideology underpinning the politico-economic conditions of global capitalism that sustain this status.[18] Neo-liberalism is the natural and logical political child of liberal humanism. In many ways it is the

---

15. Blond, *Post-Secular Philosophy*.
16. Nietzsche, *Genealogy of Morality*.
17. Durkheim, *Suicide*.
18. Greiner, "New Liberalism."

triumph of liberal humanism. Traditional transcendent values have been dispensed with so now the task of high culture is to preserve rather than critique the new entirely instrumental and inherently agonistic status quo (is this resonating with ancient Babylon's Marduk?). Neo-liberalism is also undoubtedly an intellectual improvement on liberal humanism, if, that is, one is committed to the non-transcendentally referenced world view of nineteenth-century materialistic realism. Nineteenth-century progressivism was still enamored with the absolute values of its tacitly religious cultural opposition, and so it tried—vainly—to attribute purely secular and rational absolutes to the progressive world view. Twentieth-century neo-liberalism is serious about abandoning transcendent reference points, and so the very concept of 'critique' becomes meaningless and the preservation of the existing status quo—and especially its economic underpinnings—comes to define normality, rationality and acceptability for any purely humanly constructed social cohesion and morality. There can be no prophets to denounce idolatry and violations of intrinsic value now, and there can be no final redemption, no visions of an eschatological City of God to be divinely realized against which to measure all human constructs of reality as inadequate and needing constant moral and metaphysical challenge. Instead, there is only the entirely constructed world of 'economic reality' to be fully embraced, power is now only situated in terms of manipulating 'economic reality', and we are now expected to be spiritually content with the fully realized eschatology of Money (Mammon) as the ontological frame out of which we must construct all value, meaning and reasonable aims, here and now. Political and economic power—Marduk—is now inherently about preserving the status quo's ability to impose its own order, by force, on chaos.

The transition from liberal humanism, the progressive force of yesterday, to neo-liberalism, the conservative force of today, is one propelled by neo-Kantian anti-realism, the philosophical foundation upon which both outlooks rest. So, in thinking about whether Australian universities are governed by institutional bullies who squash intellectual freedom and negate the civic role of universities, or rational and conscientious managers, it seems that both of these apparently competing evaluative frameworks are part of the same underlying belief system: modern secular reality. If modern secular reality is true then neo-liberalism, as essentially constructivist and as inherently unconcerned with the very idea of qualitative absolutes, is clearly intellectually superior to liberal humanism. But if secular reality itself is false, and some form of substantive contact with transcendent absolutes is after all intrinsic to the human condition, then in practice neo-liberalism will turn out to be inferior to liberal humanism, even though liberal humanism is premised on the same false confidence in secular reason as neo-liberalism. So, can modern secular reality itself be critiqued?

THEOLOGY AND SOCIAL THEORY

It may be that post-secular philosophy provides us with a more powerful view of the situation in which we are placed than a merely moral or merely pragmatic frame of conceptual evaluation.[19] Given the meta-contestation of evaluative frames underlying the debates about what is happening and what should be done in higher education in Australia, and given the philosophical unity underlying the apparent meta-contest between liberal humanism and neo-liberalism, a more basic understanding of social reality seems needed in order to reveal what is actually going on.

Post-secular philosophy has its origins in a seminal work by John Milbank titled *Theology and Social Theory*. In describing Milbank's thesis Fergus Kerr observes:

> Milbank . . . is struck by recent developments within social theory itself that suggest that . . . there is no socioeconomic reality which is more 'basic' than the reality of religion. Social theorists, influenced by Nietzsche, trace the formation of social structures to the will-to-power. While they mostly want to get rid of religion they acknowledge the subterranean presence of the mythic-ritual elements that social structures characteristically contain . . .
>
> . . . the Nietzschean legacy is ambivalent. On the one hand it seems the last word in post-Enlightenment rationalism, a 'truly non-metaphysical mode of secular reason'. On the other hand, for all its claimed scientific positivism and evolutionary naturalism, Nietzsche's work also embodies an ontology of non-human power and primordial conflict which is simply a return to a pagan perception of life. It looks as if something metaphysical, and thus in some sense something theological, rears its head in even the most obsessively pagan 'genealogy of morals' so far invented . . .[20]

19. Blond, *Post-Secular Philosophy*.
20. Kerr, "Milbank's Thesis," 430.

Kerr notes that "Post-Nietzschean social theorists have recognized that the mythic-religious dimension of social structures cannot be treated as superstructural."[21] Indeed, the *Verstehen* tradition of German sociology has never held itself distinct from theology, philosophy and economics. This tradition has a profound interest in the theological roots of social rationality structures and has often resisted the more dogmatically materialist tendency to separate out and subordinate the cultural and the religious to the material and the factual.[22] If this tradition is basically right about the complexities of human reality, and if—due to the counter-Enlightenment's postmodern intellectual progeny—we are indeed leaving behind the epistemologically and sociologically naïve vision of a discretely positive and material reality, then neo-liberalism itself may be on the way out with liberal humanism, and both may soon prove to be strange aberrations in the human history of reality rather than definitive modern breakthroughs forever displacing superstition and ignorance.[23]

On the other hand, the unbelief in transcendence propagated by nineteenth-century materialism may make it very hard for us to recover a more spiritually enchanted, that is, historically normal view of truth and reality. Given a tacit materialistic realism, the alliance of praxis, perception and power created by the ruling triumvirate of neoliberal economics, consumer irrealism and neoconservative politics, now constitutes the status quo underpinning our Western *Weltanschauung*.[24] These unholy three are our principalities and powers.[25] Here, as Kierkegaard saw, media image and the shameless political manipulation of the fears and base prejudices of the public, the strangely collective yet apolitical values of mere atomistic satiation, and the logic of the preservation of order and control for its own sake, are inherently conformist and are the only public realities we can collectively access.[26] Here, truth, intrinsic dignity and substantive values are notions entirely devoid of meaningful signification

---

21. Ibid.

22. Honnefelder, "Rationalization and Natural Law"; Weber, *The Protestant Ethic*.

23. Berger, *Desecularization*.

24. Pusey, *Economic Rationalism in Canberra*; Stiglitz, *Globalization and Its Discontents*; Frankfurt, *Corrupting the Youth*; Klein, *No Logo*; Kingston, *Not Happy, John!*; Maddox, *God under Howard*.

25. Wink, *Engaging the Powers*.

26. Kierkegaard, *Two Ages*.

(note the political and moral irrelevance of exposés such as Wilke and Kingston).[27]

In light of the grudging appreciation for the cultural depth of the mytho-ritualistic arising from post-Nietzschean social theory, let us not take materialism as a necessary reality given. Thinking more mytho-ritualistically, human communities, language and the moral values they produce, are always situated in a context that theology describes as worship. Worship is a function of the human condition to the degree that cosmological beliefs, symbolic meanings, desire orienting narratives and teleological practices are socio-linguistically unavoidable. Worship (worth-ship) is inherently qualitative, is always grounded in a set of cosmological and value beliefs that can never be merely materially given, and objects of worth orientate the actions and rationality of every human action. Hence, a theological anthropology holds that we are all devotees to one object of worship or another and that the mytho-ritualistic underlies all the social realities in which we live. Practical rationality, too, is always situated ontologically. What is instrumentally rational is never self-evident but is premised on cosmological beliefs that are inescapably ontological.

A good example of this way of understanding worship as central to the actual social, economic and political reality in which people live has been done by Paul Ricœur in his fascinating work *The Symbolism of Evil*. Ricœur's exposition of the Babylonian politico-ritual myth of primal and redemptive violence reveals the religious substrata underpinning the operational logic and socio-cultural meaning of the *Realpolitik* of modern Western states just as effectively as it does of Ancient Babylon. Wink, following Ricœur, points out very persuasively that this Babylonian myth of primal violence underlies the survivalism that is touted as modern realism in our politics, economics and marketing, and is thus adhered to by all modern realists be they neoliberal pragmatists or revolutionary utopian romantics. Wink argues that Babylonian redemptive violence is far more the real religion of the USA than Christianity.[28] Yet, contemporary revivals of an Augustinian primal ontology of harmony and an Anabaptist theology of the politics of peace bring modern realism, and hence the very parameters of political, social and economic possibility

---

27. Wilke, *Axis of Deceit*; Kingston, *Not Happy, John!*
28. Wink, *Engaging the Powers*, 13–31.

assumed by that realism, into fundamental question.[29] But whether one's base spiritual commitments are set in an ontology of violence or harmony, or some tense or reposed balance of the two, it seems clear that there is no pure rationality that can be instrumentally applied to reality that is ontologically neutral or objectively rational. Hence, to assume a realism that is of a modern materialist nature—where reality is falsely assumed to be ontologically void and practical rationality alone is held to be objectively valid—is to be blind to any spiritual dynamism in human affairs. This blindness, as theological phenomenologists and others point out, may render modern 'realism' hopelessly unfaithful to reality as we actually experience it.

So, when liberal humanists seek to shame neo-liberals from their critical vantage, and when neo-liberals seek to discipline and control liberal humanists from their power vantage, both typically fail to even understand the value orientation of their opponent and this gets us nowhere. (More to the point, it gets you alienated and unemployed if you are 'critical truth' seeking to speak to 'practical power'.) Explicitly contesting liberal humanism with neoliberal pragmatism as competing philosophical belief systems gets us further, but does not adequately recognize the underlying unity in a modern secular view of reality common to both alternatives, and does not address the inherent weaknesses of that reality perspective itself. So, if Milbank is right, it is theology that provides us with a deeper set of conceptual tools with which to try and understand what is going on at Australian universities.

The minute one starts to look at 'secular' economics and politics through theological lenses, a picture of remarkable clarity emerges. William Cavanaugh points out that a Milton Freidman style free market ideology is premised on the rejection of any knowable intrinsic or transcendently referenced common good that can unify modern societies in teleological truth.[30] Hence, this free market ideology understands itself to be rigorously pluralistic and secular. For the free market is (ostensibly) firmly opposed to all forms of imposed unifying worship, and is opposed to all attempts at individual formation that appeal to universally valid intrinsic human ends. However, this free market ideology's proclamation of the unknowability of true human ends is itself a knowledge claim that

---

29. Milbank, *Theology and Social Theory*; Pickstock, *After Writing*; Cunningham, *A Genealogy of Nihilism*; Hanby, *Augustine and Modernity*; Hauerwas, *The Peaceable Kingdom*; Yoder, *The Politics of Jesus*; Gingerich & Grimsrud, *Transforming the Powers*.

30. Cavanaugh, *Being Consumed*, 1–7.

unifies cultures and forms individuals towards a distinctive *telos*, and on a global scale. That is, the free market functions as a globally unifying and powerfully culturally and individually formative worship regime. Its god—Mammon—oversees a pantheon of private deities, but recognizes no power above itself when it comes to economically (and politically) ordering the way all humanity must now live as 'free'. The 'free market' approach to freedom and desire has its own mytho-ritualistic elements, its own 'liturgical' and 'salvific' dimensions, its own collective and individual disciplines and cosmological frameworks.

Whilst Cavanaugh demonstrates that thinking of economics and politics without the assumptions of 'secular reason' opens up new depths of analysis to us, it is still typically very hard for us to take this sort of analysis seriously. This difficulty, however, is not a product of the obvious superiority of the truth discourse of secular reason over religion, but is tied to the way knowledge works sociologically.

PARADIGM TRANSITION

Kuhn's sociology of knowledge notes that conceptual paradigms are always being incrementally developed until their fundamental limitations become unavoidable. But the period when a conceptual paradigm may be impossible to sustain and a better paradigm is accepted, can be a very long time.[31] Whilst the status quo of any belief system is able to keep any given paradigm alive, alternative conceptual frames are typically deemed to be the work of crackpots. However, when the status quo finally fails one of the crackpot alternatives will become the new orthodoxy.

Modern secular reality has been in serious theoretical trouble, probably for 200 years now, but as yet, and particularly after the cultural triumph of progressive nineteenth-century realism, the status quo in our Western institutions of higher learning has tended to uphold secular reality and designate all religious understandings of reality as the work of crackpots. Questioning the believability of secular materialist reality itself opens up new ways of thinking about what is happening in our universities that re-introduces the possibility of strong evaluative frameworks that are not merely human constructs and may have some contact with intrinsic or transcendent value realities. From here it may be possible to escape the liberal humanist tendency towards mere critique on

---

31. Kuhn, *The Structure of Scientific Revolutions*.

the one hand and the neoliberal tendency towards the mere conservation of power on the other hand.

If we step outside of the paradigm of modern secular and materialist reality, we move into a broad new arena of possibilities, an arena sociologists like Keenan find fascinating and fruitful.[32] Yet, to those committed to the reality frame of secular materialist academic truth, such a move can easily seem frightening. For, on one hand, such a conceptual transition may risk us encountering re-enchantment with its now very unpleasant possibility of a transcendent reality we cannot control,[33] or worse still, the possibility of some sort of revival of the notion of religious authority. On the other hand, laying aside a dogmatic commitment to secular materialism may risk us encountering the demonic.[34] Yet, many voices, such as Havel and Latour, in different ways, have told us that enchantment has never really gone away anyway, and other voices, like Bauman and Ricœur have found the demonic alive and well in modernity.[35] As profoundly non-religious a thinker as Weber carefully describes the power that religion has as a driver of broad cultural values and rationality frames, and also clearly saw the often sinister quasi spiritual life forms that human institutions themselves take on.[36] Then, Whitehead, and a stream of theoretical physicists since Einstein, and religious existentialists from Kierkegaard to Buber, branching out to the recent theological turn amongst Continental phenomenologists, have been plugging away at different non-secular truth paradigms for some time now. And as Morgan and White note, Plato's vision of truth was always religiously grounded, and his epistemology was always of a metaphysical nature, and this belief ground has been the womb of universal and absolute truth itself in Western cultural history.[37] Secular materialist truth may be but a strange aberration soon to be passed over again in the human history of truth and reality. A broad cultural transition back to a spiritually richer conception of reality may be re-asserting itself in the West, the only culture ever to briefly

32. Keenan, "Rediscovering the Theological in Sociology."

33. Tacey, *Re-Enchantment*.

34. Wink, *Engaging the Powers*.

35. Havel, "Politics and Conscience"; Latour, *We Have Never Been Modern*; Bauman, *Modernity and the Holocaust*; Ricœur, *The Symbolism of Evil*.

36. Weber, *The Protestant Ethic*.

37. Morgan, "Plato and Greek Religion"; White, "Plato's Metaphysical Epistemology."

abandon this outlook.[38] Let us speculate along post-secular lines and consider what the academy might worship and what the consequences of different worship frames might be.

THE ACADEMY AND MAMMON

To get at the belief sub-structure on which the neoliberal managerial mind set operates in the academy, a theological frame asks, 'what does this outlook worship?' Answering this question reveals the spiritual orientation that shapes the power ethos of the institution, which in turn governs the operational morality and rationality of that institution.

Whilst this sort of analysis is indeed undertaken by theological sociologists such as Jacques Ellul, this is an approach that is strangely parallel to the nineteenth-century radical heritage grounded in Marx. The difference between Ellul and Marx is not in their appreciation of the primacy of worship in the concrete reality of daily life, nor in their discernment of how worship shapes the parameters of political and economic life. Rather, Marx and Ellul disagree over Who is the true object of worship. Marx maintains that as Feuerbach and others have demonstrated that there is no God and no spirit, so all worship that is not the worship of material Man is false worship. Marx, in terms interestingly similar to Kant's conception of his epistemological Copernican revolution, proclaims:

> The criticism of religion disillusions man, so that he will think, act, and fashion his reality like a man who has discarded his illusions and regained his senses, so that he will move around himself as his own true sun. Religion is only the illusory sun which revolves around man as long as he does not revolve around himself.[39]

Ellul, however, finds the Marxist worship of economically self-created Man indistinguishable from the worship of Money. Ellul, in full agreement with Marx, finds that capitalism subordinates being to personal having, and yet Ellul notes that socialism subordinates being to doing and collective having. Both are profound alienations where the role of money itself in de-ontologising humanity is unchanged. Ellul argues that Marx's redemptive goal—the re-humanizing of Man, or the self-creation

---

38. Tacey, *Re-Enchantment*; McGrath, *The Twilight of Atheism*; Jenkins, *God's Continent*.

39. Marx, "A Contribution to the Critique of Hegel's Philosophy of Right. Introduction."

of Humanity—cannot be achieved by any politico-economic system. Ellul holds that the fallen order of reality itself must be redemptively transformed by its Creator for humanity to realize her essential dignity. Until the eschaton then, all answers are provisional—some better than others of course. But only the worship of God placed above every economic or political system allows for any real degree of economic and political justice.

For Ellul all concerns about money and politics are primarily concerns about the relationship between God and people.[40] To fail to understand this is to miss the reality vision of the Bible, and hence it is no accident that the first of the ten commandments—to have no gods before God—is pivotal to any theological understanding of money as grounded in the Abrahamic religions.

The idolatry of a praxis of life in service to the accumulation or power of money is what the Christian Scriptures call bondage to Mammon (Matthew 6:24). If we accept Dupré's argument that modern materialism's confidence in the ontic autonomy of *natura pura* is premised on the complex problematics of late medieval nominalism, and that this nominalist theology is the heart of modernism's metaphysical bankruptcy, then we can pick up Marx's fascinating religious analysis of money without needing to accept his captivity to materialism and idolatry.[41] This, in fact, Ellul does, and whilst the results are very different from Marx, Ellul makes it possible to believe that a Christian praxis of worship, when not hopelessly corrupted via its participation in the pervasive Western idolatry of Mammon, should indeed be deeply economically and politically radical.

Ellul's *Money and Power* recovers the New Testament notion of Mammon as the spiritual power that is either generated or surrendered to in the inherently idolatrous worship of money. Mammon, Ellul argues, has always been a pervasive spiritual reality in economically sophisticated societies. Indeed the worship of Mammon is, as Marx well saw, particularly evident in modern Western life.

The notion of worship carries drivers more basic and powerful than the drivers of morality and instrumental rationality; that is, worship itself empowers different moral and rational frames of belief and action. Worship involves a recognition of ultimate worth and/or authority to which one fully surrenders final loyalty. A Judeo-Christian theological

---

40. Ellul, *Money and Power*, 26.
41. Dupré, *Passage to Modernity*.

anthropology finds that worship—whether conscious or not—is basic to the practice of human life in all socio-cultural contexts.

Australian universities provide an interesting case study in the role of Mammon in the academy. Since Michael Pusey's *Economic Rationalism in Canberra* it has been evident that Mammon has been the central site of worship in Australia's national institutions of political power. Further, since the Dawkins reform of higher education in the late 1980s, that spiritual orientation has progressively come to displace the more liberal humanist and classical loyalty orientations that previously defined the moral and rational goals of universities in Australia. As Australia has little grounding in its own distinctive traditions (being a very young nation), and a nation that experienced fabulous wealth and opportunity in the post-war boom, it is not surprising that neo-liberalism is now very deeply entrenched in Australian politics and the Australian academy.

Historically three frames of worship seem operative in Australian universities. Weakest of all in the contemporary context is what could be called a classical frame, where contemplative and transcendent absolutes connected with the long and deep Christian roots of the Western university tradition defined basic loyalties and produced a particular set of moral and operational institutional characteristics. Here, the influence of the British Idealists of the late nineteenth century can still be vaguely felt in Australian universities and public institutions. Here, God (pursued in devout contemplation of the medieval *transcendentalia*—Truth, Beauty and Goodness) is, paradigmatically, the first object of worship in all knowledge pursuits. Next is progressive secular humanism with its rejection of divine transcendence, its insistence on methodological atheism and materialist realism, yet its great romantic capacity to believe in natural and humanly created truth, beauty and goodness. Here the optimism that the productive, creative and rational radiance of Man can be His own Sun, and that reason and science will provide a secular paradise on earth, places Man at the center of worship. This heritage is now increasingly marginalized in Australian universities. Finally, neo-liberalism. Here money itself is the center of worship. Worshiping not even Man, but rather the crafted idols of power and wealth than Man explicitly sets up for himself, removes even the *imago dei* within Man from worship and renders worship inherently dehumanizing, de-sacralizing, and devoid of ultimacy. Values and rationality premised on any commitment to intrinsic human dignity, inherent goodness and transcendent absolutes are, from this stance, totally incomprehensible.

The worship of Mammon is in the ascendency in Australian universities and it rolls effortlessly over all opposition because of its position of administrative power. The institutional values and rationality defined by this worship orientation are increasingly dislodging the previous two worship frames and their resultant institutional characteristics. So now universities are businesses, students are clients, academics are human resources, and marketing, branding and funding concerns attract the first attention of the planning and operational energies of our university's executives. Here Mark Lauchs' insights into the manner in which ethical procedures are now constructed in order to rationally avoid ethical responsibility and Bauman's concerns about the potential for evil in pure instrumental rationality and conformist socializing give us good reason to be worried about the future of our civilization.[42] Though Freud's fears for civilization are grounded in the very secular materialist reality frame this chapter critiques, these fears do indeed seem well grounded.[43] Once the worship of Mammon becomes the only form of life open to us then Weber's iron cage of instrumental rationality, George Orwell's politics of mere power and C. S. Lewis's understanding of the release of demonic energy, all imaginatively prophesy what our neo-liberal disconnection from the liberal humanist and classical worship heritages of Western culture will really mean.[44]

If, as Augustine claims, God has made us for Himself, and our hearts find no peace until we rest in Him, then something inherently human is lost when Mammon is the primary object of our collective culture of worship.[45] If this is the case then the banality of money as the primary object of our culture's dominant form of worship will become increasingly spiritually unendurable. If this happens we will need ever more distracting, sedating and escapist leisure (stronger narcotics, more penetrating and saturating media), ever more frenetic careers, and ever strengthening external political control to prevent our spiritually hollow life form from collapsing. The so called War on Terror may be symptomatic of the drivers of Mammon in both entertainment and power in Western culture as the globe groans under the weight of the fabulous exploitation

42. Lauchs, "Rational Avoidance of Accountability by Queensland Governments"; Bauman, *Modernity and the Holocaust*.

43. Freud, *Civilization and Its Discontents*.

44. Weber, *Protestant Work Ethic*; Orwell, *Nineteen Eighty-four*; Lewis, *That Hideous Strength*.

45. Augustine, *Confessions*.

of humanity and nature that this god demands of his Western devotees.[46] As Mammon grows in power in proportion to the number and depth of its devotees and victims—as can already be seen—evangelistic fervor for the pursuit of wealth as the first goal of true humanity and the dynamics of religious power itself promotes universal monotheism on a global scale like we have never seen before; thou shalt have no gods before Mammon.

CONCLUSION

It seems reasonable to conclude that the deepening obeisance to Mammon in the governing structures of Australia's political, economic, media and educational institutions is the best way of understanding what is really driving the sweeping cultural transition going on in our universities. If, then, there either is a God, or humanity does have an instinct for transcendence that must be carefully cultivated if we are to be humanized, then this trend lays us open as a culture to our own demonic energies and the delicate flowers of beauty, truth and goodness necessary for our collective humanity are under serious threat. If this is the case, then the contest between liberal humanist and neoliberal value frames within our universities, battled out between competing claims to morality and reason, is only a superficial symptom of a far deeper problem. The focus of our collective worship in the assumed norms, accepted practices and prevailing power structures of our way of life is the real problem.

If the above is correct, then we will only recognize the causal dynamics of our present state of transition if we stop looking at the symptoms of our present crisis as if they are its drivers. If the real drivers are indeed religious, then the entire frame of modern secular reality will have to be seriously re-considered. This is something the modern Western university is going to find very hard to do, be it of a liberal humanist or neoliberal bent. For since Russell's materialist coup,[47] English-speaking, twentieth-century universities have been the first home to what Peter Berger calls the "reality police . . . who watch over the cognitive boundaries of the culture. In their perspective transcendence in any of its historical forms is viewed as contraband goods."[48] After Russell, our universities have been becoming temples of modern secular reality, grooming and initiating the

---

46. Hauerwas & Lentricchia, *Dissent from the Homeland*.
47. Collingwood, *An Autobiography*.
48. Berger, *Facing up to Modernity*, 247.

priests of modern Western knowledge and power. And this, we have now seen, is a temple that houses and honors Mammon so naturally that we academics are unable to even identify the pervasive forms and habits of our own worship to this crass deity of our making.

Yet, now that we have Milbank's work, and now that neo-liberalism may itself be failing, and failing as a viable higher educational ideology, perhaps we can start looking at the post-secular possibilities of understanding reality and universities.[49] Escaping the secular materialist frame of reality may at last make it possible for us to not only identify how remarkably tenuous the economic theory underpinning neo-liberalism is but to develop an approach to economics that keeps it subservient to higher human ends.[50] Some notion of human society as inherently liturgical and reality as inherently sacred is needed for humane economics. And only if the ends of every human activity are humane can the science of that activity be meaningfully rational.

Perhaps we can even apply a post-secular frame of evaluation to the operational norms, cultural ethos and teleological assumptions of our universities. If Tacey is right, a cultural reality shift towards 'spirituality' is underway in the West, so it may now be the right time to ask about the worship orientation of our universities. This leads us back to John Henry Newman and re-embedding the question of the nature of the Western university in its own spiritual and theological heritage. Indeed, Pelikan of Yale demonstrates how easy it is to find gold in Newman now, even though Pelikan does not adequately address Berger's concern about the underlying non-transcendentally referenced view of reality which makes it so hard for our educated minds to grasp what Newman is really driving at.[51] For the progressive Neo-Kantian anti-realism which supports the logic and value system of neo-liberalism is premised on the wholesale dumping of our transcendently referenced past. But in a cultural environment where nineteenth-century atheistic materialism is waning,[52] a return to the traditions of spiritual orientation underlying our distinctly Western institutions of learning may well be necessary for our universities to have any future of cultural relevance to our civilization. And,

---

49. Fukuyama, *After the Neocons*; Saul, *The Collapse of Globalism*; Gallagher, "Reversing the Slide"; Davies et al., "The Rise and Fall of the Neo-liberal University."

50. Keen, *Debunking Economics*; Stretton, *Economics*; Hausman, *The Inexact and Separate Science of Economics*.

51. Pelikan, *The Idea of a University*.

52. McGrath, *The Twilight of Atheism*.

Australian Universities in Transition

as Newman points out, these traditions hark back a long way, even to Augustine of Canterbury at the close of the sixth century. Describing the religious passage of Western learning from the close of the classical era to the high middle ages Newman notes: "Such was the foundation of the School of Paris, from which, in the course of centuries, sprang the famous University, the glory of the middle ages."[53] And the University of Paris is the foundation from which sprang Western university learning, in all its richness and variety, over the past 900 years. So why should not the West seek to re-discover its own historical heritage of spirituality underpinning the very birth and development of the Western university? Why should we not again turn to the *transcendentalia*, and pursue Truth, Beauty and Goodness as acts of worship to the God in whose Being we all live and move and have our being?[54] The value and nobility of this task vastly outshines the glory of the worship of Man, the first fall of this original Western university vision in recent times. But in comparison with the second fall of Western learning into the banality of the worship of money, the McDonaldization of Higher Education reveals itself to be nothing other than a destructive prostitution of human intelligence that can only result in the degradation, exploitation and bondage of the human spirit.[55]

Let us recover true learning through a return to right worship.

---

53. Newman, *The Idea of a University*, 33.
54. Bonaventure, *The Journey of the Mind to God*.
55. Hayes & Wynyard, *The McDonaldization of Higher Education*.

6

A Post-Secular Approach to Understanding Religion and Global Security

INTRODUCTION

THIS CHAPTER IS WRITTEN in two parts. Part one looks at the big drivers of global insecurity—energy, environment and economics—so that we can put religious terrorism in its correct place as a symptom, and not a cause, of global insecurity. Part two seeks to uncover Western secularism's theological roots so that we can better understand the religious drivers embedded in the power and belief structures of the modern Western way of life. The conclusion of this chapter will then briefly link Western secularism with the real drivers of global insecurity and argue that the fostering of international peace and the transformation of the basic structures of Western power and belief—two things necessary to avert pending global cataclysm—would be advanced by the adoption of a post-secular approach to global security by the West.

PART ONE: THE CAUSES OF GLOBAL INSECURITY

For much of the first decade of the twenty-first century, George W. Bush in the USA, and John Howard in Australia maintained that our Western and free way of life was under serious external threat. This threat comes from evil foreign religious extremists who irrationally hate us and are

A Post-Secular Approach to Understanding Religion and Global Security

Hell-bent on our destruction. Not only do these terrorists hate us, they also hate the noble values of the West—freedom, the rule of law, enterprise, respect for innocent life, etc. Given this, the Bush/Howard 'war on terror' held that it is crucial that we Westerners not only resist terrorism with all available force, but that we do not entertain any doubts about the rightness of our way of life as well.[1]

Thus the Bush/Howard war on terror rested on two foundational assumptions: firstly, that any essential threat to our way of life is an external threat; secondly, that we must not doubt our Western values for our way of life is inherently good.

Both of the above assumptions are dangerously delusional. For the reality is, the biggest threats to the West's current wealth and global dominance are integral to that wealth and dominance. Further, the reason why 'conservative' and 'core' Western values have been so unqualifiedly endorsed by John Howard and George W. Bush is that Western values are in serious crisis and are on the point of collapse. In this context, religious terrorists were 'God-sent' scapegoats that Bush and Howard eagerly latched on to, for the war on terror served the purpose of propping up increasingly threatened delusions integral to the West's prevailing status quo, in which our leaders were deeply embedded.

Yet, the global status quo may well crash in the near future. Some of the big drivers of fundamental change are linked to energy, the environment, and unsustainably high levels of systemic inequality and exploitation in the global economy. Religious terrorism against Western targets is a relatively minor stress fracture that arises because of the inherently unsustainable dynamics that uphold the present world order.

Fossil Fuel Energy Dependence and Depletion

The conservative International Energy Agency (IEA) predicts a supply crunch in the global oil market in 2012.[2] That is, the IEA expects a sustained increase in the global export price of oil. We may indeed have already reached global peak oil production yet this will not slow the ever accelerating global consumption of oil immediately—at least, not in oil producing nations that subsidize their domestic markets.[3] When oil pro-

---

1. See Howard, "Sharing Our Common Values"; Singer, *The President of Good & Evil*.
2. International Energy Agency Medium-Term Oil Market Report, July 2007.
3. Campbell, *Oil Crisis*; Deffeyes, *Beyond Oil*.

duction becomes noticeably affected by scarcity, the oil that goes on to the export market will become increasingly expensive and harder to get.[4] This will have substantial economic flow-on effects for Western powers like the USA whose domestic economies are heavily dependent on cheap energy and very large oil imports. Further, very little is being done in the Anglo-American world to transition our energy supply away from oil and towards renewable energy. Nothing is being done to wean our food production process off an ever higher dependence on oil for production and transport. We are powering towards an affordability crisis in energy with profound economic implications and those implications are only the beginning of our problems.

Dale Pfeiffer points out that in the 1950s and 1960s we saw a global revolution in the industrialization of food production.[5] Essentially, by this time, all the planet's land suitable for agriculture was being used. Yet the heavy industrialization of farming, the development of new strains of plants, dependence on irrigation intensive farming methods, dependence on chemical fertilizers and pesticides, and dependence on massive international transportation networks dramatically increased the world's grain supply and pushed many of the globe's traditional subsistence farmers out of work and into the urban mega-slums of the Third World. Rich or poor, we are now globally dependent on oil to eat. Oil now powers our global way of farming and the world's population has more than doubled since 1960. So what is going to happen to our global food production if we run out of affordable oil? Even if one ignores that question, what is the post-1960s farming revolution doing to the planet? Our current methods of global food production are aggressively depleting the globe's artesian water reserves, global soil qualities are failing and we are chewing up the non-renewable fuel supplies on which our farming depends. And all the while, the First World is having the lion's share of the world's energy consumption. Speaking as an American, Pfeiffer comments:

> The United States consumes 40% more energy annually than the total amount of solar energy captured yearly by all US plant biomass. Per capita use of fossil energy in North America is five times the world average. Our prosperity is built on the principle of exhausting the world's resources as quickly as possible, without

---

4. Lardelli, "The Australia 2020 Summit."
5. Pfeiffer, "Eating Fossil Fuel."

any thought to our neighbors, all the other life on this planet, or our children.[6]

The world as we know it cannot remain on an ever upward, oil fuelled, economic growth trajectory. But what politician can seriously advocate the end of the current paradigm of non-renewable energy powered economic growth? We seem locked in on a collision course with global economic recession because we will not make serious moves towards energy source transitions until the crunch has already hit.

Environmental Stress

Environmentally, the globe is groaning under the weight of First World consumption habits and resultant global resource extraction, exploitation and industry. This is no longer a matter of serious contestation. Our way of life is radically depleting the biodiversity and fecundity of the natural environment—on which human life depends—and the stresses of this are now becoming clearly observable at a time in history when the world bears a human population far greater than at any other time. The future will not allow this way of life to continue. Yet it is now likely that Western individualism has eroded the type of collective moral framework we need to adequately address a cumulative problem of this nature and magnitude.[7] As China, India and Asia modernize, the environmental damage to the globe can only accelerate as nature is exploited by ever greater numbers of non-Western people who are also seeking to enjoy and adopt a Western consumer lifestyle. The globe is now aspiring to the West's habits of natural exploitation and consumption at a time when the globe itself is indicating it has had as much exploitation as it can take. If we persist in this trajectory nature will simply give out and pay us back with terrible global consequences and catastrophic human suffering.[8]

Systemic Economic Injustice

The global economy as it now functions is not a fair system. Joseph Stiglitz and George Monbiot point this out in a manner that cannot be seriously

---

6. Pfeiffer, "Eating Fossil Fuels," subheading, "US Consumption."
7. Northcott, *A Moral Climate*.
8. Lovelock, *The Revenge of Gaia*.

contested.⁹ The Bretton Woods Institutions and the United Nations were set up after World War Two to produce a unified global system of economic, political and military power over which the US Treasury and the Whitehouse have a uniquely powerful governing influence. Whilst postwar re-construction in Japan and Europe owes a great deal to the USA, and whilst equity is now profoundly globally mobile, the end result of post-war history has been that the USA pursues its national self-interest via the global structures of power it has a unique governing power over. This makes our global system of power inherently biased towards American national interests (as those interests are defined by powerful corporate lobbyists in Washington), and inherently biased away from the interests of everyone who is not strategically aligned with the economic, political and military interests of the USA. That is, it is not a fair system and the lack of fairness makes its long term durability unsustainable. Should the USA collapse economically our global system will rest, very briefly, on an enormous power vacuum which will most likely be replaced by a serious international scramble for global power and the system we now know will change radically or collapse completely. Further, the USA is economically unstable. Stiglitz's recent book, *The Three Trillion Dollar War*, points out the extraordinary costs of the Iraq war—all funded by the USA's national deficit—and notes the remarkable stresses this puts on the US economy.¹⁰ Throw in a sub-prime mortgage crisis and ongoing financial turmoil, add in a looming supply crunch in the global price of oil, and the mighty may well fall, and fall hard, in the near future.

Then there is the human misery of the global poor—a factor profoundly integral to the present world order. The global economy is not only unfair, it is inherently exploitative and inhumane. Back in the late 1980s Susan George documented the complex relationship between the Regan administration's massive expansion of the U.S. Army and armaments production, and the terrible debt traps of many African nations ruled by very well equipped military dictators.¹¹ By now the huge ramping up of African national debts from the 1980s has made it impossible to build, let alone sustain, basic public health infrastructure in most African nations. In 2002 Michael Fleshman's article in the United Nation's publication *Africa Recovery* points out that the under-five mortality rate for

---

9. Stiglitz, *Globalization and its Discontents*; Monbiot, *Age of Consent*.
10. Stiglitz & Bilmes, *The Three Trillion Dollar War*.
11. George, *A Fate Worse than Debt*, 21–29.

A Post-Secular Approach to Understanding Religion and Global Security

sub-Saharan Africa is thirty times higher than of the developed world. Every third child in Africa suffers from malnutrition. Three hundred million African children and their parents live in absolute poverty, on the very margin of survival.[12] Fleshman's article was written at the end of an era that sought to generate global concern from the West for Africa, and at that time, some debt relief was forced out of the G8 and the IMF by the Jubilee campaign for some of the incredibly odious debt in the worst African nations. Yet, post-9/11, Africa is, apparently, no longer much of a blight on the West's global conscience, so the horrendous trends in Africa seen in the 1990s continue apace in the first decade of the twenty-first century, and with no sign of abating in view. In this global environment of entrenched under-development and deep poverty, Stiglitz agonizingly points out how the IMF typically exerts its power in a manner that means the world's poor suffer so that speculative money markets and the interests of powerful multinational corporations can be protected.[13] For sure, African politics is a mire of violence and corruption, yet the IMF ensures that savagely in debt African nations with desperately poor people service debts produced by previous military dictators rather than providing basic health care and sanitation to their own people. This kind of entrenched human suffering is very much a part of our global economic system. Further, as Arundhati Roy points out, the USA has a sustained track record of supporting military dictators and opposing democratic grassroots movements in the Third World.[14] Paul Harrison also points out that whilst the South is producing its own expanding middle class, this actually increases the overall inequality of the globe where the absolute majority of the world's population is very poor.[15]

Inescapable debt traps, unemployment, grinding poverty, basic failures in health care and education, violence and systemic exploitation for the world's poor, has never been worse. This is the dark moral underbelly of our present global world order, and this order is morally, environmentally and financially unsustainable.[16] And when it crashes, the fall will be great for those who have benefited most from the present state of global reality, but for the world's very poor, things are already catastrophic.

12. Fleshman, "A Troubled Decade for Africa's Children."
13. Stiglitz, *Globalization and its Discontents*.
14. Roy, "The Algebra of Infinite Justice."
15. Harrison, *Inside the Third World*.
16. Pettifor, *Real World Economic Outlook*.

In brief outline, then, the above are the physical, financial and human causes of the pending collapse of the post-war global world order. Those drivers of pending collapse have actually nothing to do with Osama bin Laden. Though, bin Laden's outlook and mission does, in part, reflect a seething inchoate global sense of grievance against the West for its exploitative and unfair dominance of global wealth. And it is not untrue—as Marx saw—that all things sacred are being systematically violated by the enormous cultural inroads the Western consumer lifestyle is making on the globe.[17] Bin Laden is a stress fracture of the pending failure of the system but he is not causing the failure of the system.

Now we shall briefly examine "Western values" in order to see if these are under external threat from religious terrorists or are also simply imploding under the influence of their own inherent weaknesses.

Western Values

Many of the obvious values of modern consumerism are what our Western ancestors understood to be vices. Greed, lust, avarice, gluttony, sloth, impiety, luxury, pride, profanity, competitive self-interest etc.—these are in many ways the basic drivers of our consumer economy and its symbiotic entertainment industry.[18] Self-focused indulgent values that encourage a winner takes all attitude and that rescind on responsibilities and obligations to others and nature, and have no conception of piety or the sacred, are either simply assumed or are strongly endorsed by the main stream of our advertising and entertainment industries. Distinctly religious and moral institutional authorities that stand over and restrain individual freedom are now almost entirely eroded in the West. From infancy we are cultivated in the social norms—manufactured by our thriving popular culture industry[19]—of ignoring all responsibility and obligation to the past and the future in favor of our right to have what

---

17. See Marx & Engles, *The Communist Manifesto*, 83: "Constant revolutionizing of production, uninterrupted disturbance of all social conditions, everlasting uncertainty and agitation distinguish the bourgeois epoch from all earlier ones. All fixed, fast-frozen relationships, with their train of ancient and venerable prejudices and opinions are swept away, all new-formed ones become antiquated before they can ossify. All that is solid melts into air, all that is sacred is profaned . . ."

18. See: Hamilton & Denniss, *Affluenza*; Packard, *Hidden Persuaders*; Lasch, *The Culture of Narcissism*; Campolo, *Seven Deadly Sins*.

19. Horkenheimer & Adorno, "The Culture Industry," 120–67.

we want now, on credit. This is the value system implicit in the atomistic, market driven liberalism of our consumer lifestyle.

Western consumerism is a morally corrupting global influence that actively corrodes the traditions of obligation, restraint, authority and sacredness in all non-Western cultures of the world. Via satellite, global bill-boarding, unspeakably large marketing budgets,[20] and via the Western secular academic vision of nature divorced from spirit and instrumental reason, the West tirelessly erodes all traditional belief and value systems the tiny world over. The idea that the West is under cultural threat from external invasion is the most remarkable inversion of the realities of culture in the current global environment. Mr. Howard's belief that religious terrorists want us to abandon our good values of human decency, freedom, family, the rule of law, respect for life etc.—uniquely Western values, apparently—is remarkable. It does not seem to occur to Mr. Howard that our shameless depravity, our violence, and our self-interested and hubristic exploitative dominance of global power, culture and nature are also prominent Western values. It is these Western values and their seemingly unstoppable power to dissolve the very foundations of traditional non-Western culture that people with a strong commitment to non-Western belief systems find so invasive and corrosive. It is the very notion of the sacred and of any obligation to what stands above the individual that globalized Western consumer culture—with its political and economic life forms—seems to hunt down and destroy.

International relations pursued under Mr. Howard's convictions maintained that if we ramp up homeland security and believe unswervingly in the goodness of Western values then the world as we know it will not be moved and things will just keep improving for everyone in the globe. This is delusional, hubristic and dangerous.

The Militant West and Global Insecurity

Our world order is likely to change, soon and dramatically, and no amount of homeland security and cultural self-confidence is going to alter this fact. The Bush/Howard political strategy of focusing public attention on external threats took our attention away from the inherent weaknesses

---

20. Klein, *No Logo*, 8: "The advertising industry's astronomical rate of growth is neatly reflected in year-to-year figures measuring total ad spending in the U.S., which have gone up so steadily that by 1998 the figure was set to reach $196.5 billion, while global ad spending is estimated at $435 billion."

within our present world order and allowed us to ignore these pressing concerns that will be our demise if we simply keep pretending they are not there. After Bush and Howard, Mr. Obama and Mr. Rudd and Ms. Gillard have not turned anything around. The focus on security under Bush and Howard promoted an environment of suspicion, inconvenience and unaccountable state power, fostering a neo-fascist politics of xenophobia and curtailment of civil liberties towards cultural minorities and anyone who is a bit different. Alas, once this genie is out of its bottle it is pretty likely to run its destructive course. Further, when the remarkable underlying vulnerabilities of the U.S. economy implodes then a neo-fascist political culture pre-conditioned to suspicion, xenophobia and externally focused aggression could very easily return and produce an explosive martial era of racial and religious blood-letting. Further, Bush and Howard's merely militaristic approach to monitoring and apprehending terror cells, totally ignored the *Western* drivers of religious terrorism and easily tarred all religious adherents from other cultural backgrounds as extremists if they did not fully endorse the secularism and degenerate values of the West. This is arrogant and alienating—never a very helpful place from which to construct mutually beneficial international relationships between different culturo-religious peoples.

Yet—Mr. Howard's strategy to contain global insecurity worked for the duration of his office in the Australian domestic political context because Australians, in general, like John Howard, do not understand the theological roots of our own secularism, nor do we understand the non-secular religious global context because we see it through a modern secular lens. This ignorance makes it frighteningly easy for religious terrorism to become a fabulous distraction from the real causes of our sense of being under threat, and promotes cross-cultural antagonism in an era when we do not need any more tension points than we have already got. Global security is only possible if we first have an intelligent awareness of the real causes of global conflict and the real culturo-religious nature of the global context. In order to do this we must be able to understand and critique our own secularism.

A Post-Secular Approach to Understanding Religion and Global Security

PART TWO: A GENEALOGY OF THE RISE AND FALL OF WESTERN SECULARISM

What is Western Secularism?

The revolutionary theological idea that the supernatural can be discretely separated out from the natural, and hence that 'nature' is something free standing in its own right, is the foundation belief of modern Western secularism. This remarkable innovation—the sixteenth century concept of *natura pura*—arises out of fourteenth century Franciscan nominalism which in turn is a response to Aquinas' Herculean attempt to synthesize Augustinian Christian faith with pagan Aristotelian reason.[21] Given this very long heritage, the foundational belief of modern secularism—i.e., a purely natural nature—is so deeply historically entrenched in Western culture that is an assumed and largely unquestioned feature of the distinctly modern Western ways of thinking and living. Yet, this belief is by no means a self-evident notion to non-Western cultures, nor was it seriously entertained in the assumptions of the West's own Classical and high Medieval culture.

To Plato and Aristotle, the cosmos was enchanted. *Natura pura*, as assumed by Francis Bacon, cuts across the very grain of the divinity of reason assumed by both Plato and Aristotle, and is profoundly at odds with the reality priority of the metaphysical over the physical in Plato. Equally to Augustine and Aquinas, nature's very ground of being is God. Nature is shot through with, and entirely dependent on supernature in the Neoplatonist world view that dominated Western high culture and the West's religious belief structures, from the third to the fourteenth centuries.

William of Ockham—the great fourteenth century Franciscan nominalist—dismissed the Platonist and early Medieval notion that tangible things participate in intangible spiritual realities (ideal forms), and strongly argued that the Church should have only spiritual power and wealth, and hence secular rulers should exercise total independence from the Church in how they conducted their affairs of state, and the Church should wield no punitive civil power. This reasoned disbelief in the integration of the spiritual with the physical and its resultant political vision of the separation of church and state makes Ockham one of the

---

21. Dupré, *Passage to Modernity*, 282 points out that "the term *natura pura* was not used before Robert Bellarmine (1542–1621)."

great fathers of modernity, and his influence on us to this day is both profound and largely unknown. However, the notion of separate spheres of authority relevant to church and state are taken up to varying degrees by the Reformers, and a period of great political turbulence ensued as the old intellectual and political unifications of Medieval Christendom were torn apart at the seams. The protracted religiously tangled violence that accompanied the Reformation era finally resolved itself along nascent secularist lines in the peace of Westphalia in the mid seventeenth century and modern European state craft was born. From this time on, so the Enlightenment telling of the story goes, Western culture increasingly benefited from the peaceable and tolerant political realism of the modern secular age.[22]

Yet, by the seventeenth century, Ockham's secularism is not only affecting the political and theological culture of early modern Europe, it is making profound inroads into knowledge, for Ockham makes Descartes, and modern science as we know it, possible. Descartes' attempt to ground indubitable knowledge in the personal consciousness of his own discrete, autonomous mind, arises from Ockham's nominalist theology. Very briefly, nominalism rejects the ancient notion of ontological participation. Ontological participation holds that the physical existence of any individual thing is a derived and transitory particular manifestation of deeper, transcendent, archetypal metaphysical reality. In this way God, or the Platonic equivalent—the divine form of the Good—is the final, eternal and glorious reality upon which all transitory physical manifestations of being depend. The notion of 'participation' holds that concrete existing individuals are entirely dependent for their existence upon transcendent powers of being. Ockham's razor famously severs the transcendent and universal from the immanent and particular. Ockham

---

22. Cavanaugh (*Theopolitical Imagination*) takes a close look at this Enlightenment story and finds that the mythology of pre-Westphalian violence as inherently religious is open to serious questioning. Rather, the move towards univocal political power from the high middle ages to the modern age—the rise of the early modern state—is intimately linked with the growing power of the merchant class and the need for the aristocracy to ramp up its control. The voluntarist vision of a single head of state—political absolutism—as an incontestable repository of centralized violent power is thus taken up by Hobbes. 'Rational' and 'realist' seventeenth-century political theory is an ideology of absolute state power which centralizes violence in order, apparently, to contain it. A functional stasis, then, between states is always one of a pragmatic balance of competing forces aspiring to absolute power. Whatever the Westphalian revolution is, it is not the triumph of peaceable reason and toleration over religious and irrational violence.

maintains that all apparent individual things should be treated as if they are, in fact, genuinely individual things. That is, individual things do not have their being in any transcendent power of being.[23] Hence, God is now an existing individual whose power of being resides in His own existence, just as I am an individual being whose power of being resides within my own existence—we no longer participate in God, each other and creation ontologically.[24] Hence, the modern individual is born. So Descartes, assuming this nominalist perspective, simply believes that his own individual consciousness is a self-contained immediate reality, and this reality is the *only* reality he really participates in. Further, the warrants and rules of scientific proof that Descartes constructed out of his indubitable autonomous proof, and Descartes' interest in understanding discretely natural reality, assumes that nature is indeed a discrete reality that the religious perspective has no right to impose any dogmatic interpretive spin on. Descartes accepts the validity of the theological perspective of *natura pura*.

By the seventeenth century the separation of the natural from the supernatural and the search for discretely natural and logical causes in all observable phenomena is bedding down in the foundations of modern science. But by now many other characteristically modern separations—foreign to Classical Western culture and high Medieval Christendom—were also beginning to gain a broad cultural currency. From the Enlightenment on the separation of nature from supernature seeks to place all things supernatural in the discrete realm of faith and the church, and this is now distinct from the natural realm, which is the world of science, politics and commerce. So the church must butt out of science, philosophy, politics and economics—or else it must pursue these endeavors in discretely 'natural' and 'realistic' ways, and without any special claims to supernatural knowledge or authority. As secularism developed the now discrete realm of religious and moral belief became increasingly privatized and, by our time, religion and morality was finally separated from the realm of public legality and social norms (this is, by the way, a unique accomplishment in the history of human culture). As this process matures, Western culture has increasingly conceptually

---

23. See Flew, *A Dictionary of Philosophy*, 253. Flew gives this succinct definition for his entry on Ockham's razor: "The principle of ontological economy, usually formulated as 'Entities are not to be multiplied beyond necessity.'"

24. See Tillich, *Theology of Culture*, 10–29, for the profound implications of this shift of perspective in the underlying philosophy of religion in Western culture.

and politically separated facts from values, quality from quantity, belief from action, political reality from moral truth and economics from premodern notions of a just price and a fair wage. In all of these separations instrumental rationality becomes separated from wisdom. In Classical parlance, *scientia*—'know how,' the technological, quantitative and scientific knowledge of manipulative means—is uncoupled from the governance of *sapientia*—'know why,' the qualitative and transcendent knowledge of universal, true and good ends.

However, at the early stages of modernity few Europeans envisioned that secularism would lead to the demise of the Christian religion as the main stay of Western power and culture. The view that secularism involves the receding of religious consciousness itself is largely a nineteenth century belief. From the nineteenth century on secularism was increasingly conflated with a belief in the inevitable cultural triumph of materialistic atheism. For once the realm of the supernatural is fully separated from the natural real world, one has—as Laplace famously put it—no need for the "hypothesis" of God. Given Ockham's view of natural reality, for all practical, scientific and public purposes, God no longer exists.[25]

In the nineteenth century, highly influential social theorists believed that religion itself had no future in modern Western culture. In the light of Feuerbach's critique of religion, Marx embraced the coming end of faith with joy, and saw wonderful possibilities for a new society that was free from the tyranny, superstition and falsehood of religion.[26] Durkheim, however, whilst seeing the end of religion as embedded in the process of modernization, was not as optimistic as Marx about what the end of faith might entail. Durkheim associated the social role of the sacred with the preservation of the collective conditions of civilization, and these conditions he saw as being inherently eroded by the new personal freedoms opened up to bourgeois society after the industrial revolution.[27] Weber too, saw the demise of religion as inherent in the process of modernization, even though he understood religion as an important driver of the process of modernization. Weber saw Calvinism as underpinning the development of modern capitalism,[28] and traced the origins of mod-

---

25. See ibid. on the almost inevitability of atheism in the modern world view.

26. Marx, "Introduction to the Critique of Hegel's Philosophy of Right" (1844) in *Karl Marx, Early Writings*, 243–57; Feuerbach, *The Essence of Christianity*.

27. Durkheim, *The Elementary Forms of Religious Life*.

28. Weber, *The Protestant Work Ethic and the Spirit of Capitalism*.

ern instrumental reason to Aquinas.[29] Christian theology and Christian practices were seen by Weber as intimately formative of the modern secular world. Yet, as this world became more deeply entrenched in instrumental rationality, the strangulation of the human spirit by bureaucratic efficiency seemed inescapable. Weber liked the modern world, was agnostic about God and saw Christian Europe as forever gone, and yet he had profound fears for modernity's spiritual future.[30]

Aided by the powerful influence of the classical sociologists, by the triumph of Darwinian science and nineteenth century naturalistic cosmology,[31] and by Freud's popularization of Feuerbach's psychological understanding of religion,[32] the twentieth century saw the broad acceptance of an inherently atheistic "secularization thesis" in Western academies. This thesis holds that as societies modernize they discard religious superstitions altogether, recognizing religion as a delusion and religion itself fades away.[33] Political ideology, scientific progress and economic development become the only factors of real importance as the world modernizes. But even political ideology can cause conflict so by the end of the twentieth century—after the collapse of communism in the USSR—it is only economic and technological advancement that progresses human happiness. Thus neoliberalism tacitly maintains that we Westerners are happy and content pragmatists, who have out-grown the violence of political ideology just as surely as we have outgrown the superstitious passions of pre-scientific religion. With calm, mature realism, modern people are tolerant and moderate and have learned to live without the false hopes of salvation after death or any belief in a transcendent basis for morality.[34] But what about the non-Western peoples of the world in the current global context?[35]

---

29. Honnefelder, "Rationalization and Natural Law."
30. Weber, *The Protestant Work Ethic*, 180–83.
31. Spencer, *Essays*.
32. Freud, *The Future of a Delusion*; Freud, *The Origins of Religion*.
33. Van Krieken et al., *Sociology*, 493–99.
34. Greiner, *Australian Liberalism in a Post-ideological Age*.
35. The extent to which Western culture is now a global culture should not be under-estimated (see Harrison, *Inside the Third World*); however, neither should it be over-estimated (see Berger, *The Desecularization of the World*; Jenkins, *The New Faces of Christianity*). Particularly amongst the poor of the world, the absence of the wealth that gives access to Western ways of living excludes them functionally from Western culture, even if they are far from un-influenced by the West.

Globalization and Secularism

In the post-war era a new economic internationalism began to emerge, undergirded by the Bretton Woods Institutions, which are largely financially controlled by the USA.[36] The USA—as a champion of secular demarcations between religion and business and politics, and the champion of democracy and capitalism—was the global non-communist leader of the post-war era. The cold war saw the USSR and the USA struggle for global dominance with each other and this was typically understood as a struggle between two modern secular powers with different economic and political ideologies. By 1989 it was evident that the USSR had lost this battle for global dominance with the USA. With this American victory, modern capitalistic secular freedom—of a very American tinge, guaranteed by U.S. military might and economic dynamism—now seemed to hold an uncontested global dominance.[37] To those caught up in this spirit of American global triumph, globalization was now seen as an inherently good process furthering the freedom and prosperity of the entire globe. This triumphalism assumed that globalization would lift economically and technologically backward people into democracy, freedom, pragmatic contentment and moderate secular toleration. Globalization would hoist the world's peoples out of poverty, and thus out of the superstition, ignorance and violence of pre-modern cultural contexts too.

Yet, this expansive and self-confident global triumphalism became dramatically defensive after 9/11. The idea that now that communism was defeated not everyone in the globe wanted an unequivocally pro-American, free enterprise and secular global world order, was simply shocking to the pragmatic neocons running the Whitehouse in 2001. The idea that there might be just reasons why American global power was even hated could simply not be entertained. And now that the people of America were victims of terrorism, the moral high ground for the defense of the American way of life, at any cost, was quickly commandeered. At this point it becomes clear how profoundly unprepared for any serious analysis of the religious context of the post 1989 global world order the Whitehouse was. This, in many ways, can be put down to the assumption not only of the progressive "secularization thesis" that equates development with the demise of religion, but with the assumption that secularization

---

36. See Stiglitz and Monbiot, as previously cited, on the control of the Bretton Woods Institutions by US treasury.

37. Fukuyama, *The End of History*.

A Post-Secular Approach to Understanding Religion and Global Security

is an inherently good thing desired by all the people of the globe. As long as we cannot examine and question these assumptions the real religious dynamics of the globe, and of our own secularism, will always escape us, and foreign policy premised on illusions will result.

Secularism is an integral part of the Western capitalist, scientific, liberal, pragmatic and democratic ideological vision of a good state of human fulfillment. Post-war Western money and power created and sustains our present global world order and so the structures and rules of globalization are largely a product of Western power, but most of the people of the globe do not have a deep and long Western cultural heritage. Though modern non-Western people can be as techno savvy and as interested in Western personal freedoms as any Westerner, yet, looking a bit below the cultural surface, it is obvious that the non-Western world does not share the West's long, violent and complex developmental history of secularism and Ockhamean naturalism. Hence, the assumptions of how one should demarcate different authority spheres natural to a modern Western person, and the assumed cosmological and metaphysical belief frames of Western materialism, cannot be taken to be as unquestionably self-evident to the non-Western people of the globe—however modern and Western they may look. In this context the Western assumption that modern non-Western people are as deeply committed to a profoundly Western way of approaching economics, power and religion, is an erroneous assumption. It is also an assumption that is an easy cause of offence to non-Western people and misunderstanding by Western people. Western international relations agendas that pre-suppose this assumption, can, then, easily exacerbate inter-cultural misunderstanding and tension.

Western international relations policy, then, could really do with a better understanding of the West's secularism and an appreciation of the depth of non-secularist reality outlooks in non-Western people.[38] We could also do with a carefully differentiated understanding of the strengths and weaknesses of our own secularism. Yet, this seldom happens because belief in the unequivocal strength and validity of our secularism is, effectively, a foundational article of faith to people like Mr. Howard. However, Western culture does have a strong history of critiquing its own cultural assumptions and part of that history looks very directly at secularism. It is to this fascinating trajectory of cultural critique that we now turn.

---

38. See Quanchi, "Indigenous Epistemology, Wisdom and Tradition."

What Is Post-Secularism?

In the 1990s one of the most eminent twentieth century sociologists of religion—Peter Berger—come around to a total rejection of the atheistic secularization thesis.[39] It was now evident to Berger that whilst Western religion had been radically transformed in the twentieth century, and (generally) declined profoundly as a public socio-cultural feature of our modern Western life form—yet it had not just gone away and was transforming itself in unexpected ways. The turn of the century saw a whole new genre of literature emerge on spirituality in the West.[40] And then, if one looked outside Western culture, religion was anything but declining.[41] In fact, the weight of contemporary sociological thinking has rejected an undifferentiated 'progressive' view of secularization and many sociologists now maintain that globalization is fuelling religious dynamism in both the Western and developing worlds.[42]

In 1990, John Milbank published *Theology and Social Theory*.[43] Here secularism, and secular social theory, is seriously historically examined and critiqued at a foundational level. Tracing the origins of secularism to the nominalist theology of the fourteenth century, Milbank argues that secularism itself is a religious outlook, and what is more, it is a Christian heresy. The methodological atheism of modern social theory and the privatization of religious belief to the realm of personal freedom upheld as religious freedom in liberal Western societies, is premised not on demonstrable and objective truths but on the assumptions and lifestyle patterns of a particular, and theologically premised, belief outlook. As it is our belief outlook, we do not even notice it as an outlook—it is, in Berger's terms, simply the reality in which we live.[44] Yet this reality has been under stress in the West since at least the beginning of the nineteenth century.

---

39. Berger, *The Desecularization of the World*.

40. For example, Tacey, *Re-Enchantment*.

41. Jenkins, *The Next Christianity*.

42. Bauman, *Intimations of Postmodernity*; Giddens, *The Consequences of Modernity*; Giddens, *Modernity and Self Identity*; Lyon, "Religion and the Postmodern: Old Problems, New Prospects"; Lechner, "Fundamentalism Revisited"; Martin, "The Secularisation Issue: Prospect and Retrospect."

43. Milbank, *Theology and Social Theory*.

44. Berger & Luckmann, *The Social Construction of Reality*.

A Post-Secular Approach to Understanding Religion and Global Security

Kant's critiques—which are the high watermark of Enlightenment philosophical achievement—are driven by Humean skepticism to try and overcome the epistemological, religious, moral and metaphysical difficulties of the modern outlook, grounded as it is in Cartesian epistemology. Yet, Kant's monumental efforts did not allow the nineteenth century to re-gain its metaphysical or epistemological confidence and the whole framework of belief about what is transcendently meaningful and inherently good in the West's high culture started spiraling inexorably towards collapse.[45] Hegel's idealism reacts against Kant's rejection of any substantive knowledge of noumenal reality and thus the early part of the nineteenth century is characterized by the turmoil of the Kantian epistemological revolution and its complex philosophical responses. As the nineteenth century matured, two families of responses solidified—both shaped profoundly by adaptations and reactions to Kant and Hegel. In general terms, those who grappled with these profound theoretical problems of belief and action and who ended up convinced of the existence of a deep unresolved belief crisis in Western culture, can be called counter-Enlightenment figures. On the other hand, those who either ignored these problems, or thought they had overcome them by recourse to romantic intuition, or by replacing theory with practice, or by a pragmatic commitment to naïve positivism, can be called progressive figures. In general, Continental thinkers were more attune to the philosophical difficulties of modernism than were the more pragmatic and empirically minded Anglo-Americans. And so a direct line from the counter-Enlightenment thinkers of the nineteenth century to the European crisis thinkers of the early twentieth century—such as Heidegger—and on to the French post-structuralists of the second half of the twentieth century, and then the European "postmodernists" of today, can be seen. This counter-Enlightenment trajectory has ruthlessly explored the theoretical underpinnings of modern Western belief and practice, and, typically within a naturalist perspective, has conquered the high intellectual ground over the progressives concerning the inherently unstable nature of knowledge and meaning in a purely natural cosmos. Come the late twentieth century and the intellectual defeat of progressive confidence finally filters into the Anglo-American thought world and its influence is now becoming increasingly evident in English speaking academies.

---

45. Harrison, *The Disenchantment of Reason*.

Backing up a bit, and locking in on religion and secularism, the beginnings of a post-secular intellectual revolt against modernity can be found in two very different nineteenth century counter-Enlightenment figures: Kierkegaard and Nietzsche.

Kierkegaard probed the truth beliefs of his time—as grounded in Kantian morality, objective scientific knowledge and Hegelian idealistic reason—and found them all to raise more questions than they answered.[46] What is more Kierkegaard found modern belief structures to be irrelevant to the life that we actually live, and hence irrelevant to the most important questions of our existence.[47] To Kierkegaard, the interpersonal, both in terms of the individual's relationship to God and the relationships between people, is the sole site of our most interested concerns. It is in these most important contexts that we need truth and in these contexts the self-contained logical perfections of the Kantian mind, all questions framed discretely in the categories of natural science, and all abstracted and pure ideals, are irrelevant. Kierkegaard finds faith and sin—inherently inter-personal and religious concepts—to be the primary epistemological categories appropriate to our actual existence. Hence, if our beliefs and actions are to be meaningful and true, we must seek knowledge that is relational and spiritually connective with God and all creation through God, rather than knowledge which is merely objectively propositional or merely manipulatively useful. This is a profound rejection of the Western secularist heritage from Abelard to Hegel, and Kierkegaard greatly influenced the counter-Enlightenment existentialism of the late nineteenth century and twentieth century. To Kierkegaard, rational or scientific or ideal knowledge discretely cut off from our mode of being (i.e., relational becoming), is fatuous knowledge, and the demarcations of Western culture that have produced our modern secular way of life uphold an inherently disingenuous belief and practice frame of existence which is characteristically dis-integrated. Kierkegaard seeks to re-discover faith, truth and real life integrity in an era that does not even comprehend the very notion of integrative existential truth. Kierkegaard is thus a major turning point in an attempt to withdraw from the Ockham formed fundamental assumptions of modernity. Kierkegaard seeks to re-create a Christian and non-secular understanding of knowledge, morality, truth and lived integrity.

46. Kierkegaard, *Concluding Unscientific Postscript*.
47. Kierkegaard, *The Sickness Unto Death*.

A Post-Secular Approach to Understanding Religion and Global Security

In Nietzsche, however, we have a virulently anti-Christian rejection of secularism. Nietzsche sees clearly that in actual practice God is dead to the West, and finds this a profoundly disturbing but also potentially liberating situation. It opens up a window for the re-paganization of Europe, for Nietzsche grasps that there is no more basic social reality than the inescapable mytho-ritualistic grounds of human language, custom, belief and existence. Discarding the slave morality of Christianity, Nietzsche seeks to revitalize the Classical agonistic morality of elitist glory. As all believed realities are constructed by our own imagination, let us then imagine realities that at least offer the prospect of greatness and glory to those few souls who can climb above the despicable masses and create their own glorious humanity.[48] If God is dead we cannot settle into a complacent materialist pragmatism—at least human greatness cannot accept this groveling slavery to mere satiation—but we must strive to generate our own meaning out of nothing, and we must form our myths and practices of worship to fill the yawning vacuum that the death of God has placed at the very heart of Western culture.[49] This outlook of total constructivism rejects any attempt at the knowledge of objective factual truth or a discretely non mytho-ritualistic public space, and so erodes all the demarcations of modern secularism entirely. This outlook rejects the idea that a comfortable materialistic pragmatism is a release from superstitious pre-scientific ignorance, and is a balanced, noble and dependable cultural backdrop from which to create a good society. For Nietzsche—as followed by Freud and others—is very aware of the seething inner forces in the soul of humanity, and he sees struggle as basic to the human condition and not something that any reasonable pragmatism can cover over, let alone sustainedly contain or harness. Pragmatic, rational, soft atheism is not going to make everyone happy in the world. Rather, this inherent small mindedness will produce an entirely degenerate culture which will be the easy foil for those few elite souls, driven by the will to power, to control and craft for their own self-glorification.

Nietzsche's recognition of the ritual-mythic nature of all human existence and the intimate connection between these primal a-rational poetic belief frames and all practices of power, is a total rejection of secularism and has proved a very fruitful framework for cultural analysis. Paul Ricœur's fascinating analysis of the rituo-mythical construction of

---

48. Nietzsche, *On the Genealogy of Morality.*
49. Nietzsche, *The Gay Science.*

ancient Babylonian power is interesting precisely because of what it tells us about our own politics in modern Western contexts, today.[50] The dark vision of Freud too, gives credence to the notion that the rational ego is but a thin delusional veneer, vainly seeking to contain and control the restless and uncontainable destructive and creative powers of the id and the super ego.[51] This type of socio-cultural analysis makes the progressive vision of rational secular modern man and his peaceful control of technology and global society look terribly naïve. More to the point, it is not naïve, it is willfully delusional. For creative, destructive and self-aggrandizing forces are inherent in all human power. To believe that we Western secularists are good and rational and religious terrorists are evil and irrational is to shut one's eyes willfully to the scope and power of Western creative and destructive influence the small world over. For on a global scale, the impact of a few religious terrorists hardly registers at all when compared with Western power. And this Western cultural, political, economic and military global power is profoundly morally ambivalent and deeply irrational. The notion that modern Western civilization is the paragon of Enlightened rational man is a willful delusion that only hides the violent and exploitative will to power of the present global world order from the ordinary Western citizen. Looking at this order from outside the perspective of the dominant cultural power, this delusion is not even remotely believable.

The Nietzschean/Freudian appreciation of the mytho-ritualistic and irrational foundations of the human condition leads easily to a very dark understanding of all human power. Fictions about the enlightened, inherent rationality and universal goodness of modern Western secular power structures and our socio-political mores cannot be convincingly believed. Yet, as penetrating and insightful as this type of post-secularism is, it has a fundamental flaw. If it is true that human reality is inherently agonistic, inherently irrational, and the play thing of instinctive and social forces that it can only just functionally contain, then the very notion of critique becomes meaningless. Famously, Heidegger's refusal to fully denounce Nazism as evil is implied by his radical constructivist outlook on meaning and morality, strongly shaped, as it was, by Nietzsche. Further, what can be wrong about the violent military pursuit of glory via conquest if this is an inherently natural human desire? What is wrong

---

50. Ricœur, *The Symbolism of Evil*; Wink, *Engaging the Powers*.
51. Freud, *Civilisation and its Discontents*.

A Post-Secular Approach to Understanding Religion and Global Security

with slavery and economic exploitation? These types of relationships are all very natural. As Nietzsche points out, the moral values of Christian Europe have a particular genealogy and are constructed out of a particular cultural milieu. Nietzsche argues that as products of human culture, Christian values are not universal moral truths, in fact, Christian morality denies the reality of the human condition in relation to the high creative, sexual and destructive powers that truly and gloriously animate human civilization. Christian morals are degenerate morals to Nietzsche.

As an important aside, the Hobbesean vision of the necessity of a total control of violence by the state, and Cardinal Richelieu's philosophy of *Realpolitik* is typically assumed by the same people who espouse the goodness and rationality of modern secular global economics. Figures like John Howard want to have their cake and eat it too. They want to be enlightened, tolerant and reasonable pragmatists benefiting all mankind, at the same time as they exploit the globe and its people and apply absolute violence to all who oppose them. This apparent contradiction arises because the roots of political liberalism are grounded in the Hobbesean vision of the human condition and the reliance on overwhelming state force to uphold the structures of society that make liberal economic reality workable. The amazing erosion of civil liberties in the West after the commencement of George W. Bush's war on terror, the flagrant use of torture,[52] state endorsed xenophobia, and the determined shift towards unaccountable violent state power and pre-emptive military intervention, as seen in Iraq, Guantanamo Bay, Australia's boarder protection antics, and the Dr. Haneef case, are neo-fascist trends, natural to our Hobbesean political heritage.

But back to the fundamental flaw of Nietzschean post-secularism. This stance is not really post-secular because it still assumes Ockham's naturalism. The mytho-ritual is inherently natural in Nietzsche's outlook, as in Freud, so there is no transcendent frame of inherent value or eternal truth from which to qualitatively distinguish one culturo-moral life form from another, and there is no possibility of redemption from the inherently destructive, violent, exploitative and irrational powers inescapably embedded in the human condition. Critique is meaningless and the naturalism of its view of reality makes all human life forms mere management strategies for the meaningless forces that create and destroy human culture. As Heidegger noted, our natural life is one of being

---

52. Otterman, *American Torture*.

towards death, and this stark reality casts its pall over all the pretensions of meaning, achievement and purpose that we might construct. This outlook—as penetrating as it is in many regards—becomes an irrational and despairing outlook. The great figures of European postmodernism, such as Lyotard, Foucault and Derrida, cast a plague on all houses when they are being critical, and revel in despair, in the brokenness and dysfunctionality of the human condition when they are being constructive. A profound distrust of rationality underpins their thought; *Logos* in any transcendent sense is simply not considered. Ultimately, Nietzschean post-secularism does not provide us with a meaningful alternative to the modern secular self-confidence it so crushingly critiques. But there is an alternative form of post-secularism.

Plato, Aristotle and Plotinus all believed that unless you assume the divinity of reason—that is, that truth is an authentic revelation from a Good, True and Beautiful transcendent reality, and somehow the human mind has the capacity to receive this revelation—and that unless you assume the priority of the eternal over the temporal, no act of reasoning or observation could deliver truth. In this sense, Classical philosophy is premised on faith, for, as Aristotle—the most naturalistic of the big three—notes, one cannot prove the grounds of rational certainty and scientific observation themselves.[53] In this sense, the philosophical heritage of Western culture, Western reason itself, is grounded in the enchanted and inherently divinely animated cosmos rejected by Ockham. The Classical view is one where reality is more primary than appearance and where appearance is always grounded in the transcendent, and it is an outlook embedded in Platonist theology.[54] Ockham rejects this outlook. The real is now the merely materially apparent, and metaphysical participation is a fiction of our linguistic conceptualization. The Classical heritage of reason which birthed modern science is now subject to patricide. The new outlook kills off Classical reason and the rationality of Christian belief. Yet, it is quite possible to argue that it does not just kill Classical reason and Christian belief, it kills the very idea of rational truth and the very

---

53. Aristotle, *Posterior Analytics* 72b: "Now some think that because one must understand the primitives there is no understanding at all; others that there is, but that there are demonstrations of everything. Neither of these views is either true or necessary."

54. Burkert, *Greek Religion*, "Philosophical Religion," 305–38. Burkert notes the enormous theological inventiveness of Plato and the profound impact that had on subsequent Platonist and later Neoplatonist thinking in the Classical world.

idea of meaningful belief. The incoherent pluralism of the sophisticated intellectual dead ends of postmodernism seems to support this diagnosis. Western reason and belief is in a profound crisis. We now have unprecedented technological power but no divine wisdom to guide that power towards a truth that, as the psalmist David notes, "is higher than I."[55] The Good is now out of our reach, and all we have is blind irrational, violent, self-interested, "all too human" power—and then we die.

What if Kierkegaard is right? What if the above outlook of agonistic, meaningless despair is not scientific fact, and what if modernity's rational realism is rather an existentially unbelievable denial of the most immediate experiences of human meaning in which we are actually embedded?[56] Indeed, following through on this "what if" is the pathway of the "theological turn" in French phenomenology that can easily move towards post-secularism as pursued by contemporary thinkers like John Milbank.[57] Yet, so entrenched is nineteenth century materialistic 'progressivism' in Western academia—even though we no longer overtly believe in the doctrine of cultural progress—that the very idea that some sort of return to a Classical metaphysical outlook is possible strikes the secular intellectual ear like either a fairy tale or a regression to irrational and oppressive superstition.

Liberalism fears any threat to secularism, not because liberalism is opposed to violence—look at Hobbes; liberalism is grounded in a commitment to violent state control—but because it wishes state violence to be incontestable by any extra-state transcendently referenced authority—i.e., the church. Liberalism's model of private liberty guaranteed by the monopolization of violence by the state is indeed opposed to any liturgical and sacramental view of human society, and is, premised on Ockham's theology, nothing short of religiously committed to a de-sacralized nominalist ideology of social and cosmic atomism. And so any critique of secularism which is not of an irrationalist, agonistic, and ultimately despairing nature is inherently feared as a return to the theocratic political model of medieval Christendom, and as an essential loss of modern individual liberty. Naturalistic postmodern irrealism sits comfortably with hypermodern technophilia politically—both views being committed to

---

55. Psalm 61:2.

56. See Cunningham, *Genealogy of Nihilism*, for a close examination of the inherent difficulties of believing nihilism, i.e., the inherently contradictory construction of the belief in nothing as something which is genealogy of modern nihilism.

57. Janicaud, et al., *The "Theological Turn."*

atomistic agonism and fundamental ontological relativism—but metaphysically searching post-secularism upsets the whole post-Ockham Western reality frame.

The type of post-secularism explored by John Milbank and Philip Blond is not an attempt to return us to the pre-secular political structures of Medieval Christendom. Yet Radical Orthodoxy is relentlessly portrayed as such by its detractors who simply cannot imagine any alternative social reality to secular modernity for the West. Rather, theological post-secularism is an attempt to re-open the transcendent frame of belief to Western reason. Milbank's post secularism is an attempt to re-integrate the dis-integrated spheres of human life that modern secularism has isolated, and it is an approach that seeks to re-ground philosophy, existence and politics in the primal human realities of a theologically metaphysical mind, the practice of worship grounded in an enchanted cosmos, and community understood as sacrament and liturgy.[58]

Apart from its potential to redeem Western meaning, transcendently referenced post-secularism has a clear advantage over both naturalistic secularism and naturalistic post-secularism when it comes to understanding what is happening on the global scene in relation to politics, religion and power. These advantages flow from simply not assuming that the non-Western world is committed to secularism in any deep and basic manner, and in understanding that Western secularism is itself a profoundly problematic set of conceptual and political assumptions, without believing one has to give up on meaning and reason itself.

The basic insight of a post-secular outlook is to simply not assume that Ockham's nominalism and the belief in pure nature are self-evidently true.[59] Václav Havel's "Politics and Conscience" is a powerful illustration

---

58. See Milbank, *Theology and Social Theory*; Blond, *Post-Secular Philosophy*; Schmemann, *For the Life of the World*; Pickstock, *After Writing*.

59. Interestingly, and somewhat along Durkheim's lines, even if one assumes that religion is a 'natural' feature of human society (and what else could it be if one is a modern materialist?), then one can see what an important 'natural' role it plays in restraining power and upholding common values. Perhaps it is just a good scientific observation to hold that we exclude religion from public life, social morality and natural exploitation at our peril. Durkheim was correct to see that secular modernity creates a serious problem for modern Man. Comte was derided for his attempt to construct a modern positivist religion—and there are good reasons to be derisive of any attempt to 'create' the sacred when one has no belief in transcendence—and yet his stance is more anthropologically rational than the 'progressive' assumption that being rid of religion will open up a bold new world of freedom, rationality and human happiness. In many ways James Lovelock is a contemporary Comte, seeking to harness a materialistic understanding of 'the sacred' for rational political purposes.

of this type of post-secular outlook in action.⁶⁰ Indeed Havel demonstrates that once one takes transcendence and sacredness seriously, it is, finally, possible to see how our Western conception of purely natural reality has got our knowledge, our technology, our politics, our economics, our religion and our morality into serious difficulty. For where there is no piety restraining natural exploitation and no transcendent ground giving meaning to morality beyond its purely human construction, then mere socio-instinctive psychological necessity is the only final ground of behavior and motivation, and mere calculations of brute power are the only final grounds of rationality.⁶¹ In this 'realist' modern vision, it is human dignity that is missing. This 'realism' puts us profoundly at the mercy of the irrational and violent demons of our own inner natures. Unless we can radically re-sacralize our view of the world and human dignity, ancient pre-secular themes of hubris, impiety and apocalyptic judgment may become all too relevant to us in the near future.

CONCLUSION

Our Western way of life is under profound stress from the forces Western wealth, power and knowledge have unleashed on the globe, and from the deep internal difficulties for substantive public moral values embedded in secular Western culture. The threat of religious terrorism to the integrity and durability of our Western way of life is so small in comparison with the problems that the Western way of life itself has generated that religious terrorism is essentially a non-issue. Yet it is a wonderfully politically exploitable non-issue.

Bush's aggressive scapegoating of religious terrorism exemplified an approach to international relations that stimulated mutual mistrust between the delicately transitional, partially-secular Islamic world and the West, and which at the same time produced a smoke screen that allowed Bush and his allies to ignore the unjust and potentially catastrophic trajectory of the current pro-Western world order. This was a very unhelpful conceptual paradigm out of which to construct peaceable and visionary international relations. This framework, to the contrary, constructed

---

60. Havel, "Politics and Conscience."

61. Sophocles' play *Antigone* shows just how far back the tension between human pragmatic realism and divine authority runs in Western culture. But never has human pragmatism had such a complete upper hand as in the West now.

an aggressive, reactionary and belligerently destructive environment of global insecurity. Further, this out-look has deep roots in the theological assumptions of the West which the West itself no longer understands. In this context, conceptual clarity, keen analysis and visionary political leadership regarding global security, is very hard to uncover.

An interesting feature of the theological history of the West is the linkage between the voluntarism and nominalism in the late medieval era. That is, whilst God is withdraw from nature by nominalism and placed in the discrete realm of the supernatural, God is also increasingly seen as an absolute (though now distant) sovereign by virtue of Him possessing unlimited power and a totally sovereign will. Thus Calvin's focus on sovereignty as the first attribute of divinity comes to replace Augustine's focus on love as the first attribute of divinity. Given that anthropology was defined by theology in the culturally Christian West until very recently (i.e., people were understood to be created in the image of God) the restraints and freedoms of will, and the religious mandate to conquer the earth as an expression of Man's sovereignty over nature, and the push for singular political sovereignty by monarchs, becomes entwined in the thought and politics of the West from late medieval times to the present.[62] So, the atomism and individualism of nominalism, the quarantining of personal beliefs and values from public legality, and the 'realistic' notion of power as unrestrained will, has shaped the development of the political and economic life forms from of the West for at least the past 500 years. Even though the discretely supernatural sphere was more or less intellectually killed off by the natural sphere in the nineteenth century—as signaled by Nietzsche's famous 'death of God'—the purely natural sphere is still a theological construct that is intimately implicated in Western instrumental rationality and political pragmatism. So, the exploitative voluntarism that refuses any intrinsic restraint on our pragmatic approach to fossil fuel consumption, the instrumental imperatives of conquest and exploitation over sacredness and preservation in our approach to nature, the self-focused naturalistic anthropology of consumerism and the moral blindness of the logic of economic necessity in the global context are all profoundly rooted in the religious heritage of the West. Thus Western theology, as carried forward in the cultural life form of modern secularism, is driving us towards global cataclysm. So, not only does the blindness of Western secularism towards the beliefs and cultural situa-

---

62. Dupré, *Passage to Modernity*, 120–44.

A Post-Secular Approach to Understanding Religion and Global Security

tions of non-Western religious communities of the globe promote global insecurity, but the theology of Western secularism actually defines the power and belief norms that frame the political, economic, knowledge and military structures of the dominant global culture.

The future outlook for global security requires some basic shifts in the operational patterns of power and belief if the energy, environmental and economic structures of the present global order are to change radically enough to avert catastrophe. In order to even see the frameworks of belief that uphold the current reality assumptions of the modern secular world view, we must start to understand our own Western theological traditions.

Underpinning Bush's approach to the national security of the USA was his unconscious captivity to the nominalist and voluntarist theological innovations of William of Ockham. Australian politics, certainly under Mr. Howard, has been equally captive to the theological assumptions of Ockham's secularism. Further, in the heyday of economic rationalism and pragmatic materialism in Australian public life—from the Hawke government to the Howard government—theological illiteracy was effectively required of our political leaders. However, the dynamism of religion in the global south, and the refusal of religion to simply disappear in the West, coupled with the recent hunger for spirituality in the West, and the growing consciousness that our way of life is damaging the very biosphere, makes it possible for a new generation of political leaders to take religion, theology and cultural self-criticism far more seriously. In Australian politics Kevin Rudd gave us a brief spark of nascent theological sensibility in public office, yet he did not last long.[63] Further, it seems that Evangelical Christianity in America, now that the religious right has de-secularized it, is beginning to fracture as a merely conservative political block.[64] So something of a post-secular critical understanding of Western culture, and a greater sensitivity to the a-secularism of many non-Western global communities, may now be politically possible for Western leaders.

Ironically enough, genuine global security can only come if we embrace the profound insecurity of fundamental cultural and behavioral

---

63. Rudd, "Faith in Politics."

64. The Evangelical radical Jim Wallis' *God's Politics* has been a bestseller in the US since it was released, indicating at least a fracturing of the religious right, and potentially something of a radicalization of the Evangelical vote in the USA in the latter half of the 2010s.

change in the West. The refusal to even recognize the necessity for such change has thus far characterized the popularist political approach to ameliorating the West's inchoate sense of global insecurity. The politics of fear and ignorance is the politics of preserving the drivers of our real insecurity. Such politics will only exacerbate global catastrophe in the near future. Recognizing, with John Milbank, that the foundations of secular reason and our modern Western way of life embedded in that rationality, are theological, we need political leaders who can analyze our situation from a stance which is critically aware of the role Western secularism plays in the trajectory towards global chaos which we are currently on. Now, it seems, is the time when we need great statesmen and stateswomen of faith, like Wilberforce, Ghandi, King, Havel and Su Kee, who have deep religious sensitivity, moral power and spiritual fortitude, and who can see the terrain that we really inhabit.

7

Faith and Medicine

A Reflection on the Collision of Belief Systems and the Clash of Epistemological Power Structures

THIS CHAPTER SEEKS TO crunch through a number of complex sociological and theological concerns that can arise when Christian faith and medical care interact at close quarters. Two features of this interaction will be examined. Firstly, this chapter explores the manner in which the miraculously and eternally referenced features of Christian belief and practice are 'detoxified' and given a safe and sensible role to play within the modern secular conception of medical reality. What is of particular interest here is the extent to which the modern church readily adapts itself to the secular reality frame of modern medicine, despite its ostensible belief commitment to the miraculous and the transcendent. Secondly, this chapter explores the manner in which medical care generates its own powerful belief and practice frame which can tacitly or explicitly corrode central Christian beliefs and practices. That is, if a Christian receiving medical care is committed to a belief and practice outlook *not* defined by instrumental rationality, anti-metaphysical positivism and modern naturalism, then the hospital environment can powerfully assault central components of such a Christian understanding of healing, care, illness and death. So, this chapter focuses both on how the church is influenced by the outlook of modern medical care, and on how the larger belief and practice frame of modern medical care controls the hospital environment in ways that challenge core features of traditional Christian belief and practice. These two foci are explored from the stance of a Christian recipient of secular medical care in the context of untreatable terminal illnesses.

This chapter has two distinctive methodological features. Firstly, this chapter pursues a strongly interdisciplinary approach. That is, I seek to offer something of a theological perspective on the sociology of knowledge and power within the context of modern secular medical care, and I seek to offer something of a sociological perspective on the theology of faith, miracles and ecclesial status quo under the conditions of modern Western Christianity. The interdisciplinary nature of this approach is not simply an approach that uses multiple methodologies but is rather an approach that actively seeks to cross the boundaries separating objective medical conditions from both inter-subjective relational contexts and from beliefs that concern timeless transcendent spiritual realities and miracles. That is, it is interdisciplinary in a very strong sense, in a sense that seeks to treat human experience as an integrated whole that cannot be meaningfully reduced to any one frame of methodological exploration.[1] Secondly, this chapter draws its inferences not from the analysis of quantitative or 'qualitative' sociological data, nor is its stance one of objective rationality; rather the reflections outlined in this chapter are drawn from my own existentially interested situation. For I am a Christian father of two children who had terminal illnesses.[2] Writing in an academic voice from the stance of personal interestedness and existential commitment has, of course, many dangers. Yet perhaps the open acknowledgement of the interests and situation of the writer avoids some problems of tackling such a topic in an ostensibly objectivist manner where the interests and situation of the writer are not revealed.

This chapter is structured around the narrative of the experience of my wife and I as we interacted with our church and two hospitals in the course of the illnesses of two of our children.[3] The first half of this nar-

1. See Polanyi, *Personal Knowledge*, for a sustained argument advocating this type of strong interdisciplinary approach to meaningful knowledge.

2. See, for example, Kierkegaard, *Fear and Trembling*, wherein Kierkegaard's particular, belief committed and highly interested situation—both in relation to his broken engagement with Regine Olsen and his inner struggle for faith—does not result in solipsistic indulgence but becomes a springboard for Kierkegaard to explore the inner landscape of the human condition. I am seeking to follow this type of approach in this chapter.

3. One hospital was state run the other was a state funded Catholic hospital.

Faith and Medicine

rative looks at our experiences in relation to our church; the second half looks at our experiences in relation to the hospital environment.

THE CHURCH AND MODERN SECULAR REALITY

In March of 1998 Annette and I became parents for the first time. We named our beautiful blue eyed son Daniel. When he was six weeks old we discovered that he had Spinal Muscular Atrophy type 1 (SMA). This is a rare genetic condition where nerve signals coming out from the spine degenerate rapidly causing the loss of muscle function. When, in the typical progression of this condition, the muscle systems needed for breathing are weakened, SMA children become very vulnerable to any type of respiratory infection. This condition progresses rapidly and most children with SMA die at around the age of six months. It is a terrible condition. But Daniel—typical of SMA children—was very bright in the eyes, very mentally alert and profoundly relationally aware. He is our first born, a beautiful child, and a great joy to our hearts. Daniel, via the mystery of love, to this day is part of the very fiber of our lives and even the grief we bear from his death is precious to us for it is a part of who we, as spiritual and relational beings bonded to our son, are.

After Daniel died, Annette and I were blessed with three more children—Hannah, Claire and Aurora. They are all beautiful children, none of them have SMA, and they are all healthy and vibrant. Then, in 2006, our fourth daughter was born, Lucy—a child of rare beauty—though we quickly discovered that she had SMA.

Before we knew of Daniel's illness I had never really thought about what the Bible had to say regarding the spiritual gift of healing or miracles in general. Doctrinally I believed—so I thought—in miracles. For it seemed rationally necessary to believe in miracles if I was to believe that central Christian doctrines were true.[4] As Saint Paul himself explains, if Christ has not really risen from the dead (a miracle by anyone's standards) then all Christians are to be pitied as deluded.[5]

Both of these hospitals provided excellent intensive medical care for Daniel and Lucy, and, in our experience, there was no substantial difference between them in relation to the issues raised in this chapter.

4. From my youth I was fully persuaded by C. S. Lewis in his *Miracles* that not only is belief in the miraculous necessary for Christian faith, but that it is also reasonable.

5. 1 Corinthians 15:16–19.

When Daniel was first diagnosed I read all I could find on SMA and learnt that this genetic nerve illness could not be treated by medical science, and that as yet, medical science did not have the faintest clue about how such a condition *could* be cured. So, I concluded, if someone who has SMA is going to get better it can only be by a miracle. A miracle . . . *Now* we read the scriptures about miracles with a totally new interest and dared even to hope that what we had always believed doctrinally was really true. Oh brave new world . . .

Before going any further, I must clarify what I mean by a miracle. For, in keeping with orthodox Christian belief, whilst I do not believe in any strict dichotomy between nature and supernature, neither do I believe that a miracle is natural. This type of stance—where nature and divinity are integrated though not identical, where nature is governed by providential laws, and where God is sovereign over His own natural laws and has the power to replace the naturally universal with the miraculously singular—was taken for granted by Christianity from its beginnings up until at least the high Middle Ages.[6] Yet, coinciding with the sixteenth century theological development of the idea of *natura pura*, the outlook of modernity started to gain a greater rational and technological mastery over nature, thus nature was increasingly seen as a closed system locked off from the realm of the supernatural and as something that we can both understand and control.[7]

The allegorical outlook so richly expressed in Dante's cosmos exemplifies the typical pre-modern Christian stance well. Dante believed in a single and integrated cosmos where what we would now call nature is doxologically gifted with more than what we can adequately reduce to the categories of purely physical reality. In Dante, because this single integrated cosmos is governed by providential laws, nature itself is always more than merely *natural*. To Dante, providential laws govern the human world as much as the physical world, and these laws cannot be broken. But such natural moral laws do not prevent people from sinning or stop disasters from happening. Yet, sin will play out its folly and destruction to the apparent benefactors of injustice, brutality, malice and error, sooner or later.

In regard to the natural order, Christians through the ages have maintained that it is right to pray that Providence will support us when

---

6. Wink, *Engaging the Powers*, 3–10.
7. Dupré, *Passage to Modernity*, 167–89.

Faith and Medicine

we are acting in submission to the ways of the Lord of Heaven and Earth. Praying for God to guide doctors, to give wisdom to our leaders, to enable judges to uphold justice, to assist relief workers to get to those suffering from a disaster, and even offering up our banal daily wishes and concerns to God are, I think, genuine petitionary prayers that have faith in God's providential order and in His subtle assistance within the just bounds of that order. These daily petitions are all right and good and I do believe these prayers matter and God hears us. But praying for a miracle is a very different type of petition.

In praying for a miracle one asks God to directly intervene and over-ride the natural laws of the spatiotemporal structures that He has set up and maintains. Miracles, as typically terrifying and inexplicable singularities, happen a lot in the Bible and are often associated in the New Testament with a particular type of faith.

Modern Western people, however, do not seem to live in a cosmos where we are able to genuinely believe God *could* intervene in and over-ride nature's laws. So, whilst modern Western Christians still readily pray for God to act providentially for the good of all, and out of mercy, within what is possible in the natural order, so bizarre is the very notion of 'the miracle'—something that is naturally impossible—that we have no genuine expectation that we could even ask God to do a miracle. In reality, we only believe in God's activity where it is mediated to us through naturally understandable means. We cannot conceive of the actions of God outside of such mediation. A big part—actually, the very heart—of the worldview of the New Testament (the miraculous) is lost to us, and we tend to read the Christian scriptures largely as a collection of exotic narratives and doctrinal propositions to be interpreted in discretely moral and theological terms. We do not expect miracles to be part of the normal Christian life.[8]

---

8. Even where large sections of the modern Christian world still adhere to belief in the miraculous nature of the sacraments, the wild and free in-breaking work of God in this context is not singular and miraculous in the strong sense of the word but it is a harnessed in-breaking that can be contained and controlled by ecclesial institutions and the tangible mechanisms of ritual. Sacraments in the rites of worship do not exemplify the Spirit blowing where and how He wills, but in this context He moves only through properly authorized institutional channels, after a set pattern of movement and without any externally miraculous manifestations. The New Testament pattern of manifest singular signs and wonders being part and parcel of evangelism, worship and fellowship, speak of an era of church life before the Spirit was harnessed so to speak. Eric Dodds locates the rise of the monarchical model of the bishop towards the end of the first century as the historical juncture where the New Testament charismas of

FAITH'S KNOWLEDGE

It seems that David Hume's view of miracles has won in the West.[9] We now tend to assume that any surprising singular work of God—in time and space, yet beyond the bounds of natural possibility—is impossible, irrational, and embarrassingly naïve or worse.[10] In this sense, it is surprising, really, that modern Western Christians read the Bible

---

the Spirit were institutionally tamed. Dodds, in noting the institutional quenching of prophetic utterance, makes these comments: "[Prophecy was sidelined in keeping with] the sage advice whispered by the Holy Spirit to Ignatius: 'Do nothing without the Bishops.' In vain did Tertullian protest that the Church is not a collection of Bishops; in vain did Irenaeus plead against the expulsion of prophecy. From the point of view of the hierarchy the Third Person of the Trinity had outlived his primitive function. He was too deeply entrenched in the New Testament to be demoted, but he ceased in practice to play any audible part in the counsels of the Church. The old tradition of the inspired *prophet* who spoke what came to him was replaced by the more convenient idea of a continuous divine guidance which was granted, without their noticing it, to the principal Church dignitaries. Prophecy went underground to re-appear in the chiliastic manias of the later Middle Ages and in many subsequent evangelical movements..." Dodds, *Pagan and Christian*, 67–68.

9. David Hume argued ("On Miracles") that the probabilistic credibility of natural laws makes any belief in miracles inherently improbable and so faith cannot be supported by reason when it comes to believing any report of a miracle. Thus faith (and miracles) inherently part company with the rationally and practically believable. This seems to describe the reality of our modern approach to miracles even if many modern Christians still tend to assert the importance of miracles doctrinally. I do not find Hume's argument convincing, even so, broadly empiricist concerns that religious faith should be tied in some manner to God's concrete and particular in-breaking actions in His world, such as argued in Anthony Flew's essay "Theology and Falsification," are, I think, well justified from the stance of the Christian Scriptures themselves. The Classically low (i.e., roughly empiricist) epistemological categories of *doxa* (opinion derived from appearances), *pistis* (conviction based on experience and demonstrated relational reliability), and *semeion* (an observable miraculous singularity that signifies a specific divine communication) as embedded in historical particularity and the ongoing practices and modes of the Christian community, are basic to the New Testament approach to both believing the gospel and witnessing to the truth. Conversely, where there is no ongoing and demonstrable manifestation of the miraculous work of God amongst the people of God, the argument that Christianity is delusional has great force.

10. Since the nineteenth century any belief in transcendent realities—as Paul Ricœur has famously noted—is also inherently suspicious. In the West's high culture, Feuerbach, Strauss, Marx, Nietzsche and Freud hurl their hermeneutic of suspicion with great force against any belief in the miraculous. Under this hermeneutic, belief in the reality of the miraculous is symptomatic of psycho-sexual pathologies, of emotional weakness, and of superstitious ignorance. Only ignorant and backward people, and only ruthless manipulators of lower class ignorance, can still seek to present any inherently miraculous religious belief or practice as credible. See Feuerbach, *The Essence of Christianity*, and Ricœur, *Freud and Philosophy*.

Faith and Medicine

at all considering how heavily miraculously laden it is at its very core. Yet, Annette and I did read our Bibles, and we read what it had to say about miracles of healing, and we read with the entirely interested gaze of desperation.

In the book of James the Christian Scriptures instruct believers to call the elders of the church to anoint the sick with oil, for confession and forgiveness to transpire, and then "the prayer offered in faith will make the sick person well" (James 5:15). Annette and I are 'Bible Believing Baptists' so when we knew Daniel was terminally ill we asked the 'Bible Believing' elders of our church if they would anoint him with oil, in accordance with the Scriptures, and pray for a miracle of healing for our son. Our elders took our request very seriously and in prayer and counsel sought discernment on how to proceed. In the end they told us that they did not believe it was God's will that Daniel should be healed. So they did not anoint him with oil and pray for his healing. While we certainly felt jilted, we knew praying seriously for a miracle was a hard call for our leadership, so we tried to fit in with what our church understood to be "God's will"; but we secretly kept asking God to have mercy on us and heal our son.

We knew, just as our elders knew, that we were asking them to seek God for a miraculous intervention that was simply not naturally possible. This is a very big ask in our modern secular day and age—even for clergy and even for Christian leaders of deep piety and compassion. In fact, as impossible for us parents as it was not to hope for a miracle, having faith, as a gift from God for a miracle of healing, is something that we were never able to grasp, and yet it was something that our reading of 1 Corinthians 12 led us to believe should be available to us within the local incarnation of the Spirit enlivened Body of Christ—our church congregation.

Searching our hearts in retrospect it seems clear that we and our congregation did lack a very basic sort of belief in any tangible manifestation of the properly miraculous power of God. That is, despite our doctrinal commitment to the miraculous we probably lacked the ability to believe that a miracle of healing for Daniel was even a remote possibility.[11] We are, after all, modern, scientifically realistic people, who rely

---

11. This is a very disturbing revelation for orthodox Christian doctrine is premised entirely on the miraculous action of God. If we cannot functionally believe in this miraculous action now, then why should we believe in the immaculate conception, in the physical resurrection of Christ, in the power of the Holy Spirit being given

on science and markets (things we can see, control and understand to some extent) to mediate God's gift of our daily bread and health to us. Take such natural and tangible mediations out of the picture, and, at the level of functional daily life, our modern reality assumptions simply do not believe in miracles.

Given this fundamental difficulty, it seemed reasonable to accept the judgment of our elders, and so we sought to weather the terrible storm ahead of us as best as we could. And in the storm that came the medical assistance we received was a true blessing; in this storm, we did find divine companionship and a divine sharing of our grief, and, holding onto the hope of resurrection, we were not simply obliterated by death itself—but we received no miracle of healing. Yet, eight years later when Lucy was born, we simply could not make ourselves believe that it was "God's will" for her to go through this terrible path of suffering too.[12]

---

to the Church, in the work of Christ in our world and our own life now, or in the resurrection from the dead of our loved ones and ourslevels at some time in the future? Put another way, if the miraculous happens at all then there is no doctrinal difficulty in believing in miracles, but if we cannot actually believe in miracles within the reality structures in which we live, then our belief in miracles is *merely* doctrinal and one would have to suspect that all of our religion operates in purely natural terms, and is, after all, just a work of our own making. If this is the case then liberal Protestants who 'de-mythologize' the Scriptures are simply more honest than conservative Protestants, and again, one would have to wonder why both liberal and conservative Protestants bother with orthodox Christian belief at all.

12. Holding to a somewhat Augustinian outlook on 'evil' (see Hauerwas, "Seeing darkness, hearing silence") the question of 'why bad things happen to the innocent' never occurred to us. Indeed, Kierkegaard's "Gospel of Sufferings" (*Upbuilding Discourses*, 213–341) was of profound help to us as a call to follow Christ in the midst of our own suffering. Yet, the heart of a parent to protect one's children from the physical suffering of illness and death as far as one can is a human love motive that Jesus responded to with universal healing compassion in the gospels (e.g., Mark 5:21–43, even John 4:43–53). Jesus teaches us to pray to God as Abba Father so that an intimate paternal care—with its delighted, protective and life nurturing love—is clearly a valid way of understanding something about God. Whilst God most assuredly is not a 'divine object' to be bargained with and manipulated and merely used as a magical technology to protect us from the frailties of the human condition, yet the degree of Christ's sympathy with 'natural' human infirmity shown in the continuous stream of miraculous healings in the gospel narratives—also displaying His redemptive Lordship over the principalities of sickness and death—illustrates that the 'pagan' desire for divine help in the face of human frailty is in not, in itself, at odds with Christian faith. Given this, it does not strike me as idolatrous sentimental egoism to maintain that the belief that God could actively will terrible suffering on helpless babies is profoundly dissonant with the Abba Father revelation of who God is that Jesus proclaimed. Indeed, Jesus' healing compassion on the sick is at least as striking as his sympathy with the poor and the outcast in the gospel accounts.

Maybe we were calling this passage of suffering "the will of God" simply because we did not have the type of faith James was expecting the fellowship of believers to have? Truth be told, the idea that God *could* actively and inscrutably will this terrible suffering on our son simply did not jell with us from the beginning and we could not accept that as valid the second time around.[13] The Lord's Prayer teaches us that things happen on earth that are not God's will and the Sermon on the Mount teaches us that God has a father's heart and he will not give us a stone if we ask for bread. So, if—at least hypothetically—it was not God's will that our children should suffer and die in this terrible way, and if Our Father does indeed expect us to ask Him for things we need, then if we ask and do not receive (unlike Matthew 7:7) it seems that there are three explanatory possibilities. Either God is powerless, or a myth of our own making, or we are deficient in faith. Rather than accuse God of being sadistic or

---

13. This is where Anthony Flew's essay—"Theology and Falsification"—has extraordinary power. If God is like a father and yet the most basic features of father love as we experience and understand father love do not apply to God—like life nurturing care—then the revelation of God as our Father becomes qualified into meaninglessness. If God is Our Father then trusting Him to care for our most essential needs and looking expectantly to His nurture is surely what it means to have faith in God as Our Father? Some high Platonic or Stoic God, who is not "Our Father," but is Good, whom we love, and whom we trust as having ordained spiritual purposes for us 'beyond' the immediate, contingent, transitory context of our enfleshed life experience, might be believed in and resignedly 'trusted' in the face of the tragedy of a dying child. But such a remarkably Greco-Roman *Theos* is not the emotive, passionately loving and hating, historically interventionist and dramatically delivering God of the Hebrew religion, and is certainly not the Abba Father that Jesus prayed to and taught us to pray to. Whilst there is astonishing and paradoxical dialectical subtlety involved for Christian theology here—see Gavrilyuk, *The Suffering of the Impassible God*—a merely impassible God whose fate we simply accept is Greek, not Hebraic, and not Christian. The traditional Greek gods are immortal, and the Greeks did partition them, but they are not the eternal *Theos* of Greek philosophical theology. For the immortal gods, like us, and like the natural cosmos, are profoundly bound by fate. Fate rules the spatio-temporal realm and the eternal *Theos* is some universally pure and non-interventionist Divine Mind who, at least to Aristotle, is not at all interested in us. Indeed, it would be theologically offensive to approach the eternal *Theos* for some tangible deliverance from any natural fate. So belief in some lofty divine mind, in a fixed cosmic fate, and hence in our spiritual struggle being independent of contingent material determinates, is not compatible with belief in God who is Our Father and whose Son is enfleshed and is redemptively engaged with all creation so as to transform sin, darkness and death into love, light and life. If God does not intervene in history and nature, and does not care about our very human cares, then the Greco-Roman vision of God alone makes sense and Christianity is indeed a debased pagan myth. For these reasons, Flew's reasoning cannot be lightly laid aside by Christians via a 'high' theology that might work for Classical Greek philosophy.

refusing to believe in Him at all, we thought we should seriously examine the question of whether we were deficient in faith.

So when we discovered that Lucy had SMA, we told our local church that we could no longer believe that it was God's will for Lucy to suffer in this terrible way, so could we please consider what would be involved in our request for the elders to anoint her with oil and pray for her healing. Interestingly, it seemed obvious to Annette and I that repentance, reconciliation and forgiveness within our congregation was integral to following James 5 through, and these were things we had a deep need of anyway.

Eventually the elders decided they would anoint Lucy with oil and pray for her healing. Because we were adamant, they were prepared to give it a go—but they rejected outright the idea that we as a congregation needed serious relational healing and reform, and they were very loathe to pray for Lucy's healing under the terms in which we approached the matter. For if she died, would we not then hold ourselves and the church as lacking in faith and as accountable for her death? So they prayed and they anointed, but within a scope carefully limited only to Lucy's illness and staunchly committed to the escape clause of Calvinist voluntarism. That is, God is sovereign and if He, for His inscrutable reasons, has ordained to allow Lucy to have this terrible illness and not to heal her, that is His business and we will accept His will in good faith knowing it is the action of our loving Father and believing it to be for our good, beyond our ability to understand. And—God forbid!—we will not presume to dictate to God what He must do for us.

Essentially our elders understood Christian faith to be a kind of blanket passive trust in divine goodness, whatever apparently terrible fate God, in His inscrutable sovereign will, has dished out for us. This did not strike us as a credible New Testament understanding of faith, of miracles, of petitionary prayer, or of God's character and sovereignty. But our church was not interested in crunching through these Scriptural and theological matters with us. Such matters were all a bit too threatening, all a bit too unhinging and had the potential to seriously ruffle the existing status quo within our congregation. And our leaders most definitely did not wish to ask the question, 'what if we have just been playing at faith all along?' What if we knew nothing, really, about the Spirit empowered, miraculously enabled Body of Christ that Jesus promised, that Paul talked of and that James assumed?

After anointing Lucy with oil—to no apparent effect—prayer for her healing bubbled down into a quiet background issue for the leadership of our congregation. As her condition progressively deteriorated the leadership started positioning itself to read her pending death as some sort of a triumph of faith and Christian witness. Whilst we understood the theological complexity of our situation, in the final analysis it seemed to us that the status quo in our church was very concerned to preserve the appearance of triumphant Christian normality in the face of obvious impotency. We, on the other hand, were endeavoring to confess our impotence in the hope that collective humility, repentance and reconciliation would lead us to spiritual renewal. In this way we hoped that we might recover—in our time and place—the environment of faith and miraculous empowerment sketched in the New Testament. So we found ourselves at cross purposes with the leadership of our church.

When Lucy died our church felt terribly wounded by us, for despite all the practical care some members of our congregation had shown us, and despite their prayers for Lucy, we were so ungrateful as to believe that we—our church—had collectively failed in faith. They felt we were blaming them for Lucy's death. But to us, the issues Lucy's death opened up for our church were far more fundamental than blame. We did not understand what we saw as our collective failure of faith as having anything to do with finding someone to blame for Lucy's death. Yet we understood the total absence of unmistakably miraculous acts of God in our midst, in our time, in our place, as a disturbing and obvious fact that needed to be looked at very seriously.[14] For if Christianity is only a fair-weather religion—which is great for doing community things, affirming doctrinal beliefs and being busily engaged in "the things of God" when your life is ticking over OK, but is of no more-than-human help to you when the wheels fall off—then it is hard to explain what is so fundamentally different about being a member of a church compared to being a member of

---

14. See Whitehead & Tyson, *Rumors of God*. If the work of God is only a rumor in the modern secular world, then the Christian faith indeed is, in Karl Barth's terms, merely a religion. If church life in the First World is merely a function of well-run human ministries, well-taught doctrinal systems, slick entertainment experiences, talented leaders, well-conceived and executed programs, and high tech presentation, then we are in fundamental trouble as First World Christians. If the surd of the work of God is absent, then the glory of the Lord has departed. Whitehead and Tyson's book is about the search for a manifest but humanly inexplicable work of God within the modern secular world, which, because it is not a human work, profoundly challenges the reality boundaries of the modern secular world.

a football club or a local choir. In the ten years we were members of this congregation, by and large people whose wheels seriously fell off—marriage breakdown, mental illness, protracted unemployment, etc.—simply fell out of the church when this happened, and the church had no way of holding on to them or meeting their needs. Thinking of the many damaged and suffering people who had faded out of our congregational community in their extremity, we were now aware of a large body of evidence which demonstrated that the power of God was not present in our church to save people whose lives were crashing. And for the already crashed—the ruined people who floated around the edges of our church life and whom the church tried to help in some manner—they simply remained ruined, and did not find any transformative power of God in our midst. Further, in many ways our church was a comfortable place for chronically pathetic people, but a sinister co-dependence between the apparently together and spiritual leadership and the pathetic and determinedly juvenile flock was also evident. And when the dysfunction of the way of life of our marginal people of ruin meant that they moved on from our community, no one went after them. In fact, no one went after anyone when they left, for our ecclesiology seemed to assume that we were a society of individual believers who were free to come and go and live as we pleased, rather than a local concrete expression of the interdependent and spiritually integrated Body of Christ. Is this the Body of Christ that Paul talks of and that James assumes? Did our congregation embody the miraculous life of Jesus incarnate through us by the Holy Spirit? Was this 'body' positioned in dynamic redemptive tension with what John calls "the world"? If not, we seriously wondered, were we just a middle class religious social club that thought we were God's gift to the world and tried to 'minister' to people as best as we could with entirely natural (and rather mediocre) resources? If we were not able to access the life giving redemptive power of the Holy Spirit—if we had no faith for miraculous transformations that could not be achieved by normal human means—then, Annette and I wondered, what in heaven's name were we playing at in our religious life?

Asking these sorts of questions not long after Lucy died was very offensive to our church. So we were left alone in our grief and theological struggles and they simply did not know how to deal with us anymore. We were cast adrift ecclesially in our turmoil.

In short, our church was comfortable operating within the bounds of a modern secular vision of reality and we were not. This meant that we

Faith and Medicine

became alienated from our church in our attempt to find the miraculous power of God. This also made us very alone and vulnerable as Christians in the pervasively non-Christian environment of the modern secular hospital.

THE HOSPITAL AND CHRISTIAN BELIEF

When Lucy was in hospital the head doctor of the intensive care unit responsible for Lucy—let us call her Dr. Brown—would 'chair' a kind of end game planning meeting shortly after every near fatal medical crisis Lucy went through (we had all too many of these). Dr. Brown would continually remind us that these meetings were designed to ensure that we were all "on the same page" in relation to Lucy's medical care. But it was as hard for us to be "on the same page" with Dr. Brown as it was for us to be "on the same page" with our church.

The book Dr. Brown was reading from was endeavoring to treat a patient with a terminal medical condition, and this only gave our doctor palliative options for proper care. The book we were reading from was endeavoring to find faith in order to experience the healing power of God for our beloved daughter.

The radical differences between the medical book and our book made the notion of being "on the same page" with Dr. Brown totally unconvincing. If Dr. Brown could accept that we were in a different book, and that some middle ground between the beliefs, goals and rationales of each book was necessary for a dialogue between us that did not seek to force us out of our book and into hers when we are on her turf (medicine), then the challenge would not be that we were all on the same page, but that she understand our book, and we understand her book, to the degree that they needed to overlap each other for us to work together. We were not trying to convert her to read from our book, but whilst she was totally unaware of it, she was certainly trying to convert us to read from her book. When the rubber hit the road in terms of treatment plans and end game procedures, Dr. Brown displayed no comprehension of the difference between our two books.

We could not read from Dr. Brown's book. Dr. Brown did not have any hope for Lucy's healing and was personally detached from her death. Lucy's death was a clinical certainty for her that must be accepted and managed as humanely as medical science permitted. Yet, it was totally unnatural for us to have no hope for Lucy—however scientifically absurd hope here was—and it was totally unnatural for us to have an attitude of clinical, resigned matter of factness about her death. Dr. Brown could, and to a large extent, should be detached and 'realistic', but she should not expect us to be detached and 'realistic' too.

Her manner—as well intentioned and genuine as it no doubt was—was one of maternal reassurance. She smiled gently all the time, she had concerned expressions of face, and she used small words and spoke in reassuring tones. And what was she trying to reassure us about? It was that her detached and hopeless outlook was necessary for the best management of Lucy's condition, and our attached and hopeful outlook was not for the best management of Lucy's condition and was bad for our psychological health. If we accepted her outlook then we were all on the same page and Lucy would get the best palliative care and we would be being both reasonable and 'normal'. I was genuinely respectful and appreciative of her medical expertise but this reduction of Lucy's care to sit within medical determinism, and our sense that Dr. Brown was on a maternal mission to help us get to where she was at, was received by us as deeply patronizing, profoundly ignorant of our beliefs and values, and—despite the smiles and kind tones—very forceful. In fact, we experienced her condescending assertiveness against our most basic belief commitments as a type of doctrinal violence, foisted on to us from a position of assumed moral and intellectual superiority.

Dr. Brown was very concerned that we should not prolong Lucy's suffering so she seemed to assume that a detached (clinical) and realistic (hopeless) outlook for Lucy was more humane and caring than our attached (non-medical) and hopeful (unrealistic) outlook. And as the medical expert—a figure of power and authority who determined what the medical system would give and withhold from us—we were not on an equal negotiating footing with her if we wanted something she had determined not to give us. That is, when we had meetings with her there was a strong and continuous pressure for us to get on the same page and in the same book as she was on and in.

Yet, Dr. Brown, though a highly trained medical doctor, had no expertise in the sociology of knowledge. Hence, she was not consciously aware that the belief structures of secular medical science are supported by specific historically embedded social institutions, maintained by entrenched communities of belief, status and practice, and are underpinned by a tacit and—within that discourse—shared worldview. I begrudged her none of these things, excepting that she simply assumed that I should accept the matrix of knowledge, belief and practice that she accepted. But she was gentle and patronizing with me—yet firm where needs be—if I did not seem to quite get the picture. If she was happy that I got the picture, then she was happy that we were on the same page.

Dr. Brown's approach to death was embedded in the knowledge paradigm of modern medical reality. This paradigm sits within an assumed pragmatic and materialistic cosmology. Death, to this model, is reduced to a medical state, and this state sits within a view of facticity and inevitability determined by the current limits of medical science. Annette's and my approach to death was not medically reductive and neither was it defined by medical determinism. With such profound differences in the manner in which we understood death itself, the expectation that we could be on the same page was profoundly unreasonable.

On the one hand, we did not fear death because we were not materialists. Living in a very materialist culture, death is typically treated narcotically. For the materialist, the extinction of a person in the end of biological life is, on the one hand, entirely natural and normal, and, on the other hand, just too horrible to look at squarely. We need to escape it somehow, we do not want to be there when it happens, and, we want some professional to deal with it for us so that we do not have to look at any dead bodies and contemplate what mortality might really mean (i.e., its meaninglessness within a naturalistic outlook is overpoweringly bleak and crushing).[15] Funeral parlors, chaplains and grief counselors have their work cut out for them in assisting us to not really come to terms with the meaning of mortality within a naturalistic social life form.[16] We

---

15. Put the other way around, human love, situated within the spatiotemporal manifold, is transient and contingent. Yet, human love participates in the eternal and intrinsic reality of the very nature of God (love) for the Christian. Love gives meaning to our lives and it is a meaning that transcends the flux and contingency of space and time, yet our experience of this meaning is profoundly savaged by death. Thus meaning is intrinsic and enduring only within a belief context that allows the immanent to participate in the transcendent, and which allows the eternal to triumph over the temporal (Plato argues this way too; see *Phaedo* and *Apology*). Death is the ultimate negation of any human participation in intrinsic and enduring meaning when approached from a modern naturalistic stance.

16. See Budde & Brimlow, *Christianity Incorporated*. This book makes a persuasive argument that chaplaincy—religious service to non-religious institutions—usually comes at the price of Christianity being adapted to the culture, beliefs and values of the institution it serves. Such chaplaincy is encouraged (or tolerated) by its mother institution to the extent that religion endorses and even legitimates the values and

must escape any strong awareness of death, and we must escape physical pain because death is the end of all that we are and protracted mortal suffering is a meaningless trauma of pointless agony. Or we seek to rationalize and control death so that it is a mere medical fact to be managed and accepted; as if technical knowledge somehow makes death manageable. Yet, Annette and I believe love—God's love—is stronger than the grave; this is the central tenant of Christian belief.[17] We do not believe death is the end and we understand the horror of death as being there precisely because there is something deeply spiritually wrong and even physically unnatural about death. So we do not want to manage death so as to make it free of pain and sweep it away as soon as possible. Further, we have some handles of belief to hold on to regarding the triumph of love and meaning, even directly in the face of death. In short, we do not have a modern secular conception of what a humane death management plan is.

Further, just because current modern science knows SMA is medically incurable this does not mean that God cannot heal Lucy. So, from our perspective, we have: (1) an outlook on death that does not need narcotic escape; (2) a non-reductive view of death that keeps spiritual and relational ties alive beyond physical death; and (3) a hope for healing beyond medical science that the materialist outlook does not permit. Our

---

goals of the institution it is serving. For what army is going to employ pacifist chaplains who will practice and preach against the art of war itself? What school principal is going to employ a chaplain who will take him aside and question the way he treats his staff and manages his school? Our experience of chaplains in both State and Catholic hospitals was that the outlook of medical naturalism was accepted and endorsed by priests as much as by social workers and doctors. Here, belief in God's miraculous healing power is shameful and delusional, and even though rituals of healing prayer are performed on request, the practice of miraculous healing is absent. Further, where both hospital chaplains and patients are embedded in the life form of "modernity's fear of death . . . death becomes removed from its place in the primary Christian narrative of life, death and resurrection, and [is] made over into grief management and therapeutic interventions for the living, making death even more tragic, and definitely more final, than it is in the larger Christian tradition," *Christianity Incorporated*, 101–2.

17. Because of the example of Christ we also believe that love and fear are incompatible and that love does not make decisions premised on a cost to benefit analysis that weighs pleasure against suffering, or social acceptance against shame (see 1 John and Hebrews 12:2). This is why, though Annette and I have a one in four probability of conceiving a child with SMA, we did not stop having children after Daniel was born. This Christian logic of setting intrinsic values as primary in a decision making process seems irrational, possibly indulgent, probably cruel, and certainly reckless and costly by the dominant naturalistic logic of our larger secular culture where physical securities are considered primary and values and beliefs are considered secondary add-ons.

Faith and Medicine

view of death itself is definitely not found in the same book as secular medical knowledge. But we discovered that the belief system that governs the practical reality assumptions of the hospital environment privileges the secular medical view of death as normal, realistic and correct, and all other views of death are hence abnormal, unrealistic and, well, false.

Peter Berger and Thomas Luckmann's classic text in the sociology of knowledge points out that reality is socially constructed.[18] That is, our most basic beliefs about the nature of reality are not even seen by us as beliefs but just as reality, even though all reality beliefs are embedded in a community that forms and legitimates those beliefs. Sociologically, there is no reality without belief and no belief without a community that forms and legitimates those beliefs.[19] This means that knowledge and reality structures are as essentially believed for Dr. Brown as they are for us.[20] And yet, it was clear that Dr. Brown saw our belief in God's healing for Lucy as psychological denial, metaphysical infantilism and as an impossible and destructive fantasy. Indeed, because Dr. Brown knew a great deal about medical science she felt entitled to guide us away from actions premised on our religious beliefs and plans premised on the love logic of parental hope. But what expertise did she have in religion and parental love logic in this context?

The social theorist Bruno Latour points out that the neat reductionism of modern pragmatic instrumental logic has not actually made us neatly compartmental beings.[21] We are a whole. In fact, we cannot separate the physical from the spiritual or the emotional. In practice we do integrate facts and values, *scientia* and *sapientia*, religion and politics, economics and morality, the objective and the subjective, even nature and supernature. Modernity's demarcations are legal fictions. No medical issue is not also a spiritual issue, not also a sociological issue, not also a relational issue.

Medical expertise is, even so, often very helpful. I am very glad Dr. Brown had such a distinguished degree of medical expertise in an area that was of direct practical help to Lucy. I very much wanted to talk with

---

18. Berger & Luckmann, *The Social Construction of Reality*.

19. This is as true of scientific belief/knowledge as it is of any type of belief/knowledge. See Polanyi, *Personal Knowledge*; and Kuhn, *The Structure of Scientific Revolutions*.

20. This, as Polanyi (*Personal Knowledge*) seeks to demonstrate, does not relativize all truth claims. Yet it does make all claims to knowledge humble and dependent.

21. Latour, *We Have Never Been Modern*.

her and cooperate with her. But I did not want to have to come into her book to talk with her, and I would have greatly valued the very real effort she would need to make to understand as much about our book as we understood about her book so that we could negotiate a middle space in which to contact each other. But in our meetings we did not talk at length about either her or our book—yet, it was her book that set the agenda. And she was a busy and important woman saving people's lives so we could not expect to chew up too much of her valuable time. It was 'only' the social workers who took the time and effort to try and understand our book. And we were lucky, for one of our social workers—a mother and a woman of some Christian belief herself—pretty well understood where we were coming from and tried to act as a go between for us. But even here, a social worker who is prepared to try and understand a parent's religious perspective without the professional secular reality assumptions of clear demarcations between objective facts and subjective beliefs, comes up hard against the epistemological power structures of medical institutions. For even though our social worker could tentatively enter the reality space in which we were struggling with our faith, when she then tried to mediate a middle space between the belief books of faith and medical science she too discovered that these are remarkably hard books to negotiate—and in some areas they are simply incommensurable.[22]

From the stance of religious faith, human knowledge and medical technology, as acts of worship, are beautiful exercises of God's gifts to us in the service of love. Western hospitals are born of this type of worship and this type of love for people.[23] However, where human knowledge asserts itself as the only thing people can rely upon, to the Christian, it becomes an idol supplanting the rightful place of God in our lives. From this belief outlook then, Modern Secular Reason is thus the great idol of our times and the hubris of science without humility before God is a deeply idolatrous spiritual stance, even where its practitioners have very serious 'private' religious beliefs.

Well, Annette and I struggled through and in the end, when Lucy died, we were totally alone. The church refused to understand us and the

---

22. See Milbank, *Theology and Social Theory*, for a probing account of the complex theological history of secular reason and its deep and powerful influence on modern life. In our experience social workers (and even more so, doctors) are typically conceptually formed in the assumptions of modern secular reason even if they are people of deep personal religious conviction.

23. See Porterfield, *Healing in the History of Christianity*.

medical profession and professional carers—who did assist us wonderfully in facilitating the best physical care that Lucy could have in her short sojourn with us—never understood us. We were not only deeply grieved, profoundly theologically unhinged, emotionally, spiritually and physically exhausted, but we were also bizarre nutters that no-one could reach.

Intellectually, I knew enough about sanity and madness from a sociological and a literary perspective to find being a nutter, in some important ways, quite noble.[24] But, in the end, as a nutter, you are a threatening social pathology to be contained and treated, if you will accept the compassion offered to you, or you must be driven out of town as demonic if you refuse 'help'. Thus ejection from our ecclesial community was the icing on our trauma cake, after a long and grueling road of anguish.[25] But, after the grief and exhaustion that accompanied the death of Lucy, the humiliation of being a nutter even to our church did not mean much anymore. In fact, nothing seemed to mean much anymore. But we had our other children to love and this, and the love of family and friends who stood with us whether they understood us or could help us or not, gave us life. And so it was through love that God alone—so it seemed to us—held onto us, and so we did not perish.

CONCLUSION: SOME QUESTIONS ABOUT CHRISTIANITY AND REALITY

Reality, as we experience and live it, is always embedded in shifting and layered collective structures of belief, knowledge, practice and power. Many of these different layers are not neatly commensurable and are not organically unified or logically coherent. Thus, background reality dissonance is a normal feature of the human condition. It can often be a creative background that throws up wonderful and interesting new imaginations and insights—talk to any child. And yet, we can only operate sanely and normally as adults by believing that the reality environment

---

24. See Foucault, *Madness and Civilisation*; Shakespeare, *Hamlet*.

25. We were not kicked out of our church—but we had so stretched the limits of their 'ministry' to us that out of consideration for their feelings we had to leave in order to deal with our grief and grapple with our theological issues in a manner that was interpersonally safe for both them and us. To the view point of modern medicine we were always reality refusing nutters, but to our fellowship, very quickly after Lucy died, we flipped over from being valiant victims of a terrible circumstance whom they could help, to being ungrateful, maladjusted and threatening weirdoes who upset everyone.

that we inhabit is stable, concrete, controllable and, simply—real. But this adult view is a practical fiction, for belief is a profoundly dynamic process that in a very fundamental way does indeed generate the reality in which we live.[26] Reality is not as stable as we must functionally believe, and what and how we believe can indeed open up entirely different reality frames to us. So faith and belief—as the New Testament so insistently proclaims—are indeed tied to what we can and cannot see and experience as real.[27] This is a much more complex and 'realistic' view of reality than reductive secular naturalism can offer.[28] This is why, I suspect, faith and medicine have the capacity to clash so violently. For the Christian understanding of reality—in a strange harmony with some penetrating postmodern insights[29]—insists that belief is dynamically and contestedly related to reality, whereas medicine, embedded as it is in reductive and decidedly modern secular naturalism, only allows one frame of approaching reality beliefs any real currency. The modern secular and pragmatic outlook allows you to 'believe' whatever personal fictions you like, but only lets reductive materialism define true, powerful and final reality. Further, the materialist functionalist outlook on reality is such a comfort to us

---

26. See Matthew 18:3. Jesus said "I tell you the truth, unless you change and become like little children, you will never enter the kingdom of heaven." The capacity to allow novelty and dissonance to play in our minds is characteristic of childhood. The plasticity and openness of the child's mind to the astonishingly rich environment in which she forms beliefs seems to harden as we grow up, so that things which are dissonant and novel no longer register within the established and central structures of our perception and reflection (maybe this is why we cannot perceive angels after about two years of age). Trusting dependency also characterizes the relational context in which children form their beliefs. Jesus seems to be saying that we have to trust God and allow our fallen reality frame to be disturbed by God's rich and subtle dissonances that can break into our world at any moment if we are to enter the kingdom of heaven and see God. But the adult mind rebels against such trust and fears dissonance because our very identity as self-directed autonomous individuals relies on our ability to understand reality and to control our environment within an (apparently) dependable and coherent reality structure.

27. See John's Gospel in particular for a sustained account of the relationship between a responsive openness to the in-breaking Word of God—belief, surrender and love—and the ability to see and enter into the reality of the Christian gospel (i.e., John 7:20—8:59). See also (selected at random) Mark 9:23; John 11:40; Matthew 9:2; Mark 10:52.

28. See Goetz & Taliaferro, *Naturalism*, for a careful examination of some of the fundamental difficulties with framing one's reality beliefs within the structure of naturalist doctrines.

29. See Smith, *Who's Afraid of Postmodernism?*

Faith and Medicine

because it takes all the stress and storm out of our messy and incommensurate belief contexts and offers us control, certainty and simplicity. And it offers us status, of course, as masters of reality.[30] This knowledge makes us our own god, and, as Marx well understood, progressive modern man revolves around the sun of what our own hands can make in a captivated state of self worship.[31] Yet, ironically, this frame of modern scientific 'realism' now so deeply assumes the centrality of the worship of Man that it has entirely lost awareness of worship itself. It cannot understand its own idolatry or the blasphemous gospel it proclaims to the ears and way of someone who is seeking to worship the Christian's God.

I have experienced a head-splitting reality dissonance between my Christian faith and medical secular naturalism, and this dissonance has moved out of the background of my awareness and has exploded into the foreground of my consciousness, rupturing the very fabric of my believed reality outlook in the process. I experienced that rupture in the context of medical care for Daniel and Lucy, but my medical interlocutors, and, ultimately, my church, did not experience any rupture. Reality beliefs did not become unstable for them in their encounter with Daniel or Lucy's illness, or in their encounter with our struggle of faith. One expects the secular medical profession not to be unhinged by the mystery of suffering and death, hope and life, but to just get on with doing what they can do to protect and prolong physical life. That is no surprise. But that the church would not become unhinged with us is a much bigger problem. Does this mean that secular naturalism—the respectable dominant knowledge outlook of our times—is the reality frame we too really believe in the modern Western church?

Walter Brueggemann notes that those who receive the prophetic Word of God breaking in and upheaving the realm of human control are typically "those ill schooled in explanation and understandings. It comes to those who will settle for amazements they can neither explain nor understand."[32] Conversely, those who are deeply invested in the reality frame derived from the dominant human structures of power and control typically resist all divine in-breaking and all disruptive reality dis-

---

30. Kierkegaard's relentless assault on the vanities of the aspirations of a non-faith approach to truth, reason and reality, pervades his corpus. See his *Unscientific Postscript* for his most sustained work on the relationship between faith and the reality that is found only in the gospel as lived truth.

31. See Marx, "Hegel's Philosophy of Right."

32. Brueggemann, *The Prophetic Imagination*, 104.

sonance as vigorously as they can. Typically, the rich, the powerful, the knowledgeable and the respected are invested heavily in the prevailing status quo. So it is largely with the outcasts that any genuinely prophetic gospel of liberation finds reception.[33] It is to those who yearn for a different reality and who are prepared to imagine radically alternative orders of power, knowledge and wealth that the disruptive, the shockingly particular, and the incomprehensibly singular in-breaking Word of God speaks to. Jacques Ellul notes how the categories of necessity within all fallen orders of power and knowledge are inherently controlling, exploitative and violent, and are fundamentally subverted by the gospel.[34] Ellul argues that Christians should live at cross purposes to the dominant reality structures of what is natural in the fallen world order. In this light, it is not surprising to find that Philip Jenkins and Simon Chan have noticed that it is in the global underclass that the ancient spiritual dynamism and in-breaking power of the Holy Spirit is being re-discovered in our times.[35] So it seems that we Christians in the modern West may be in serious trouble with God. Our actual way of life is deeply invested in the knowledge, wealth and power of the First World, with all its violence, exploitation and injustice. And what if it is this 'reality'—the reality that our status, knowledge and comfort is so deeply invested in—that God is going to break open and release His totally different kingdom into? Are we modern Western Christians ready for God to do something like that? Would this be an in-breaking of apocalyptic destruction for us, ruining our "all too human" religion and our "all too human" attempt to create paradise with our own hands? Or would such a divine in-breaking be a world re-creating redemptive deliverance from the death accepting realism of Modern Scientific Man for those who are resident aliens struggling to live as Christians in a faithless and idolatrous age?

---

33. This challenge to imperial power, the prevailing status quo, and the knowledge and deities of that social order, is a central feature of the exodus account in the Hebrew Scriptures.

34. Ellul, *Violence*.

35. Jenkins, *The Next Christendom*; Jenkins, *The New Faces of Christianity*; Chan, *Pentecostal Theology*.

Faith's Knowledge

THE EXPLORATIONS OF THESE pages leads me to the conclusion that while an absolute indubitable certainty of the truth is not something human knowledge can obtain, this does not mean that genuine (though never complete) truth is intrinsically unknowable. Indeed, I am inclined to believe that truth, and faith in truth, are indispensable for the proper flowering of the human condition. Or, to state a similar point more Platonically, it seems that confidence in the knowability of truth—truth that is the *ground* for whatever reality we apprehend via logic, experience, action, intellection, imagination and intuition—is indispensable for the meaningfulness of human reason. That is, those who approach human reason without any confidence in human meaning's ability to touch, in some manner, true reality, do not take human reason or meaning itself seriously. But if this is true then all known truth remains a venture of faith that needs to retain both the seriousness and confidence appropriate to our commitment to that which is 'above' or 'prior to' ourselves, and the humility and openness of faith in relation to that which we can never finally master and which stands over us. Hence truth is always understood—we stand under truth. Truth is not a mere tool of our creation and crafting, even though creativity, crafting and use are not removable from the complex process of the act of knowing. Further, whilst truth is always embedded in the coherence defying shifting feast of historically, culturally and politically contextualized linguistic meaning, yet, the centrality of truth to the way we engage with others and the world means that interpersonally and practically we *must* have beliefs that we have faith in. Hence, we must have a degree of confidence—of faith—in our knowledge for it to be knowledge, and liveable knowledge, at all. Thus, faith cannot be removed from knowledge. There is no meaningful relationship between the separate things 'faith' and 'knowledge' but faith and knowledge are always present together. Hence the title of this book is not *Faith and Knowledge*, but *Faith's Knowledge*.

It seems that the glory and pathology of modern Western knowledge is tied up with its desire for indubitable certainty; its hankering to separate knowledge out from faith and hence to demarcate proven, objective, absolute and 'closed' philosophy and science from believed, participated, relative and 'open' religion, culture and community life. The glory of the modern epistemological endeavor is the scientific method and the vast fields of natural knowledge and technological power it has opened up to us. The pathology of this endeavor is the tendency to reduce valid knowledge either to the sphere of mechanical certainty appropriate to modern reductive scientific enquiry, and—in philosophy and religion—to seek to construct truth only in terms of indubitable proof. Where indubitable proof cannot be found (and it cannot, finally, be found anywhere) then we tend to drop the notion of 'high' truth altogether. The net effect of this situation is that we have enormous instrumental power over nature and over our own societies but we have destroyed our confidence in 'high' truth and thus we relativize and trivialize all substantive values and all spiritual bearings. We are now somewhat like busy pragmatic cockroaches scurrying around doing whatever comes 'naturally' to us (so we assume) with few cultural institutions left that might enable us to seriously consider what any high human meaning or *telos* might be. Knowledge itself becomes purely instrumental in such an environment, as does power, so the high reasons which birthed the Western university tradition are becoming increasingly incomprehensible to many of the powerful people who control our knowledge institutions.

Yet, the intellectual trajectories that run from the counter-Enlightenment through to postmodernism find the modern quest to ground universal and indubitable truth in the scientific method both unbelievable and, often enough, oppressive and destructive. Even so, the idea that high truth—*without* demonstrable and absolute certainty—might still be genuinely knowable seems to occur to few who react against the knowledge/power structures of modernity. But why—if certainty cannot be had—should truth beliefs that are openly and humbly grounded in faith be so unthinkable? Is secular postmodernism captive to the *failed* modern meta-narrative of epistemological certainty? For, given the postmodern critique of modernity, there is nothing intellectually that would

Faith's Knowledge

make the grounding of high truth in faith—as embodied in communities of belief and practice—inherently invalid.[1]

But Christian theological epistemology goes further than simply being a possible alternative to postmodern epistemological nihilism. The outlook on faith's knowledge that I have given in this book starts out approaching the notion of faith in philosophical terms but becomes increasingly more theologically, and specifically Christianly, focused. For, from the theological perspective, knowledge is an inherently spiritual affair—that is, it has to do with one's relationship to God and others, and so with all aspects of life—nothing can be marked off from its domain. In recent times a bigger contextual understanding of knowledge has been well advanced by sociologists like Peter Berger and renegade epistemologists like Michael Polanyi, but still, it is theologians who understand this breadth best.

Kierkegaard, in agreement with the age-old understanding of the church, understood that sin is inherently a function of pride and that knowledge, sin and status/power are intimates in the normal course of human existence. It is pride that seeks—in such a ridiculous manner—to stand over, create and own reality, and to capture truth via abstracted, indubitable, universal knowledge.[2] And it is an inverse form of this same pride that fears being out of control and that leads to either indulgent narcissistic withdrawal or tyrannical pragmatic mastery. To have faith in truth we cannot master is basic to Christian knowledge (and any love), and this epistemological outlook of love and subordinate joy (the genuine opposite rather than the mere inversion of mastery and domination) reads the dominant Western epistemological tradition as an expression of a deep seated cultural hubris in attempting to either master and enslave truth or, failing that endeavor, of reverting to mere will and power without truth. Love and fear, confidence and suspicion, faith and unbelief, hope and despair—these are opposite spiritual orientations that shape the very conception of what knowledge and truth is within Chris-

---

1. This point is made well in Smith, *Who's Afraid of Postmodernism?*

2. I do not mean to imply here that rulership and understanding are not inherently good and human endeavors. Theologically, Humanity's participation in the ruling, reasoning creativity of God's own nature is in itself both good and beautiful. Yet, our very capacity to participate in the fullness of the human condition in these regards is hindered by pride, by the determination to be our own god and the desire to distortedly play God over others and creation. This pride is our way of (vainly, but destructively) seeking to cut ourselves off from the ontological grounds from which our highest fulfillment springs; the free and open handed love of God.

tian theology. Thus, in Kierkegaard, faith is the trusting and integrative knowledge outlook of love, confidence and hope, and sin is the fearful and autonomous knowledge outlook of pride, fear and despair.[3]

This framing of epistemological categories in explicitly theological terms, then, has a rich Christian heritage which, thanks to theologians like John Milbank, is alive right up until the present. Yet the dominant modern knowledge heritage seeks to separate knowledge from faith, seeks to separate philosophy from theology, seeks to separate the intellect out from one's spiritual relation to God, and from the heart, the body, and the relational and personal situation of the knower, in history and in culture. Hence, modernity creates that most strange apparition, the ghost of knowledge; information.

In the secular age of high modernity, political separations between church and state have established a form of life in which abstract and often artificial delineations of power, knowledge and reality have become assumed.[4] Thus, purely rational or purely empirical objectivist notions of true knowledge have prevailed in the modern discretely secular philo-

---

3. Kierkegaard, *Unscientific Postscript*.

4. My hunch is that something very big happens, in broad cultural terms, in the way truth itself was conceptualized by Western Christians between the fifty and the seventh century. After Pope Gregory the Great—accompanied by a profound shrinking of the intellectual environment and a collapse of Imperial power and unity—doctrine and faith and the ecclesial institution had come to provide the only framework of certainty, meaning and order within Western culture. The manner in which indubitable doctrine then comes to define and guarantee truth gives rise to a culture of certainty in which logical coherence, cosmic order, institutional integration (church and state) and ontological clarity flower in the high middle ages. Whilst this flower had many virtues, yet the petals quickly fall from this fragile bloom, and the fruit of such a conception of the indubitably certain proofs of truth is late medieval nominalism, the parent of modernity. The rise of knowledge independent of the truth claims of the church produces huge political upheaval and the fragile environment of high medieval cohesive certainty breaks up. However, the distinctly modern assumption that truth is provable, can be mastered and gives controlling power seems to me to still demonstrate the meta-epistemological cultural developments of the early medieval period. It also seems to me that this development is a serious degradation of the primitive Christian understanding of the approach to being under truth that is granted by the knowledge of faith. This primitive Christian understanding is never lost from the theological traditions of the West, yet even where it is given expression in great theologians like Aquinas, the broader cultural verities of the context in which he lives means that his outlook on truth and proof feeds, in the end, into the separation of that which can be *proven* doctrinally, from that which can be *proven* by 'unaided' natural reason. Yet in both cases, proof and truth are epistemologically linked, and proof is the tool used in the attempt to master and own truth.

sophical context in which professional epistemology has been typically done. Yet, as Kołakowsky reminds us, religion and 'secular' philosophy have never really been independent—nor can they be.[5] These neat delineations of the modern secular mind are useful fictions, they are the *mythos* which legitimates and facilitates our way of life; yet they are not, in any necessary sense, just how things really are. In fact, whilst in sociological terms the belief assumptions of modern secularism define the dominant reality frame in the contemporary world, and whilst they have many attractive features to Modern Man, their artificiality and inadequacy is increasingly hard to ignore. For all acts of knowledge are, inescapably, acts of faith. All acts of power enabled by knowledge are equally embedded in a belief frame that is trusted. So the modern epistemological project—the pursuit of pure and objectively demonstrable true knowledge—is inherently fraudulent. If such a conclusion is valid, then why do we not re-open the possibility of what Bradley characterizes as an incomplete but fundamentally important apprehension of the truth that is prior to appearance,[6] but via faith's knowledge? And if we take faith seriously as inseparable from all knowledge, then the explicitly theological approach to epistemology—such as seen in Milbank and Pickstock[7]—is an inherently reasonable, as well as importantly hopeful, pathway to the recovery of high truth in Western intellectual culture. Given the destructive social life forms that accompany the assumption that high truth is unknowable in Western culture,[8] it seems to me that we are at risk of

---

5. See Kołakowski, *Why Is There Something Rather Than Nothing?*

6. "I am so bold as to believe that we have a knowledge of the Absolute, certain and real, though I am sure that our comprehension is miserably incomplete. But I dissent emphatically from the conclusion that, because imperfect, it is worthless." Bradley, *Appearance and Reality*, 3.

7. See Milbank & Pickstock, *Truth in Aquinas*. Whatever the merits or difficulties of Milbank and Pickstock's reading of Aquinas, this text is a bold endeavor in theological epistemology that seeks to re-fire a theological yet high understanding of truth for us in our times.

8. See Cavanaugh, *Being Consumed*, 1–7, for a brilliant exposition of Milton Friedman's linkage of the inability to know higher teleological truths with the "freedom" of the "free market" and hence, with the political core of the secular consumeristic way of life. Atomism, anomie, depressive illness, delinquency and identity anxiety within modern Western culture, and the entrenched structure of oppression and exploitation that sustain the First World consumer life-style are all premised on Friedman's *telos*-less "freedom." But is this "freedom" really good for us? Is such "freedom" culturally and socially sustainable? Could it be that without some shared frame of high human meaning and some communally upheld understanding of a truly good human *telos*,

casting off all that is of substantive value in our heritage unless we can recover faith in the knowability of high truth.

It is my hope that this book makes some contribution towards the recovery of the knowability of high truth in Western culture. This book endeavors to aid this end by seeking to contribute to three aspects of the Radical Orthodoxy literature—a body of literature that seems to me the most hopeful contemporary intellectual movement that aims at the recovery of high truth via the theological roots of Western culture.

Firstly, this book supports the endeavor of reviving the British tradition of Christian Platonism,[9] focusing on a theological appropriation of Plato's tacit approach to faith and his onto-epistemology vision of reality, in our postmodern context. Radical Orthodoxy, via fresh and powerful readings of Augustine and Aquinas, has a clear interest in recovering metaphysics in the spirit of what might clumsily be called a post-postmodern Christian Platonism. Here Plato is interpreted without reference to modernist assumptions about the independence of philosophy from theology, without reference to the modern secularization and sublimation of theology into philosophy, *and* without the postmodern suspicion of every metaphysical truth claim due to an often cynical and sophistic aporia which results from a wistful disillusionment with modern epistemology. This type of Christian Platonism is also inherently situated within the very human, very historically, linguistically and inter-personally grounded reality of the actual human knower. Thus, this type of Platonism—in harmony with both Plato and the Patristic worldview—is neither a 'pure' idealism nor an onto-theological hubris. That is, this book affirms Radical Orthodoxy in pointing out the genuine continuity between Classical philosophy and orthodox Christian theology regarding the need to trust truths that are the warrants of human perception and reason (hence undemonstrable) and thus affirms the metaphysical and ontological traditions of Western theology and philosophy up until the parting of the ways of 'faith' and 'reason' in fourteenth century nominalism. This approach to true knowledge escapes the conundrums of modern epistemological foundationalism, but, unlike secular and atheistic forms of postmodernism, is also able to affirm a genuinely metaphysical vista on truth where truth is both independent of the limitations of hu-

---

we are less than human and cannot be humanly free? Cavanaugh, via Augustine, argues that this is indeed the case.

9. In more recent times, this theo-philosophical spirit can be clearly recognized in C. S. Lewis.

man knowledge and yet—analogically, and inherently shaped by our own language, culture, relationships and imagination—also knowable.

Secondly, this book seeks to fill a gap in Radical Orthodoxy scholarship that as yet has little emphasis on faith understood in a New Testament manner—i.e., a somewhat Hebraic[10] and Classically low[11] manner—as the pathway to the distinctly holistic and redemptive Christian understanding of truth. Thus, the area which I seek to push the boundaries of the current Radical Orthodoxy literature concerns the degree to which a New Testament outlook on faith and truth is, in important regards, distinct from the dominant Greco-Roman heritage of our Western philosophical and theological traditions. This emphasis does not contradict the degree to which Greco-Roman approaches to truth and faith are compatible with much of Western Christianity's theological traditions, but does seek to nuance the relationship between Greco-Roman culture and Christian faith.[12]

Thirdly, this book seeks to further round Radical Orthodoxy's interest in making its theological concerns engage concretely with the world in which we live (as well, of course, as letting the world in which we live speak to and engage the theological concerns of Radical Orthodoxy). Essays by John Milbank on the 'War on Terror' and on geopolitical concerns, and Stanley Hauerwas' writings on politics, the university and the medical profession, illustrate this applied concern in Radical Orthodoxy

---

10. See Moltmann, *Theology of Hope*. Moltmann describes how the extent to which the God of the Hebrews is a God of promise who acts radically and transformatively in history, and is faithful to His promise, and whose people trust in His faithfulness, shapes the Hebraic understanding of divinity, of faith, of history, of creation, of the future, and of the role of the 'heart' in knowledge in ways that render it distinct from Hellenistic conceptions of the same.

11. See Brueggemann, *The Prophetic Imagination*. Brueggemann points out that whilst the Hebrews have a tradition of "royal consciousness" that is committed to the perpetuation of the status quo, this perspective is always checked by the outside "alternative consciousness" of the prophets, the oppressed, the powerless, the uneducated, who hope for a radically different order of reality brought about not by king, cultus, wealth, power or learning, but by God Himself. Brueggemann powerfully situates Christianity within this alternative apocalyptic consciousness, which must of necessity be in conflict with 'high', sensible, practical, respectable outlooks on reality and power.

12. See Kerr, *Christ, History and Apocalyptic*, 127–60. Kerr looks at the manner in which the historical singularity of Christ, the most radical event of divine breaking into history, places a Christian understanding of apocalyptic history quite radically at odds with the universalist and ever the same notions of Greek divinity and history, and reason.

well.[13] The chapters I have written on these same topics focus on the epistemological framing of practical concerns in such a manner as to challenge the credibility of secularist perspectives on knowledge assumed by modernity's dominant sociological life form, and approaches knowledge in the university, the global context, and in the hospital, through the categories of faith and worship. That is, the focus and situatedness of my approach is quite distinct from the brilliant approaches of Milbank, Hauerwas and other Radical Orthodoxy scholars, and so my work seeks to complement the work of other post-secular critiques of these important areas of lived practice in the contemporary world.

I would like to close this book up with a short reflection on two brief passages in the New Testament. Paul says:

> The man who thinks he knows something does not yet know as he ought to know. But the man who loves God is known by God. (1 Corinthians 8:2–3, NIV)

The writer of the letter to the Hebrews says:

> By faith we understand that the universe was formed at God's command so that what is seen was not made out of what was visible. (Hebrews 11:3, NIV)

I am not going to exegete these passages here. This is not because I have no regard for exegesis but rather it is because what I want to say is not exegetically invalid simply because it has nothing to do with matters pertaining to food sacrificed to idols or first century Greco-Roman cosmogony. Rather I want to very briefly point out—in a kind of Hamannean gesture—the incredible power of the words of the Scripture and the manner in which they can speak to us today on what I see as the two crucial theo-epistemological matters facing us in the post-Christian West in the early twenty-first century.

Paul claims that being known by God is more important than any 'thing' we might claim to know. Human knowledge in propositional terms—even when it is right—is relativized by the relational knowledge of love and this love for God (which must itself be a gift of the Spirit and must be existentially and praxiologically transformative) opens up a passage from the Divine to the human where Truth knows and transforms

---

13. See Hauerwas & Lenticchia, eds., *Dissent from the Homeland*. See Hauerwas, *The State of the University*. See Berkman & Cartwright, eds., *The Hauerwas Reader*, 539–622.

us. Being known by God is to be transformatively grasped by Truth that we can never contain or master or—in the modern sense of the word—know. So to be known by God is to be grasped by Truth yet that 'being grasped' is the truest (and intrinsically relational, intrinsically transformative) knowledge that the human knower is capable of.

Only from within a place of 'being grasped' by God can we adequately know what to rightly make of human knowledge. So it is no coincidence that Thomas Aquinas was a saint. If we want to think well, know well, act well—to the extent that we can and not presumptuously further, yet not fearfully less, yet even so, always through a glass darkly—we must love God with all our heart, soul, mind and strength. Centrally then, theological epistemology is not a discretely intellectual enterprise. And to the extent that the discrete intellectual enterprise (a very modern idea) oh so easily displace the life of prayer, the disciplines of reflection, the practices of Christ-like living, the mission of being the people of God in the world bearing witness to the Kingdom of God now and yet to come, then even ever so brilliant theological epistemology—as a discrete intellectual project—will be an empty idol. We must love God if we are to know truth. We must recover an integrative understanding of true knowledge where who we are, who we love and how we live cannot be separated from what we claim to believe and know. Yet the entire cultural pattern of modernity is one premised on the separation of faith from knowledge, beauty from truth, religion from science, objective facts from subjective values, power wealth and reality from morality teleology and meaning.

Modernity is a profoundly disintegrative politico-religio-epistemic life form. If we are to be faithful to the integrative vision of knowledge Paul talks about then we must be prepared to run radically against the grain of the very life form we inhabit. Thus, if we are being faithful to the knowledge that arises out of the love of God, we cannot expect to be taken seriously by our own cultural life form because to be taken seriously would actually mean to abandon that life form. Only when we are worthy of being radically denounced by the life form of disintegrative modernity will we have any real alternative to offer to spiritually dying, morally impotent, meaninglessly pragmatic, late modern consumer irrealism.

The writer to the Hebrews makes the point with devastating simplicity that the grounds of what we can see and grasp are not themselves seeable and graspable. That is, the human capacity to understand cannot be its own epistemic foundation, for human understanding is premised on divine meaning which is fundamentally prior to human understanding. So human understanding only comes through faith in the meaningful grounds of that understanding which that understanding itself cannot establish. Without any confidence in an unseen meaningful reality prior to human understanding, human intelligence itself must be unintelligible.

A foundational faith in the reality of divine meaning was unproblematic in ancient times—at least for Platonist and Aristotelian trajectories—but since Descartes the distinctly modern Western enterprise has sought to establish indubitable foundations for true knowledge out of the 'purely natural' epistemic capabilities of the knowing subject. Further these foundations are sought in a distinctly philosophical manner where what we mean by philosophy precisely excludes faith. To this outlook, that which establishes the knowing subject—and that which establishes the reality of the cosmos itself—is bracketed out.

Within the artificially small and supposedly autonomous world of supposedly self-justifying human knowledge, knowledge without cosmic meaning has become a formidable power. Knowledge as empirical provability, mathematical comprehensibility and observational objectivity is knowledge deemed independent of foundational cosmic belief, and this knowledge has unleashed the vast and metaphysically aimless, cosmologically agnostic technological powers of Modernity. And sadly, the destructive potential of these powers and their structural un-coupling from the wisdom traditions of the West make the old fashioned dogs of war in pre-modern times look like harmless puppies in comparison.[14]

The writer to the Hebrews is claiming that we understand foundational meaning by faith, and faith—trusting confidence in God who is the invisible origin and destiny of all that is visible—is the only basis of foundational understanding you can have. Conversely, without foundational understanding knowledge itself is either piecemeal or meaningless, and logos and episteme reduce finally to mere epiphenomena and arbitrary power. So the entire modern enterprise—the aim to establish by rational and empirical proofs, without faith, the foundations of valid knowledge/belief/value—can only end in the fragmentation of meaning itself; the curse of Babel. This curse is only visited (self-inflicted?) upon great and powerful civilizations who aspire to build a tower from earth to heaven and to take all reality by the force of what we can build on entirely human

---

14. See P. W. Singer, *Wired for War*; and *Corporate Warriors*. See Fisk, *The Age of the Warrior*. See Otterman, *American Torture*. See Otterman, Hil, and Wilson, *Erasing Iraq*.

foundations. So if we will not believe in what we cannot see, if we will not have faith in a cosmic and transcendent meaning that is essentially prior to human knowledge, then knowledge itself will become our destroyer, and meaning itself will be destroyed. Conversely, if Western civilization is to be redeemed before catastrophe becomes irreversible, then a recovery of faith in the divine meaning of reality—beyond what we can see and grasp—is essential. We must recover the basic faith of Hebrews 11:2–3 which is very much harmonious with the basic Platonist faith—confidence in the unseen transcendent goodness, beauty and truth of God. And whilst the knowledge of God can never be a modern knowledge—proof constructed in the terms of empirical, rational and linguistic structures of human perception, thought and words—modern knowledge was always a far too small and intrinsically unbelievable notion to begin with. Let us return to a bigger and more believable vision of meaningful reality.

I do not think it is meaningful to talk of foundationless knowledge. However, knowledge grounded in *faith* is a type of foundation that is inherently different to the notion of knowledge grounded in foundations which are either proven certainties or pragmatic possibilities premised entirely on human epistemic capabilities, naturalistically understood. Modern foundationalism is self-destructive. But postmodern non-foundationalism must abandon the notion of truth altogether and thus falls relentlessly into a-rationality.

It seems that the Scriptures are right: we must believe in the Divine Logos if we are to reason at all. As the writer to the Hebrews puts it, we understand by faith. Again, this is a way of thinking about meaning that the Modern life form rejects. Again, only when we are rejected by Modernity because we unashamedly *believe* in the unseen fount of real meaning, real value, real truth etc., will we have the authority to prophetically speak *for* reason, meaning, beauty, truth and goodness in our times.

The Scriptures speak to us—people removed from the original hearers by thousands of years, thousands of kilometers, by language, morality, culture, science, life form, politics, basic reality outlook etc.—with great power. But this power is only revealed to those who have ears to hear; to those whose spirits have been made alive in faith; to those who can somehow see eternity through the fragile human tissue of revelation. This paradox of the eternal Word of God being powerful and pointed, though it is mediated to us by a seemingly endless sequence of contingent and contextually specific human words and practices, is the very signature of God to the Christian. Thus does God sign his Unspeakable Name on the letters of love with which he would woo Humanity. With Hamann and Saint Paul we might well gape in wonder at God's rash and dashing self-emptying so that what God would say is fitted to what we can hear. Even so, the Glory of the Lord remains, but hidden within (yet also beyond) human flesh, within (yet also beyond) history, creation, words, actions, and the Church. Thus there is a surpassing wisdom in the foolishness and self-debasing ardor of God for the small and oh so fragile world of human understanding. Indeed, how much wiser is the folly of God than the hubris or nihilism of the faithless knowledge of Modern Secular Reason? How much wiser is the knowledge of faith than the epistemic futility of skeptical and instrumental unbelief?

Bibliography

Adorno, T. *The Culture Industry: Selected Essays on Mass Culture*. London: Routledge, 1991.
Alighieri, D. *Divine Comedy*. 3 vols. Translated by Dorothy Sayers and Barbara Reynolds. London: Penguin, 1949 (vol. 1), 1955 (vol. 2), 1962 (vol. 3).
Althusser, L. *For Marx*. London: Cox & Wyman, 1969.
Arendt, H. *Between Friends*. London: Secker & Warburg, 1995.
Aristotle. *The Complete Works of Aristotle*. Edited by Jonathan Barnes. Princeton: Princeton University Press, 1995.
Augustine. *Against the Academicians and The Teacher*. Translated by Peter King. Indianapolis: Hackett, 1995.
———. *The Confessions of Saint Augustine*. London: Hodder & Stoughton, 1983.
Barnes, J. *Aristotle*. Oxford: Oxford University Press, 1986.
Bauman, Z. *Intimations of Postmodernity*. London: Routledge, 1992.
———. *Modernity and the Holocaust*. Cambridge: Polity, 1989.
Beasley-Murray, G. R. *John*. 2nd ed. Word Biblical Commentary 36. Nashville: Nelson, 1999.
Benedict XVI. *Deus Caritas Est*. Vatican, 2006.
Berger, P. L., editor. *The Desecularization of the World: Resurgent Religion and World Politics*. Grand Rapids: Eerdmans, 1999.
———. *Facing up to Modernity*. New York: Penguin, 1977.
Berger, P. L., and T. Luckmann. *The Social Construction of Reality*. London: Penguin, 1971.
Berkman, J., and M. Cartwright, editors. *The Hauerwas Reader*. Durham: Duke University Press, 2001.
Blond, P., editor. *Post-Secular Philosophy*. London: Routledge, 1998.
Bok, D. *Universities in the Marketplace*. Princeton: Princeton University Press, 2003.
Bonaventure. *The Journey of the Mind to God*. Translated by P. Boehner. Edited by S. F. Brown. Indianapolis: Hackett, 1990.
Bonhoeffer, D. *Ethics*. Translated by N. H. Smith. New York: Macmillan, 1965.
Bradley, F. H. *Appearance and Reality*. 2nd ed. Oxford: Clarendon, 1930.
Brueggemann, W. *The Prophetic Imagination*. 2nd ed. Minneapolis: Fortress, 2001.
Brunschwig, J. et al. *Greek Thought*. Cambridge: Harvard University Press, 2000.
Buber, M. *I and Thou*. Translated by R. G. Smith. Edinburgh: T. & T. Clark, 1937.
Buckley, M. *The Origins of Modern Atheism*. New Haven: Yale University Press, 1987.
Budde, M. L., and R. W. Brimlow. *Christianity Incorporated: How Big Business is Buying the Church*. Grand Rapids: Brazos, 2002.
Burkert, W. *Greek Religion*. Translated by J. Raffan. Cambridge: Harvard University Press, 1985.

Bibliography

Burnett, D. *World of the Spirits: A Christian Perspective on Traditional and Folk Religions*. London: Monarch, 2000.

Cain, J., and J. Hewitt. *Off Course: From Public Place to Market Place at Melbourne University*. Melbourne: Scribe, 2004.

Callinicos, A. *Against Postmodernism: A Marxist Critique*. Cambridge: Polity, 1989.

Campbell, C. J. *Oil Crisis*. Brentwood, UK: Multi-Science Publishing, 2005.

Campolo, A. *Seven Deadly Sins*. Wheaton, IL: Victor, 1987.

Casey, M. A. *Meaninglessness: The Solutions of Nietzsche, Freud, and Rorty*. Melbourne: Freedom Publishing, 2001.

Cavanaugh, W. T. *Being Consumed: Economics and Christian Desire*. Grand Rapids: Eerdmans, 2008.

———. *Theopolitical Imagination*. Edinburgh: T. & T. Clark, 2002.

Chan, S. *Pentecostal Theology and the Christian Spiritual Tradition*. Journal of Pentecostal Theology Supplement Series 21. Sheffield, UK: Sheffield Academic, 2001.

Coady, T., editor. *Why Universities Matter: A Conversation about Values, Means, and Directions*. Sydney: Allen & Unwin, 2000.

Coady, T., and S. Miller. "Australian Higher Education and the Relevance of Newman." *Australian Universities Review* 36/2 (1993) 40–44.

Coaldrake, P., and L. Stedman. *On the Brink: Australia's Universities Confronting their Future*. St. Lucia: University of Queensland Press, 1998.

Collingwood, R. G. *An Autobiography*. London: Penguin, 1944.

Connell, R. W. "Core Activity: Reflexive Intellectual Workers and Cultural Crisis." *Journal of Sociology* 42/1 (2006) 5–23.

Cooper, S. et al. *Scholarship and Entrepreneurs: The University in Crisis*. Melbourne: Arena, 2002.

Copleston, F. *A History of Philosophy*. London: Continuum, 2003.

Cornford, F. M. *From Religion to Philosophy*. Princeton: Princeton University Press, 1991.

———. *Principium Sapientiae: The Origin of Greek Philosophical Thought*. Cambridge: Cambridge University Press, 1952.

Crouzel, H. *Origen*. Edinburgh: T. & T. Clark, 1989.

Cunningham, C. *Genealogy of Nihilism*. London: Routledge, 2002.

Davies, B. "The Impossibility of Intellectual Work in Neoliberal Regimes." *Discourse* 26/1 (2005) 3–16.

Davies, B. et al. "The Rise and Fall of the Neo-liberal University." *European Journal of Education* 4/2 (2006) 305–19.

Dawkins, S. J. *Higher Education: A Policy Statement [white paper]*. Canberra: Australian Government Printing Service, 1988.

Deffeyes, K. S. *Beyond Oil: The View from Hubbert's Peak*. New York: Farrar, Straus & Giroux, 2005.

Dodds, E. R. *The Greeks and the Irrational*. California: University of California Press, 1951.

———. *Pagan and Christian in an Age of Anxiety*. Cambridge: Cambridge University Press, 1990.

Dupré, L. *Passage to Modernity: An Essay in the Hermeneutics of Nature and Culture*. New Haven: Yale University Press, 1993.

Durkheim, E. *The Elementary Forms of Religious Life*. Translated by J. W. Swain. New York: Free Press, 1965.

---. *Suicide*. Translated by J. A. Spaulding and G. Simpson. Edited by G. Simpson. New York: Free Press, 1966.
Ellul, J. *Money and Power*. Translated by L. Neff. London: Pickering, 1986.
---. *The Technological Bluff*. Translated by G. W. Bromiley. Grand Rapids: Eerdmans, 1990.
---. *Violence: Reflections from a Christian Perspective*. Translated by C. G. Kings. New York: Seabury, 1969.
Esolen, A. "The Freedom of Heaven and the Freedom of Hell." *First Things* March (2009) 37–41.
Feuerbach, L. *The Essence of Christianity*. New York: Harper & Row, 1957.
Fish, S. "God Talk, Part 2." *New York Times*, 17 May 2009. Online: http://fish.blogs.nytimes.com/2009/05/17/god-talk-part-2/?ref=opinion.
Fisk, R. *The Age of the Warrior*. London: Harper Perennial, 2009.
Fleshman, M. "A Troubled Decade for Africa's Children." *Africa Recovery* 16/1 (April 2002. Online: www.un.org/ecosocdev/geninfo/afrec/vol16no1/161child.htm.
Flew, A. "Theology and Falsification." In *Philosophy of Religion*, edited by C. Taliaferro and P. Griffiths, 105–6. Oxford: Blackwell, 2003.
Foucault, M. *Madness and Civilisation: A History of Insanity in the Age of Reason*. Translated by R. Howard. London: Routledge, 1971.
Frankfurt, H. G. *On Bullshit*. Princeton: Princeton University Press, 2005.
Franklin, J. *Corrupting the Youth: A History of Philosophy in Australia*. Sydney: MacLeay, 2003.
Freud, S. *Civilisation and Its Discontents*. London: Penguin, 2002.
---. *The Future of a Delusion*. The Standard Edition of the Complete Psychological Works of Sigmund Freud 21. London: Hogarth, 1968. Online: www.adolphus.nl/xcrpts/xcfreudill.html.
---. *The Origins of Religion*. Pelican Freud Library 13. London: Penguin, 1985.
Fukuyama, F. *After the Neocons*. London: Profile, 2006.
---. *The End of History*. New York: Free Press, 1992.
Gadamer, H.-G. *Heidegger's Ways*. Translated by John W. Stanley. SUNY Series in Conemporary Continental Philosophy. New York: SUNY Press, 1994.
Gallagher, M. "Reversing the Slide." *Australian Universities Review* 48/1 (2005) 10–15.
Gardiner, D. "Change Proposal: School of Humanities and Human Services, 31 May 2007." Online: www.chancellery.qut.edu.au/dvc/ltd/hhs.studentstaff/HHS%20Change%20Proposal.pdf.
Gavrilyuk, P. L. *The Suffering of the Impassible God*. Oxford: Oxford University Press, 2006.
George, S. *A Fate Worse than Debt*. London: Penguin, 1989.
Gersh, S., and D. Moran, eds. *Eriugena, Berkeley and the Idealist Tradition*. Notre Dame, IN: University of Notre Dame Press, 2006.
Gerson, L. P. *Aristotle and Other Platonists*. New York: Cornell University Press, 2005.
Giddens, A. *The Consequences of Modernity*. Cambridge: Polity, 1991.
---. *Modernity and Self-Identity: Self and Society in the Late Modern Age*. Cambridge: Polity, 1991.
Gilson, E. *History of Christian Philosophy in the Middle Ages*. London: Sheed & Ward, 1980.
Gingerich, R., and T. Grimsrud, editors. *Transforming the Powers*. Minneapolis: Fortress, 2006.

Bibliography

Goetz, S., and C. Taliaferro. *Naturalism*. Grand Rapids: Eerdmans, 2008.
Greiner, N. *Australian Liberalism in a Post-ideological Age*. Melbourne: The Alfred Deakin Lecture Trust, 1990.
Hadot, P. *What Is Ancient Philosophy?* Cambridge: Harvard University Press, 2002.
Hamilton, C., and R. Denniss. *Affluenza: When Too Much is Never Enough*. Sydney: Allen & Unwin, 2005.
Hanby, M. *Augustine and Modernity*. London: Routledge, 2003.
Harrison, P. *Inside the Third World*. London: Penguin, 1993.
Harrison, P. R. *The Disenchantment of Reason: The Problem of Socrates in Modernity*. SUNY Series in Social and Political Thought. New York: SUNY Press, 1995.
Hauerwas, S. *The Peaceable Kingdom: A Primer in Christian Ethics*. Indiana: University of Notre Dame Press, 1983.
———. "Seeing Darkness, Hearing Silence: Augustine's Account of Evil." In R. Grant, ed., *Naming Evil, Judging Evil*. Chicago: University of Chicago Press, 2006.
Hauerwas, S., and F. Lenticchia, editors. *Dissent from the Homeland: Essays after September 11*. Durham: Duke University Press, 2003.
Hausman, D. M. *The Inexact and Separate Science of Economics*. Cambridge: Cambridge University Press, 1992.
Havel, V. *Open Letters*. New York: Vintage, 1992.
Hayes, D., and R. Wynyard, editors. *The McDonaldization of Higher Education*. Westport: Greenwood, 2002.
Heidegger, M. *Being and Time*. Translated by J. Macquarrie and Edward Robinson. New York: Harper, 1962.
Hil, R. *Whackademia*. Sydney: NewSouth, 2012.
Honnefelder, L. "Rationalization and Natural Law: Max Weber's and Ernst Troeltsch's Interpretation of the Medieval Doctrine of Natural Law." Review of *Metaphysics* 49 (December 1995) 275–94.
Horkenheimer, M., and T. Adorno. *Dialectic of Enlightenment*. Translated by J. Cumming. New York: Continuum, 1993.
Howard, J. "Sharing Our Common Values." Irving Kristol Lecture, delivered at the Gala Dinner for the American Enterprise Institute, in Washington, DC, 5 March, 2008. Online: www.theaustralian.news.com.au/story/0,25197,23328945-5014047,00.html.
Huebner, C. K. *A Precarious Peace: Yoderian Explorations on Theology, Knowledge, and Identity*. Polyglossia 1. Waterloo, ON: Herald, 2006.
Hume, D. *Inquiry Concerning Human Understanding*. Chicago: Open Court, 1988.
Huxley, A. *Brave New World*. London: Grafton, 1983.
International Energy Agency Medium-Term Oil Market Report, July 2007. Online. wsj.com/public/resources/documents/iea20070707.pdf
Jaensche, D. *The Hawke-Keating Hijack*. Sydney: Allen & Unwin, 1989.
James, P., editor. *Burning Down the House*. Melbourne: Arena, 2002.
Janicaud, D. et al. *Phenomenology and the "Theological Turn": The French Debate*. New York: Fordham University Press, 2000.
Jenkins, P. *God's Continent: Christianity, Islam, and Europe's Religious Crisis*. Future of Christianity Trilogy. Oxford: Oxford University Press, 2007.
———. *The New Faces of Christianity*. Oxford: Oxford University Press, 2006.
———. *The Next Christendom*. Oxford: Oxford University Press, 2002.
Keen, S. *Debunking Economics: The Naked Emperor of the Social Sciences*. Annandale, NY: Pluto, 2001.

Keenan, W. J. F. "Rediscovering the Theological in Sociology." *Theory, Culture & Society* 20/1 (2003) 19–42.
Kerr, F. "Milbank's Thesis." In *Theology and Sociology: A Reader*, edited by R. Gill, 429–34. London: Cassell, 1996.
Kerr, N. R. *Christ, History and Apocalyptic: The Politics of Christian Mission.* Theopolitical Visions. Eugene, OR: Cascade Books, 2008.
Kierkegaard, S. *Concluding Unscientific Postscript to Philosophical Fragments.* Princeton: Princeton University Press, 1992.
———. *Fear and Trembling.* London: Penguin, 2005.
———. *The Point of View.* Princeton: Princeton University Press, 1998.
———. *The Sickness Unto Death.* Princeton: Princeton University Press, 1980.
———. *Two Ages.* Princeton: Princeton University Press, 1978.
———. *Upbuilding Discourses in Various Spirits.* Princeton: Princeton University Press, 1993.
King, P. "The Metaphysics of Peter Abelard." In *The Cambridge Companion to Abelard*, edited by J. Brower and K. Guilfoy, 65–125. Cambridge Companion to Philosophy. Cambridge: Cambridge University Press, 2004.
Kingston, M. *Not Happy, John! Defending Our Democracy.* Melbourne: Penguin, 2004.
Klein, N. *No Logo: No Space, No Choice, No Job. Taking Aim at the Brand Bullies.* London: Flamingo, 2000.
Kołakowski, L. *Why Is There Something Rather than Nothing?* London: Penguin, 2007.
Kuhn, T. H. *The Structure of Scientific Revolutions.* Chicago: University of Chicago Press, 1970.
Lasch, C. *The Culture of Narcissism.* London: Norton, 1991.
Latour, B. *We Have Never Been Modern.* Translated by C. Porter. Cambridge: Harvard University Press, 1993.
Lauchs, M. "Rational Avoidance of Accountability by Queensland Governments." Doctoral thesis, Queensland University of Technology, School of Justice Studies, 2006.
Lechner, F. J. "Fundamentalism Revisited." In *In Gods We Trust: New Patterns of Religious Pluralism in America.* Edited by T. Robbins and D. Anthony. 2nd ed. New Brunswick, NJ: Transaction, 1990.
Lewis, C. S. *The Abolition of Man.* 1947. Reprinted, London: Fount, 1999.
———. *Miracles.* London: HarperCollins, 1974.
———. *That Hideous Strength.* New York: Simon & Schuster, 1996.
Lewis, H. *Excellence without a Soul: How a Great University Forgot Education.* New York: Public Affairs, 2006.
Lovelock, J. *The Revenge of Gaia: Earth's Climate Crisis and the Fate of Humanity.* New York: Basic Books, 2006.
Lyon, D. "Religion and the Postmodern: Old Problems, New Prospects." In *Postmodernity, Sociology and Religion*, edited by K. Flanagan and P. C. Jupp, 14–29. London: Macmillan, 1996.
Lyotard, J.-F. *The Postmodern Condition: A Report on Knowledge.* Translated by G. Bennington and B. Massumi. Minneapolis: University of Minnesota Press, 1979.
Lubac, H. de. *Paradoxes of Faith.* San Francisco: Ignatius Press, 1987.
MacDonald, G. *The Princess and the Goblin.* London: Puffin Classics, 1997.
Macmurray, J. *Persons in Relation.* The Form of the Personal 2. London: Faber & Faber, 1961.

Bibliography

Maddox, M. *God Under Howard: The Rise of the Religious Right in Australian Poltics*. Sydney: Allen & Unwin, 2005.

Malins, I. *Prepare the Way for Revival*. Grand Rapids: Baker, 2004.

Manning, R. "The Oil We Eat: Following the Food Chain Back to Iraq." *Harpers Magazine* (February 2004) 4–7.

Marcus, R. A. *Christianity and the Secular*. Blessed Pope John XXIII Lecture Series in Theology and Culture. Notre Dame, IN: University of Notre Dame Press, 2006.

Marrone, S. P., editor. *The Cambridge Companion to Medieval Philosophy*. Cambridge Companions. Cambridge: Cambridge University Press, 2003.

Martin, D. "The Secularisation Issue: Prospect and Retrospect." *British Journal of Sociology* 42/3 (1991) 465–73.

Marx, K. "Introduction to A Contribution to the Critique of Hegel's Philosophy of Right." In *Karl Marx, Early Writings*. Translated by R. Livingstone and G. Benton. 1844. Reprinted, London: Penguin, 1975.

Marx, K., and F. Engles. *The Communist Manifesto*. London: Penguin, 1988.

McGrath, A. *The Twilight of Atheism*. London: Rider, 2004.

McGrath, S. *The Early Heidegger and Medieval Philosophy*. Washington, DC: Catholic University of America Press, 2006.

Milbank, J. "Reason, Faith and Imagination: The Study of Theology and Philosophy in the 21st Century." Posted on 8 January 2007. Online: www.theologyphilosophycentre.co.uk.

———. *Theology and Social Theory: Beyond Secular Reason*. Signposts in Theology. Oxford: Blackwell, 1990.

Milbank, J., and C. Pickstock. *Truth in Aquinas*. Radical Orthodoxy Series. London: Routledge, 2001.

Moltmann, J. *Theology of Hope: On the Ground and the Implications of a Christian Eschatology*. Translated by J. W. Leitch. London: SCM, 1967.

Monbiot, G. *Age of Consent: A Manifesto for a New World Order*. London: Flamingo, 2003.

———. *Captive State: The Corporate Takeover of Britain*. London: Pan, 2000.

Morgan, M. L. "Plato and Greek Religion." In *The Cambridge Companion to Plato*. Edited by R. Kraut. Cambridge: Cambridge University Press, 1992.

Newbigin, L. *The Open Secret: An Introduction to the Theology of Mission*. Grand Rapids: Eerdmans, 1995.

Newman, J. H. *The Idea of a University*. Chicago: Loyola University Press, 1927.

Niehoff, M. R. "Did the Timaeus Create a Textual Community?" *Greek, Roman and Byzantine Studies* 47 (2007) 161–91.

Nietzsche, F. *The Gay Science*. Translated with commentary by W. Kaufmann. New York: Random House, 1974.

———. *On the Genealogy of Morality*. Translated by C. Diethe. Edited by K. A. Pearson. Cambridge Texts in the History of Political Thought. Cambridge: Cambridge University Press, 1994.

———. *Will to Power*. Translated with commentary by W. Kaufmann. New York: Random House, 1967.

Northcott, M. S. *A Moral Climate: The Ethics of Global Warming*. London: Darton, Longman & Todd, 2007.

Norton, A. *The Unchained University*. St Leonards: The Centre for Independent Studies, 2002.

Bibliography

Orwell, G. *Nineteen Eighty-Four*. London: Penguin, 1954.
———. *Why I Write*. London: Penguin, 2004.
Otterman, M. *American Torture: From the Cold War to Abu Ghraib and Beyond*. Melbourne: Melbourne University Press, 2007.
Otterman, M., R. Hil, with P. Wilson. *Erasing Iraq: The Human Costs of Carnage*. London: Pluto, 2010.
Packard, V. *Hidden Persuaders*. 1957. Reprinted, Ringwood: Penguin, 1986.
Partenie, C. and T. Rockmore, editors. *Heidegger and Plato: Toward Dialogue*. Topics in Historical Philosophy. Evanston, IL: Northwestern University Press, 2005.
Pascal, B. *Pensées*. London: Penguin Classics, 1966.
Pelikan, J. *The Idea of a University: A Re-examination*. New Haven: Yale University Press, 1992.
Peperzak, A. T. *Platonic Transformations: With and After Hegel, Heidegger and Levinas*. Lanham, MD: Rowman & Littlefield, 1997.
Perrier, E. "Duns Scotus Facing Reality: Between Absolute Contingency and Unquestionable Consistency." *Modern Theology* 21/4 (2005) 619–43.
Pettifor, A., editor. *Real World Economic Outlook—The Legacy of Globalization: Debt and Deflation*. London: Palgrave, 2003.
Pfeiffer, D. A. "Eating Fossil Fuels." From *The Wilderness Publications*, 2004. Online: www.fromthewilderness.com/free/ww3/100303_eating_oil.html.
Pickstock, C. *After Writing: On the Liturgical Consummation of Philosophy*. Oxford: Blackwell, 1998.
Pieper, J. *Scholasticism: Personalities and Problems of Medieval Philosophy*. Translated by R. Winston and C. Winston. South Bend, IN: St. Augustine Press, 2001.
Pimentel, D., and M. Pimentel, eds. *Food, Energy and Society*. Rev. ed. Niwot: University of Colorado Press, 1996.
Plato. *The Dialogues of Plato*. Translated by B. Jowett. 3rd ed. Oxford: Oxford University Press, 1892.
———. *Perseus* 2.0 (CD-ROM) Newhaven: Yale University Press, 2000.
———. *Plato*. Vols. I–XII. Loeb Classical Library. Various translators and dates. New Haven: Harvard University Press.
———. *Plato, Complete Works*. Edited by J. J. Cooper. Indianapolis: Hackett, 1997.
Polanyi, M. *Personal Knowledge: Towards a Post-Critical Philosophy*. Chicago: University of Chicago Press, 1958.
Popkin, R., and C. Schmitt, eds. *Skepticism from the Renaissance to the Enlightenment*. Wiesbaden: Harrassowitz, 1987.
Porterfield, A. *Healing in the History of Christianity*. Oxford: Oxford University Press, 2005.
Prince, D. *Re-Discovering God's Church*. New Kensington, PA: Whitaker House, 2006.
Pusey, M. *Economic Rationalism in Canberra*. Cambridge: Cambridge University Press, 1991.
Quanchi, M. "Indigenous Epistemology, Wisdom and Tradition: Changing and Challenging Dominant Paradigms in Oceania." A paper presented to the "Social Change in the 21st Century" Conference, Queensland University of Technology, 29 October 2004. http://eprints.qut.edu.au/archive/00000630/01/quanchi-max.pdf.
Radcliffe, T. *What Is the Point of Being a Christian?* London: Burns & Oates, 2005.
Ratzinger, J. *Introduction to Christianity*. Translated by J. R. Foster. Communio Books. San Francisco: Ignatius, 2004.

Bibliography

Readings, B. *The University in Ruins.* Cambridge: Harvard University Press, 1996.
Reimer, A. *Sandstone Gothic.* Sydney: Allen & Unwin, 1998.
Ricœur, P. *Freud and Philosophy: An Essay on Interpretation.* Translated by D. Savage. New Haven: Yale University Press, 1970.
———. *The Symbolism of Evil.* Translated by E. Buchanan. Religious Perspectives 17. New York: Harper & Row, 1967.
Rorty, R. *Contingency, Irony and Solidarity.* Cambridge: Cambridge University Press, 1989.
———. *Objectivity, Relativism and Truth.* Philosophical Papers 1. Cambridge: Cambridge University Press, 1991.
Roy, A. "The Algebra of Infinite Justice." *The Guardian, Saturday Review*, September 29, 2001. Online: www.guardian.co.uk/saturday_review/story/0,3605,559756,00.html.
Rubenstein, R. E. *Aristotle's Children: How Christians, Muslims, and Jews Rediscovered Ancient Wisdom and Illuminated the Dark Ages.* Orlando, FL: Harcourt, 2003.
Rudd, K. "Faith in Politics." *The Monthly* 17 (October 2006). Online: www.themonthly.com.au/tm/?q=node/300.
Ryckmans, P. *The View from the Bridge.* The 1996 Boyer Lectures. Sydney: ABC Books, 1996.
Saul, J. R. *The Collapse of Globalism: And the Reinvention of the World.* Toronto: Viking Canada, 2005.
Schindler, D. C. "Mystery and Mastery: Philosophical Reflections on Biblical Epistemology." In *The Bible and Epistemology: Biblical Soundings on the Knowledge of God.* Edited by M. Healy and R. Parry. Carlisle, UK: Paternoster, 2007.
———. *Plato's Critique of Impure Reason.* Washington, DC: Catholic University of America Press, 2008.
Schmemann, A. *For the Life of the World.* New York: Saint Vladimir's Seminary Press, 1997.
Schmitt, C. *Aristotle and the Renaissance.* New Haven: Harvard University Press, 1983.
Shakespeare, W. *Hamlet.* Oxford: Oxford University Press, 1989.
Simpson, C. B. *The Truth Is the Way: Kierkegaard's Theologia Viatorum.* Eugene, OR: Cascade Books, 2011
Singer, P. *The President of Good & Evil: The Ethics of George W. Bush.* New York: Dutton, 2004.
Singer, P. W. *Corporate Warriors: The Rise of the Privatized Military Industry.* Cornell Studies in Security Affairs. Ithaca, NY: Cornell University Press, 2003.
———. *Wired for War: The Robotics Revolution and Conflict in the Twenty-first Century.* New York: Penguin, 2009.
Smith, J. K. A. *Introducing Radical Orthodoxy: Mapping a Post-Secular Theology.* Grand Rapids: Baker Academics, 2004.
———. *Who's Afraid of Postmodernism? Taking Derrida, Lyotard, and Foucault to Church.* The Church and Postmodern Culture. Grand Rapids: Baker Academic, 2006.
Smith, P. *Killing the Spirit: Higher Education in America.* New York: Viking, 1990.
Sophocles. *The Three Theban Plays.* London: Penguin Classics, 2000.
Spencer, H. *Essays: Scientific, Political and Speculative.* London: Williams & Nogate, 1890.

Bibliography

Stiglitz, J. E. *Globalization and its Discontents*. UK: Allen Lane, 2002.
Stiglitz, J. E., and L. J. Bilmes. *The Three Trillion Dollar War: The Real Cost of the Iraq Conflict*. New York: Norton, 2008.
Stretton, H. *Economics: A New Introduction*. London: Pluto, 2000.
Surber, J. P., editor and translator. *Metacritique: The Linguistic Assault on German Idealism*. Amherst, MA: Humanity, 2001.
Tacey, D. *Re-Enchantment*. Sydney: HarperCollins, 2000.
———. *The Spiritual Revolution*. Sydney: HarperCollins, 2003.
Taylor, C. C. W. "Aristotle's Epistemology." In *Epistemology*, edited by Stephen Everson, 116–42. Companions to Ancient Thought. Cambridge: Cambridge University Press, 1990.
Tertullian. *De Carne Christi*. In *Ante-Nicene Fathers*. Edited by A. Roberts and J. Donaldson, Vol. 3. 1885. Reprinted, Peabody, MA: Hendrickson, 1995.
Tillich, P. *Theology of Culture*. Oxford: Oxford University Press, 1964.
Tolkien, J. R. R. *The Lord of the Rings*. London: HarperCollins, 1991.
Tyson, P. "Western Culture and the 'Hypothesis of God.'" *Appraisal* 5/4 (2005) 169–76.
Van Ophuijsen, J. "Making Room for Faith: Is Plato?" In *The Winged Chariot: Collected Essays on Plato and Platonism in Honour of L. M. de Rijk*, 119–34. Edited by M. Kardaun and J. Spruyt. Leiden: Brill, 2000.
Wallis, J. *God's Politics: Why the American Right Gets It Wrong and the Left Doesn't Get It*. New York: Harper, 2005.
Weber, M. *The Protestant Work Ethic and the Spirit of Capitalism*. Sydney: Allen & Unwin, 1987.
Weil, S. *Gravity and Grace*. London: Routledge Classics, 2002.
———. *Waiting for God*. Translated by E. Craufurd. New York: Harper & Row, 1973.
Westphal, M. *Overcoming Onto-Theology: Toward a Postmodern Christian Faith*. Perspectives in Continental Philosophy 21. New York: Fordham University Press, 2001.
White, N. P. "Plato's Metaphysical Epistemology." In *The Cambridge Companion to Plato*, edited by R. Kraut, 277–310. Cambridge: Cambridge University Press, 1992.
Whitehead, D., and J. Tyson. *Rumors of God: Experience the Kind of Faith You've Only Heard About*. Nashville: Nelson, 2011.
Wilke, A. *Axis of Deceit*. Black Inc. Agenda Series. Melbourne: Black Inc. Agenda, 2003.
Williams, C. *The Greater Trumps*. Vancouver, BC: Regent College Publishing, 2003.
Winefield, H. W., et al. "Occupational Stress in Australian Universities: A National Survey." A Report to the Vice-Chancellors, National Tertiary Education Union, Faculty and Staff of Australian Universities, & the Ministers for Education, 2002.
Wink, W. *Engaging the Powers: Discernment and Resistance in a World of Domination*. The Powers 3. Minneapolis: Fortress, 1992.
Woolcock, J. *Within the Hollowed Halls of Learning*. Brisbane: Copyright Publishing, 2006.
Yannaras, C. *Elements of Faith: An Introduction to Orthodox Theology*. Translated by K. Schram. Edinburgh: T. & T. Clark, 1991.
———. *On the Absence and Unknowability of God, Heidegger and the Areopagite*. London: T. & T. Clark International, 2005.

Bibliography

Yoder, J. H. *The Politics of Jesus: Vicit Agnus Noster*. Grand Rapids: Eerdmans, 1972.
———. *The Priestly Kingdom: Social Ethics as Gospel*. Notre Dame, IN: University of Notre Dame Press, 1984.

www.ingramcontent.com/pod-product-compliance
Lightning Source LLC
Chambersburg PA
CBHW051059230426
43667CB00013B/2364